Spanking the Yankees

To Christopher:

I hope you enjoy reading
this as much as I enjoyed
writing it!

Your friend,

Gabriel Schechter

About the Author

Born in the hospital where Roy Campanella was taken after his accident, Gabriel Schechter is just old enough to remember seeing the New York Giants at the Polo Grounds. Raised in New Jersey, Gabriel grew up when he headed west and was the Damon Runyon of Las Vegas before turning to baseball history. His first book, *Victory Faust*, was a finalist for SABR's Seymour Medal in 2001. From 2002-2010 Gabriel was a researcher in the library at the Baseball Hall of Fame in Cooperstown, the baseball experience of a lifetime. He wrote the captions for two Taschen collections of photos by the legendary Neil Leifer: *Ballet in the Dirt* (baseball, 2008) and *Guts and Glory* (football, 2011). Their collaboration on Leifer's boxing photos will be published in 2020. Gabriel lives in Oregon.

Other Books by Gabriel Schechter

VICTORY FAUST: The Rube Who Saved McGraw's Giants (2000)
UNHITTABLE! Baseball's Greatest Pitching Seasons (2002)
AMERICA'S PASTIME: Historical Treasures From the Baseball Hall of Fame (2006)
THIS *BAD* DAY IN YANKEES HISTORY: A Calendar of Calamities (2008)

Spanking the Yankees

366 Days of Bronx Bummers

By Gabriel Schechter

SUMMER
GAME
BOOKS

ISBN: 978-1-938545-96-2 (pbk)
ISBN: 978-1-938545-97-9 (ebook)

For information about permissions, bulk purchases, or additional distribution, write to

Summer Game Books
P. O. Box 818
South Orange, NJ 07079

or contact the publisher at www.summergamebooks.com

Some of the content in this book is derived from material written by the author that appeared in a calendar published in 2008.

Dedication

To my father, Harold Schechter, who taught me to love baseball.

Sources

The original calendar, in which some of the material in *Spanking the Yankees* first appeared, reflected research mainly utilizing the clippings files and other archival material at the Giamatti Research Center at the Hall of Fame in Cooperstown. More recent research benefited from online sources including newspapers.com, PaperofRecord.com, and the *New York Times* online archive. Special thanks to Professor Michael Haupert of the University of Wisconsin-LaCrosse, for sharing his research on Yankees business ledgers during Jacob Ruppert's ownership. The following books are cited in the text:

Blomberg, Ron. *Designated Hebrew: The Ron Blomberg Story.* Champaign, IL: Sports Publishing, 2006.

Bouton, Jim, and Leonard Shecter. *Ball Four.* New York: World Publishing, 1970.

Carmichael, John P. *My Greatest Day in Baseball.* New York: Grosset & Dunlap, 1951.

Golenbock, Peter. *Wild High and Tight: The Life and Death of Billy Martin.* New York: St. Martin's Press, 1994.

Katz, Jeff. *The Kansas City A's & the Wrong Half of the Yankees.* Hingham MA: Maple Street Press, 2007.

Leavy, Jane. *The Last Boy: Mickey Mantle and the End of America's Childhood.* New York: Harper, 2010.

Lyle, Sparky, and Peter Golenbock. *The Bronx Zoo.* New York: Crown Publishers, 1979.

Reichler, Joseph L. *The Baseball Trade Register.* New York: Collier Books, 1984.

Torre, Joe, and Tom Verducci. *The Yankee Years.* New York: Anchor, 2010.

Winfield, Dave, with Tom Parker. *Winfield: A Player's Life.* New York: Avon, 1988.

Contents

Introduction

I don't know how you can have more fun writing a book than I had with this one.

Walt Friedman at Summer Game Books turned me loose on my 2008 publication, *This BAD Day in Yankees History*. That spiral-bound desk calendar presented one page per date, celebrating the worst things that happened *to* the Yankees or were perpetrated *by* them *on that date*. The only frustration during that labor of love came when I had to compress or even jettison juicy items because I simply didn't have the room. There was *too much* good material about bad Yankees days.

Join me in this expansive, unfettered celebration of Yankees misfortunes in *Spanking the Yankees: 366 Days of Bronx Bummers*. Although I still cover all 366 calendar dates here—with more than 550 items—the joy of writing this book was telling great stories for all they're worth, rather than simply recording a collection of delicious disasters.

For instance, Joba Chamberlain's visitation from the Fourth Plague in the 2007 ALDS didn't make the cut for the calendar because several important World Series losses occurred on the same date. The attack of the midges gets the coverage it deserves here, along with *all* the lowest points in franchise history. The Yankees spared nobody, and neither do I.

I come by my hatred of the Yankees honestly, by inheritance. My father's antipathy toward them fit the 1950s cliché that rooting for the Yankees was like rooting for General Motors, but for him it was personal. In 1957, he won a brand-new Cadillac in a raffle. A brand-new lemon. The thing broke down every three weeks, and after a year of aggravation and repairs, he traded it in for a Ford. But not Whitey. My father was a National League fan who could never root for the Yankees.

I am not a Yankee-hater. I'm a *Yankees*-hater; I hate the whole damn franchise. But say to me, "I'm a Yankee fan. Are you?" and my answer will be, "Yes, I like Giancarlo Stanton. Which one do you like?" I've almost always had one or two individuals in pinstripes I liked and rooted for.

The first two were Moose Skowron and Jim Bouton, both of whom I was pleased to meet decades later. I particularly enjoyed watching Mel Stottlemyre pitch during my teens. But I've always wanted the *team*, the Yankees, to lose every game. Every year.

In Part I, the Regular Season, I took the best item or two from each date—on the field or off—and put the story in greater perspective, making room for more damning details, cringe-worthy quotes, and general derision. Or, as I thought of it, adding more cowbell.

Part II spans nearly a century of postseason play, arranged chronologically by year, covering every game they lost in every series they lost. Each series is a separate narrative—all 27 of them (plus one wild card game), a good baseball number for Yankees postseason failures. October 5 is a magical date on which the Yankees lost games in ten of those series.

October 5 was a day off in 1976, my favorite World Series. My father was born in Cincinnati in 1906, so I'm a lifelong Reds fan, sort of a congenital defect except during the 1970s. Harold Schechter attended the 1919 World Series in Cincinnati and the 1939 sweep by the Yankees in New York, where he lived during the 1930s. So it was mighty sweet in 1976 when our Big Red Machine stomped the Yankees to sweep the World Series. I watched the finale with my father, who beamed at me after the last out and exclaimed, "I've been waiting seventy fucking years for that!"

Part III, the Off-Season, was the most enjoyable part of writing this book. My mission here was to assemble each narrative's ingredients— scattered among assorted dates in the calendar—into a deliciously malicious meal. I could dig into the bizarre Steinbrenner-Winfield feud, prosecute the case for Jacob Ruppert as the Yankees' most heartless owner, and remind people of the assorted victims of a century of Yankees bullying, from Babe Ruth and Lou Gehrig down to batboys and ushers.

The great irony of my life is that so many of my friends have been Yankees fans. Even my soulmate, Linda, was a Yankees fan when we met, though I soon cured her. Five of her six brothers were Yankees fans; the youngest became a Red Sox fan just to piss them off. Dennis, the most rabid, stayed up until almost 2:30 AM one Saturday night in 2011 to watch a tense, extra-inning battle from Seattle. Tied 4-4 in the 12th inning,

Mariano Rivera came in, gave up three quick hits, the Yankees lost, and Dennis fired his remote control right through the television screen. I trust he wasn't the only one.

When Hank Steinbrenner replaced his fading father as the loud-mouth-piece of the franchise in 2008, he declared, "This is a Yankee country. We're going to put the Yankees back on top and restore the universe to order." This sense of entitlement offends me more than anything about the Yankees, this delusional assumption that they'll have a yearly October romp to a title.

Don't tell a Yankees fan that according to the laws of probability, they're not due to win another World Series until 2039. George Steinbrenner used to panic when they lost a few games in a row *in spring training*; two years without a title burst the limits of his patience.

We have just passed the first *decade* without a Yankees appearance in a World Series since the decade *before* they got Babe Ruth. What a treat it has been to add fresh failures to the litany of outrages that is the true legacy of baseball's most-hated franchise.

So pull up a chair and enjoy my smorgasbord of schadenfreude. For dessert, there's an Index like you've never seen before, in case you wonder how I really feel.

Bon appetit!
Gabriel Schechter
Salem, Oregon, April 2020

Part I

The Regular Season

Opening Day

For the baseball fan, Opening Day brings the long-awaited escape from a gameless winter, heralding a time of infinite hope and renewal. You can start paying close attention; it all counts again, and for the next two hundred or so days, your life will be full of old favorites and new marvels, of familiar patterns punctuated by things you've never seen before.

For those of us who root for whichever team is facing the Yankees, it is never too early to gloat over the Yankees' misfortunes. When they began the 1966 season with an atrocious 1-10 record, this dynasty which had won the pennant every year from 1960-1964, it seemed too good to be true. In 1965, they had fallen out of the first division for the first time in 40 years, but could they possibly be this bad? It was no illusion, as the Yankees did a spectacular free-fall to last place for the first time since 1912. There's always the hope that an Opening Day loss can propel them into an irreversible tailspin.

Some of the Yankees' most embarrassing Opening Day performances have come on important dates in franchise history, including a couple of home openers after they began the season on the road. These gave the Yankee Stadium fans a chance to be disappointed in person. Here's a spring bouquet of my favorite Opening Day failures in Yankees history, in chronological order:

April 22, 1903 In the first game in franchise history, the New York Highlanders lose at Washington, 3-1. Jack Chesbro, whose wild pitch will cost the Highlanders the 1904 pennant, loses to Al Orth, who has the Highlanders "at his mercy," according to one reporter. The Highlanders start their existence 15-22, take until

August to get over .500, and finish a humdrum fourth, 17 games behind the pennant-winning squad from Boston.

April 10, 1913   In their first game since making "Yankees" their official name, they play the opener at Washington again and lose, 2-1. President Woodrow Wilson throws out the ceremonial first ball on a cold, raw day, but Walter Johnson has the honor of stifling the Yankees. He hits the first batter, Bert Daniels, who scores, but shuts them down the rest of the way—and shuts them out the next three times he starts against them.

April 16, 1935   In their first game as the post-Babe Ruth Yankees, they lose, 1-0, to the visiting Boston Red Sox. Wes Ferrell two-hits them while walking and striking out nobody, embarrassing their future Hall of Famers, who go 1-for-15. Ruthless. The only run off Lefty Gomez is unearned, thanks to errors by three of those immortals: Gomez, Bill Dickey, and Lou Gehrig, whose wild throw allows the run to score. Meanwhile, in Boston, Babe Ruth drives in three runs to lead the Braves to an Opening Day win.

April 16, 1964   Yogi Berra, one of the most popular players in franchise history, was named Yankees manager when Ralph Houk kicked himself upstairs into the GM post. In Berra's debut, his buddy, Whitey Ford, pitches all 11 innings against the visiting Red Sox, but it doesn't do him any good. In the 11th, Mickey Mantle shies away from the center field wall, playing Bob Tillman's blast into a triple, and Ford's wild pitch brings in the winning run. The 4-3 loss is one of three straight extra-inning losses to start a Yankees season in which they lose 15 times in extra innings—plus Game 5 of the World Series to Bob Gibson and the St. Louis Cardinals.

April 12, 1965   After Yankees legend Yogi Berra is fired for losing the 1964 World Series, the winning manager, Johnny Keane, makes the fateful decision to be lured into managing the Yankees. His tenure begins with another ugly loss. Five errors help the Yankees lose, 5-4, in 11 innings, with the key error made by a guy who didn't even enter the game until the ninth inning, as a pinch-runner. Art Lopez, making his major league debut as Mickey Mantle's legs, finds himself lost in left field, staring up into the sun as wind gusts send the baseball into his vicinity. Lopez's three-base error sets up the winning run. The Yankees finish sixth, and Keane is fired after the Yankees start off 4-16 in 1966. Eight months later, Keane dies of a heart attack.

April 12, 1966 The Yankees' worst season since 1912 begins in disheartening fashion at Yankee Stadium as Whitey Ford loses a tough duel to Mickey Lolich, 2-1. It's 1-1 going to the ninth inning, and a different era as Lolich, a career .110 hitter who went to the trouble of switch-hitting, leads off against Ford with a single. Joe Trimble of the *New York Daily News* describes Ford's ordeal in the 50-degree chill as Norm Cash comes to bat with two outs and the go-ahead run on third. "The Tigers made him desist from using a small plastic hip flask containing hot water to keep his pitching hand warm," a problem that plagued Ford after surgery in 1964 for a circulatory problem. "Ford didn't want to pitch to him. Whitey stood with his back to the plate, staring into the outfield and working the fingers of his left hand to get some feeling. Eventually he had to throw and there was nothing on the ball. Cash lined the first pitch." What was Johnny Keane thinking about as he watched Ford suffer? Why did he wait until Ford yielded the game-winning hit to replace him? No wonder the Yankees set Keane free three weeks later, finishing last without him.

April 9, 1973 The Yankees expect this home opener to be a big deal, celebrating the 50th anniversary of Yankee Stadium's opening. With the widows of Babe Ruth and Lou Gehrig on hand, Mayor John Lindsay throws out the ceremonial first pitch before an appreciative crowd of history-minded Yankees fans totaling . . . 17,028. At that, it's better than their average crowd that whole season, 15,562. It's the kind of desultory day when the most interesting thing the *Daily News* reports is the crowd's supportive response to the introduction of starting pitcher Fritz Peterson, who swapped wives and families with teammate Mike Kekich a few weeks earlier. Peterson loses to the Indians, 3-1. Forget the celebration, folks, nothing to celebrate here—the Yankees finish fourth and exile themselves from the Stadium for two years so it can get a tawdry facelift.

April 16, 2009 After nine games on the road, the Yankees get to unleash their gazillion-dollar replica of Yankee Stadium on the baseball world. CC Sabathia faces Cliff Lee of the Indians, and it's a calm 1-1 game in front of 48,271 paying customers until the seventh inning. Jose Veras comes in and ignites the Yankees' demise by giving up a leadoff walk followed by back-to-back doubles. He leaves with the Indians ahead, 3-1, replaced by Damaso Marte. Manager Joe Girardi makes sure Marte gets all three outs, but by that time it's 10-1. Marte hits the first batter, messes up a bunt play, walks another guy with the bases loaded, and torches the proceedings by serving up a grand slam to Grady Sizemore.

Now that we have the Yankees off to a lousy start, let's dig into their worst days in the regular season.

April

April 6, 1973 At Fenway Park, Yankees first baseman Ron Blomberg becomes the first designated hitter in MLB history, but the local fans are more interested in watching the Red Sox administer a 15-5 whupping. Batting sixth, Blomberg—who titled his memoir *Designated Hebrew*—walks with the bases loaded in the top of the first inning and later gets the first hit by a DH with an infield single off Luis Tiant. Red Sox DH Orlando Cepeda goes 0-for-6 but it doesn't matter to the 32,882 Fenway faithful, who see Carl Yastrzemski homer off Mel Stottlemyre in the first inning and Carlton Fisk drive in six runs with two homers. The Red Sox sweep the season-opening series as Cepeda wins the finale with a homer off Sparky Lyle in the bottom of the ninth. Thus the Yankees usher in a losing season and a fourth-place finish.

April 8, 1991 "Yankees' Defense Wastes No Time Reaching Mediocrity," reads a *New York Times* headline after Opening Day in Detroit. Tied 4-4 in the seventh inning, the Tigers have runners on first and second with one out. Both runners break with the pitch; both hesitate and are trapped midway between the bases. Yankees catcher Matt Nokes has his choice of dead runners to nail—and he doesn't get either one! Instead of running at Milt Cuyler, the lead runner, Nokes makes a long, low throw to second base which allows Cuyler to reach third safely. Given an extra out, the Tigers cash in two runs on Cecil Fielder's two-out double to win, 6-4. Yankees manager Stump Merrill, showing the firm leadership that carries the team to a 71-91 record that season, muses, "He got excited. It's the first game, and the whole bit. Those things happen. If you execute, you've got a chance to win." Astute, Sherlock. . .

April 8, 1989   There's nothing as giddy as watching a Yankees season go down the drain in the first week. Hammered today by the Indians, 11-1, the Yankees have been outscored, 36-10, in losing four of their first five games. They'll lose three more, dropping to 1-7 and prompting manager Dallas Green to tell the truth: "We stink. We're playing dumb baseball. . .We've done some dumb things offensively, and we've pitched like Little Leaguers."

April 9, 1986   The Yankees have signed few free agents who incited Yankee Stadium fans to the bursts of wild hatred that Ed Whitson did. Signed for $4.4 million, the right-hander allowed 29 runs in his first 22 innings as a Yankee in 1985 and was booed mercilessly by Stadium critics all season. In September, he got in a fist-fight with Billy Martin IV, but Martin is gone now, and Lou Piniella gives Whitson his first home start of 1986. He allows a run to the Royals in the first inning, another in the second, and George Brett leads off the third with a home run. Whitson is gone three batters later, and the next day, Piniella takes the extraordinary measure of announcing that Whitson will start only road games from now on, to avoid the slings and arrows of his hometown fans. It doesn't help, and he sports a 7.54 ERA that July when he is traded back to San Diego, where his 14-8 record in 1984 sucked the Yankees into wasting money on him in the first place.

I've made it easy for you to keep Billy Martin's managerial messes straight: each stint is designated the way you would indicate a monarch or pope, with a Roman numeral.

Reign	First Game	Last Game	When Fired
Martin I	August 2, 1975	July 23, 1978	Resigned July 23
Martin II	June 19, 1979	September 30, 1979	October 28
Martin III	April 5, 1983	October 2, 1983	December 16
Martin IV	April 29, 1985	October 6, 1985	October 27
Martin V	April 5, 1988	June 22, 1988	June 22

April 10, 2015 At Yankee Stadium, it takes 19 innings to lose to the Red Sox, 6-5. Blame it on Chase Headley, whose homer with two outs in the bottom of the ninth ties it. In the 16th inning, David Ortiz homers, but Mark Teixeira matches it. Both teams score again the 18th, but the Yankees have no answer in the 19th for Mookie Betts' game-winning sacrifice fly off Esmil Rogers. . . .

April 10, 2018: The Red Sox rip the Yankees, 14-1, at Fenway Park, including a beautifully ugly nine-run sixth inning. The parade of Sox includes four walks, a hit batter, another one safe on an error, two hits, and to cap it off, a grand slam by Mookie Betts off Chasen Shreve.

April 11, 1961 The Minnesota Twins inaugurate their franchise with a 6-0 win over the Yankees in front of 14,067 chilled fans *on Opening Day* at Yankee Stadium. Whitey Ford, 24-5 against this team when they were the Washington Senators, is in a scoreless duel with Pedro Ramos until the seventh inning. Bob Allison's leadoff homer gives the Twins the lead, and later in the inning, Ramos strokes a two-run single that knocks Ford out. Ramos polishes off a three-hitter to win, 6-0, and, as an overheated Minneapolis reporter notes, "make the Yankees look like just another team."

April 13, 1962 Joe Trimble of the *New York Daily News* calls it "a travesty which bordered on the ridiculous," a game at Tiger Stadium that is delayed for an hour and shouldn't have been played. It's raining when they begin, and snow begins in the third inning, whipped by strong winds and a 36-degree chill that assails a crowd of over 29,000 wolverines. Some fans light fires in the stands. The Yankees lead, 3-2, when someone in the right field grandstand throws a bottle at Roger Maris. Maris races in, brandishing the bottle, finds shelter in the dugout, and refuses to come out. Finally the Tigers send some detectives up there, and the umpire tells Maris he has to bat; he gives the booing fans the finger, but they decline to pelt him with firewood. Meanwhile, Luis Arroyo falls apart, allowing a game-tying triple to Detroit pitcher Frank "The Yankee Killer" Lary and later walking in two runs that are the difference in a 5-3 loss.

April 14, 1967 Making his major league debut at Yankee Stadium, Red Sox left-hander Bill Rohr comes within one out of a no-hitter, yielding only a two-out single to Elston Howard in the bottom of the ninth, two batters after Carl Yastrzemski saves the day with a spectacular catch of Tom Tresh's drive. "It was the first time I ever got a base hit and got booed in New York," Howard marvels. Reggie Smith's leadoff homer off Whitey Ford to start the game is all the support needed by the 21-year-old Rohr, who walks five and strikes out two. Rohr beats the Yankees at Fenway Park a week later with another complete game, then wins only one more game in his major league career.

April 15, 1980 The abiding irony of Jim Kaat's reputation catches up with him today in one of only four appearances he makes with the Yankees in 1980. From 1962-1977, Kaat won the Gold Glove Award for pitchers every season. The irony is that Kaat never led his league's pitchers in fielding percentage, and in fact led twice in errors, including a whopping eight in 1969, with a fielding percentage of .826. He led in assists once and double plays twice—all in his first four full seasons. Entering in the 14th inning of this game at Comiskey Park, Kaat puts Yankees fans through an excruciating inning before finally losing. It starts with a walk and a stolen base, followed by Harry Chappas' bunt to the right of the mound. The 41-year-old Kaat reaches down, bobbles the ball, slips on the turf, and runners are safe on first and third. After an intentional walk, Kaat gets a 1-2-3 double play, but Chet Lemon introduces a new element—a base hit—that wins the game.

April 16, 1940 Although 66 of 77 writers polled picked the Yankees to win their fifth straight championship, the season gets off to an inauspicious start in Philadelphia. Red Ruffing goes the distance but can't beat 181-pound "Chubby" Dean, who's embarking on a 6-13 season for the last-place Athletics. Not only do the Yankees manage just a meager six hits and an unearned run off Dean, but

Ruffing allows Dean, originally a first baseman in the majors, to drive in the winning run in the tenth inning with a sacrifice fly. This unexpected loss throws the Yankees off-balance, and their sluggish 7-14 start is enough to ruin a September run, leaving a third-place finish.

April 17, 1966 A September call-up in 1965, rookie Bobby Murcer is thrilled to start the 1966 season splitting the shortstop job with Ruben Amaro. The 19-year-old Oklahoman grew up idolizing Mickey Mantle, and now he's heralded as Mantle's successor. Well, not so much after today, when Murcer's three errors cost them a game at Baltimore. Trailing 4-3 in the eighth inning, the Orioles have two men on when Yankees pitcher Pete Ramos fields a bunt and throws it to Murcer, who drops it. The two runs that follow give the Orioles a 5-4 win. A few days later, Murcer, after committing 11 errors in 29 games, is sent back to the minors, like Mantle a failed shortstop who later manages to hang on as an outfielder.

A raw 17-year-old in his first year as a pro, Mickey Mantle brought back memories of the days before fielders wore gloves in his first two seasons. The budding shortstop committed 102 errors, earning this assessment by scout Dutch Zwilling in a 1950 report: "Don't believe he is capable of playing short in AAA. If must play shortstop would recommend Class B – possibly A." The brass noted Zwilling's statement that Mantle, a "great hitter," was ready to play AAA ball at 18, and a year later he debuted with the Yankees as a right fielder.

April 18, 2009 In the worst inning in franchise history, the Yankees are battered by a 14-run second-inning punishment administered by the Cleveland Indians at Yankee Stadium. Chien-Ming Wang, after giving up seven runs in his first start of the season, does even worse this time. His second inning goes thusly: single, single, home run, out, double, single, double, double, wild pitch, and, somehow still in the game, one last single before Joe Girardi mercifully hooks him. (Wang, incredibly, is allowed to give up 23 runs in 6 innings in his first three 2009 starts.) Girardi brings in Anthony Claggett, making his big league debut, who follows neatly in Wang's footsteps: double, walk, single, out, homer, homer. That makes it 14-2, and the Indians pound out 25 hits in a giddy 22-4 drubbing. Thanks to that scintillating debut, Claggett's career lasts just three games, with an ERA of 27.00.

April 19, 1979 In the near corner (of the shower): Goose Gossage, raging reliever, 6'3" and 220 pounds. In the far corner: Cliff Johnson, combustible catcher, 6'4" and 225 pounds. Some routine locker-room ribbing about whether Johnson could hit Gossage's fastball escalates into a slippery shoving match and then a fist-fight. The result is a torn ligament in the thumb of Gossage's pitching hand which sidelines him for almost three months. By that time, the Yankees are in fourth place—where they will finish the season—and Johnson has been exiled to Cleveland. Two days after the fight, Gossage admits, "I can't believe it. I just screwed up, that's all."

April 20, 1993 The Yankees think they've pulled off a miracle when they rip Dennis Eckersley for five runs in the top of the ninth inning, erasing a 6-2 deficit. Not so soon. Steve Farr blows the save in the bottom of the ninth at Oakland, and in the tenth inning, John Habyan surrenders a game-winning, two-run homer by Rickey Henderson. . .

April 20, 1997 Displaying some truly dreadful bullpen prowess, Yankees relievers Mike Stanton and Brian Boehringer walk seven White Sox in four innings and pay the price. Stanton walks two batters who come around to score and tie the game, 7-7. In the 11th, a two-out double precedes two Boehringer walks to load the bases and, just for lagniappe, one more walk to force in the winning run.

April 21, 1987 It was bad enough a few weeks earlier when the Yankees screwed their fans with the team's new cable network, SportsChannel. Today, the fans are doubly outraged. It happens that SportsChannel also owns the rights to the Mets,

Islanders, Devils, and Nets, and adding a second channel (available to only 430,000 paying customers) doesn't help much, especially on this day. The network bumps one of its sacred Yankees telecasts to show a playoff hockey game and—the horror!--a Mets game.

April 22, 1938   The celebration at the home opener goes awry at Yankee Stadium, where 25,000 fans are enraged by the time the ceremonial first pitch takes place. Why? Mayor LaGuardia delegated that responsibility to acting mayor Newbold Morris, President of the City Council. Morris, joined by Bronx Borough President James Lyons, find their entrance into the Stadium blocked by picketing members of Local 90 of the Stadium and Sport Center Employees Union. The politicians, ever mindful of the labor vote, refuse to cross the picket line, listening to the (former Stadium) employees' complaints. After twenty minutes of palaver, a promise to look into things Monday morning at City Hall persuades the picketers to let them pass. Meanwhile, do you suppose anybody on the Yankees thought to tell the fans inside the park what was going on? They never do. The spectators sit on their thumbs for a half-hour, and when they finally get a glimpse of the politician they assume has been kissing babies and asses, they serenade him with boos and genuine Bronx cheers.

April 24, 1971   "At the end it looked like the climax of a Fellini movie," reports Murray Chass in the *New York Times.* "Rain falling heavily, lightning flashing, papers swirling around haphazardly, people standing around feeling frustrated and empty." He's talking about the Yankees and their fans after a four-hour fiasco in the Bronx, though only a scattering of the 10,204 paying customers remain. The Yankees leave 20 runners on base in an 11-inning, 11-8 loss to the Twins. They get 17 hits and draw 11 walks, but leave the bases loaded three times. Their four pinch-hitters strand eight runners on base. Manager Ralph Houk is ejected midway through, and with all those pinch-hitters and a pinch-runner, Houk's stand-in runs out of players after Bill Burbach gives up three runs in the top of the 11th. With two outs and two men on, the Yankees send the tying run to the plate—Burbach, a career .085 hitter, who grounds out weakly to end the ordeal.

| April 25, 1933 | Bad blood between the Yankees and Senators erupts into a 15-minute brawl at Griffith Stadium. It has boiled over from **July 4, 1932**, when Bill Dickey broke the jaw of Senators outfielder Carl Reynolds. Today, it's the fault of Yankees left fielder Ben Chapman, who literally goes out of his way to spike Washington's second baseman Charles Solomon "Buddy" Myer, a well-known Jewish player who waited until after his playing career to mention that he wasn't. Chapman spiked Myer three times in 1932 and detours well left to spike him as he turns a double play. Myer has finally had enough, and after a moment of grappling, they're both ejected. In what could happen only at an old-time ballpark, Chapman has to walk through the Senators' dugout to get to his own locker room. En route, he tries to cold-cock Earl Whitehill, and this time the brawl is on. Both teams spill onto the diamond, where they are soon joined by hundreds of fans, five of whom are arrested. Chapman is suspended for just a few games, his biases encouraged, and he gains lasting notoriety for his vitriolic and racist taunting of Jackie Robinson as the Phillies manager in 1947.

| April 26, 1931 | In another embarrassment at Griffith Stadium, Lou Gehrig is bamboozled out of the home run title by teammate Lyn Lary. It was ridiculously difficult to hit a home run there; from 1926-1931, the Senators *team* averaged fewer than a dozen home runs per season. So there's Lyn Lary at first base with two outs when Lou Gehrig rockets a shot to dead center field, an impossible-to-reach 441 feet from home plate. Lary trots around to third base with his head down and veers into the dugout, assuming the ball was caught. Gehrig, also running with his head down after watching the ball disappear into the bleachers, reaches home plate and is informed that he's out for passing Lary on the basepath. In the short run, it costs the Yankees two runs in a game they lose, 9-7. However, in the long run it leaves Gehrig not only tied with Babe Ruth at 46 that year but stuck forever in a career deadlock with Fred McGriff at 493. Damn you, Lary!

April 27, 1967 The *New York Daily News* serves up this juicy headline: "Houk Claims No-Hitter as MacRae Hits the Deck." It seems that the Yankees manager and his wife, Betty, visit the Waldorf-Astoria last night to take in the show of his pal, singer Gordon MacRae. After performing, MacRae joins them, Toots Shor, Shor's wife, and another couple for drinks. Properly lubricated, MacRae takes each of the wives for a spin on the dance floor. Recently divorced from his singing partner, Sheila, MacRae also favors each dance partner with a hearty kiss. Just as he plants one on Betty, ex-Marine Ralph arrives with her coat. He drops the coat. Then he drops MacRae, knocking him unconscious for two minutes. When MacRae comes to, Toots Shor tells him, "you slipped," and MacRae agrees. They're all buddies again the next day, as Shor chirps, "If anybody gets credit, I want it. Say I flattened them both."

April 29, 1966 After dropping to sixth place in 1965, the Yankees suspect that their dynasty is toast, and today provides clear proof. Averaging a sickly 2.6 runs per game during a rollicking 2-11 start in the American League, they travel to West Point for the annual exhibition game against the Army team. The Yankees' sad state is revealed by the pre-game agreement to play just seven innings—but if the Yankees are losing, the soldiers will give them a chance to catch up. They almost need it. They do score a run in the top of the first inning on two singles and a ground out by Mickey Mantle. But that's it. They get just four hits off Army's Barry DeBolt, who strikes out eight and walks nobody. Jim Bouton hurls six shutout innings for the Yankees, who escape with a 1-0 victory. Then they return home and get back in their groove, getting shut out three times in the next five days.

April 30, 1946 After losing nearly four seasons to World War II service in the Navy, Bob Feller takes a 1-2 record to the mound at Yankee Stadium before 38,112 fans. The game is scoreless to the ninth inning, and Feller has a no-hitter going. With one out, his battery-mate, catcher Frankie Hayes, makes things much easier by belting a home run off Bill Bevens. In the home half, George Stirnweiss tries to bunt his way on, and he succeeds when the first baseman fumbles it. With the announcement that it has been scored an error, the Yankee Stadium crowd erupts with cheers. Henrich also bunts, this one good for a sacrifice. Joe DiMaggio works the count full and hits a ball sharply to shortstop Lou Boudreau, who secures the second out. Next comes Charlie "King Kong" Keller, who grounds out to second to give Feller his second no-hitter. Feller walks five Yankees and strikes out 11, throwing 133 pitches, and an awed Joe DiMaggio claims, "Anybody who had the stuff Feller had today deserved a no-hitter. We didn't hit the ball solid all day."

May

May 1, 1969 Augmenting a paltry paid crowd of 7,170 at Yankee Stadium, the Yankees give away 8,000 free tickets to children and senior citizens. The spirit of giving continues as they hand a 6-2 victory to Cleveland, which had lost 15 of 16 games before enjoying the hospitality in the Bronx. Stan Bahnsen takes a no-hitter to the seventh inning, but Bobby Murcer, proving that he's an even worse third baseman than a shortstop, commits a key error (one of 14 in 31 games there), and it's 2-2 to the ninth. Steve Hamilton gives up four runs, three on a Duke Sims home run following an intentional walk. This is the Yankees' third straight loss during a gloriously dismal stretch during which they lose 13 of 14 games while scoring just 29 runs (1-0-2-1-4-3-2-2-2-2-3-0-4-3) and allowing 77.

May 2, 2014 Chris Leroux had a 1-2 record with a 5.56 ERA in the majors when the Yankees claimed him on waivers last winter. Today the 30-year-old's big league career comes to a crashing halt against Tampa Bay at Yankee Stadium. Leroux enters in the 14th inning, walks the leadoff man, and after fanning Evan Longoria, he fails to retire any of the next six hitters. Credit one run to manager Joe Girardi, who, observing this batting practice, makes Leroux walk one batter intentionally. Two singles later, the Rays lead, 10-5, and Leroux winds up his career at 1-3 and 6.03, never rising above the minors again.

May 3, 1912 The 1912 season was as jam-packed with low-lights as any in franchise history, their 102 losses unchallenged in more than a century. Here's a deliciously frustrating loss that drops them into a comfortable 4-11 record. They spot the hometown Athletics a seven-run first inning, then lull them through the middle innings, arriving at the ninth with an 18-5 deficit. Connie Mack auditions two pitchers who retire just one of a dozen Yankees, until he brings in a real pitcher, Eddie Plank, who ends the burlesque one batter later on a strikeout plus a pickoff. The Highlanders become the only team ever to waste a ten-run ninth inning, losing 18-15, en route to the highest ERA in the league and a last-place finish, 55 games behind the first-place Athletics.

May 4, 1984   The Yankees' lineup today is full of solid professional hitters: Don Mattingly, Dave Winfield, Ken Griffey Sr., Willie Randolph, Oscar Gamble, Steve Kemp, Roy Smalley, and Butch Wynegar. Don Baylor is ready on the bench. Yet they are shut out for the seventh time already this season, falling to an 8-16 record. Yesterday they were held to a Mattingly single by LaMarr Hoyt in Chicago. Today they explode for three hits off Chuck Porter and Rollie Fingers at Milwaukee. Tomorrow they'll get a run, lead 1-0 with two outs in the ninth inning, and lose again. The offense has vanished, and Phil Niekro takes today's tough loss on an error, a walk, a hit batter, and a sacrifice fly. "I was once on a team that lost 16 in a row," says a philosophical Niekro, "so I know I've seen bad before." It's deja vu all over again.

May 5, 2016   The Yankees have lost 14 of their last 19 games, dropping into last place as they tackle the Orioles at Camden Yards. It's Masahiro Tanaka vs. Kevin Gausman, and neither man gives up a run in eight innings. Displaying their penchant for trusting ballgames to unknowns who wind up with 1-3 career records, the Yankees hand the ball to Johnny Barbato in the bottom of the ninth, still scoreless. He promptly surrenders two singles, and Andrew Miller comes in to serve up the game-winning sacrifice fly. It's a desultory symptom of a fourth-place season.

May 6, 1915 Making his sixth start in the major leagues, 20-year-old Red Sox southpaw Babe Ruth is sabotaged by two unearned runs and loses to the Yankees, 4-3, in 13 innings. Along the way, he pounds his first home run in the American League, along with two singles, making Yankees right-hander Jack Warhop the answer to an enduring trivia question. "Ruth, who impressed the onlookers as being a hitter of the first rank," reported the *Boston Globe*, "swatted a low ball into the upper tier of the right-field grandstand and trotted about the bases to slow music." He becomes famous for his mincing home-run trot, with skinny ankles holding up his ever-increasing bulk.

May 7, 1957 It's an accident, but it's still the worst injury inflicted by a Yankee on an opposing player since Carl Mays killed Ray Chapman with a beanball back in 1920. Third baseman Gil McDougald nails Indians pitcher Herb Score in the eye with a line drive, and neither player is ever the same. Score, a 23-year-old southpaw who was better in his second season than Sandy Koufax was in his seventh, has won 36 games and two strikeout titles in those seasons, but he wins just 17 games the rest of his career, battling arm problems and psychological issues. McDougald can't shake the horror and the guilt, fades after 1957 and retires three years later at age 32, having wrecked two careers with one swing of the bat.

May 8, 1990 The Yankees lose to the A's for the fifth time already this season, a 5-0 pasting in Oakland. "This is tough," admits Yankees manager Bucky Dent. "I've never seen anything like this." Get used to it, Bucky. The A's sweep all 12 games from the Yankees this season, outscoring them 62-12 in the process (0-2-0-1-0-1-0-1-1-1-2-3). On second thought, Bucky, never mind. Four weeks later, he is liberated from his Bronx bondage, ending his managing tenure with a record of 36-53. Some guy they call "Stump" takes his place, and the Yankees finish dead last in their division with a 67-95 record.

May 9, 1997 The screwiest play of the season ends with a neat piece of baseball karma. It isn't even covered in the rules, so the umpires get it wrong at least twice. See if you're as confused as they were: 3-0 Yankees, bases loaded with Royals in the sixth inning, one out, grounder to third, step on the bag for the force, wild throw to first, runner races from first to third, rounds the bag too far, rundown looming, and suddenly the third-base umpire calls him out for passing another runner, ending the inning, teams change sides, umps quickly confer, and crew chief sends Yankees back on field, letting the run score and putting runners on second and third, huh? The runner he passed was the guy already forced at third, dawdling in the vicinity, not in play and thus okay to pass, ah. Naturally the next guy singles to tie it, and the Royals win thanks to a Derek Jeter throwing error. Manager Joe Torre whines, "I can't see how the umpires stop the play and then we get penalized because they screwed up." The explanation is quite simple: karma. The crew chief improvising this call is Richie Garcia, the same ump who cowered on the warning track in right field in the 1996 playoffs instead of calling interference on Jeffrey Maier.

May 10, 1980 Here's an unlikely but great pitching duel between southpaws Darrell Jackson (Twins) and Tom Underwood (Yankees). Underwood pitches into the ninth inning but can't match Jackson, who gives the Yankees just five hits in ten innings. The Yankees get a runner across the plate on a failed double play, but it isn't a run. Yankees great Eric Soderholm is called out for interference when—after being forced at second—he veers well out of his way to clobber shortstop Roy Smalley, making the pivot. This targeting was still tolerated into the 21st century and was rarely called forty years ago, but Twins manager Gene Mauch notes, "It was a dumb play because Roy wasn't even going to throw to first. . .I understand Eric's intention, but he was ill-advised." Yankees manager Dick Howser says simply, "I like aggressive play, and that was an aggressive play." The Twins win, 1-0, in the 11th inning.

May 12, 1961 Bronx native Rocco Domenico "Rocky" Colavito is enjoying life at Yankee Stadium on a lovely Friday evening while his Tigers teammate, Frank "Yankee Killer" Lary, beats them for the umpteenth time. Rocky always has a big cheering section in left field, and his wife, father, and brother are there tonight. Trotting off the field after the eighth inning, he's shocked to spot his father fighting with some drunken fan. "I always look up there," Colavito explains later, "and when I saw my father struggling with somebody, I went right over the rail. My father is 60, and nobody is going to hit him while I'm there." Colavito races up the aisle, knocking fans over in his frenzy to get at his father's foe. More Tigers race after him, and they restrain him about the time the minor scuffle breaks up. The drunken Yankees fan (pardon the redundancy) harassed Colavito's wife until her in-laws came to the rescue. Colavito is ejected, and American League president Joe Cronin has a predictably paternalistic explanation for not suspending the slugger: "It wasn't the right thing for the boy to go up into the stands," says Cronin. "But I guess it was natural for him to want to help his father."

May 13, 1991 Yankee Stadium fans display their innate compassion by mercilessly harassing Jose Canseco of the A's. He's having a tough time, what with the whole steroids thing coming to light, his marriage difficulties, and that much-publicized, late-night visit to Madonna after his arrival in Manhattan. What drives him nuts are the taunts that he should go home to Cuba, and the profanity, which he describes as "so disgusting, you can't even write it." He doesn't pull a Colavito, but he does accost his tormentors and succeeds in getting one schmuck from New Jersey ejected. Teammate Rickey Henderson sympathizes with him. "You start talking about the family and other people, and them is fighting words."

May 14

May 14: It's time to commemorate this particularly miserable calendar date in the baseball
life of Billy Martin:

- **1950:** Unable to win the second base job from Jerry Coleman,
  Martin is shipped back to the minor leagues. He takes it personally, screaming at GM George Weiss, "I'll make you pay for
  abusing me like this! I'll get even!"
- **1977:** After badmouthing George Steinbrenner and GM Gabe
  Paul, Martin I is fined $2,500 by the team. Martin wants a
  catcher, they give him an outfielder, and he explodes. Steinbrenner fires back, "Martin lied about the whole situation. He
  has been in violation of his contract four distinct times. He
  could be fired right now." Paul persuades The Boss to hold that
  thought.
- **1978:** That thought returns after an incident on the flight
  home from Kansas City after a tough, 10-9 loss. Several players
  complain to Martin about Mickey Rivers' lack of effort. Martin
  tells them to settle it themselves and wants Thurman Munson,
  the Captain, to be the heavy. Munson prefers to do his own
  bullying, not Martin's, and when he balks, Martin goes nuts,
  berating him and nearly making the mistake of trying to fight
  him. This soap opera marks the beginning of the end for
  Martin's first roller-coaster ride as Yankees manager.

May 15, 1957

In the most infamous night out on the town in
baseball history, a half-dozen Yankees and
their wives make the rounds to celebrate bachelor Billy Martin's birthday,
which starts at midnight. At 2:30 AM, at the Copacabana nightclub,
heckling by a nearby group of drunks bothers the Yankees, and pretty
soon there's a procession to the men's room, where outfielder Hank
Bauer, a former Marine known to his teammates as "Bruiser," breaks a
delicatessen owner's nose and knocks him out. This provides fodder for
the newspapers for days, and all six Yankees, including Mickey Mantle,
Yogi Berra, and Whitey Ford, are fined $1,000 by the team. George Weiss

blithely assumes that Martin threw the punch and uses the bad publicity as an excuse to exile Martin to Kansas City. Martin never does get revenge on Weiss, dumped by the Yankees in 1960, but he takes his anger out on plenty of other New Yorkers over the next three decades.

May 16, 1968 The Yankees are cruising at Fenway Park with a 10-5 lead in the eighth inning and ace Mel Stottlemyre on the mound. Rookie third baseman Bobby Cox is thinking about his .194 batting average three weeks after being handed the job. He's 0-for-3 today with two strikeouts, and he has a measly two extra-base hits in his first 67 at-bats. Leadoff batter Jose Tartabull hits an easy grounder to Cox, whose throw sails wide for an error. That opens a floodgate—four hits, two walks, and two pitchers later, it's 10-10 with a runner on third. The Red Sox win on a squeeze bunt, and Cox senses a growing awareness that his future is not in playing baseball.

May 17, 1981 The managers spin themselves dizzy with mid-game stratagems that add up to a 1-0 Mariners win before a crowd of 54,223 fans on "Bat Day" at Yankee Stadium. It starts as a duel between left-handers Floyd Bannister and Ron Guidry, who leaves after five innings with a foot injury. In comes Ron Davis, who gives up two hits and a sacrifice fly. In the bottom of the sixth, with two outs and runners on second and third, Mariners manager Rene Lachemann brings in righty Dick Drago, who walks Barry Foote to load the bases. Yankees manager Gene Michael sends up lefty Jim Spencer to pinch-hit, and Lachemann counters by bringing in southpaw Shane Rawley, who gets Spencer for the third out. In the seventh inning, with two outs and a runner on second, Lachemann walks Dave Winfield intentionally to let Rawley challenge Reggie Jackson, who takes a called third strike. Game, set, match, Seattle.

May 18, 1962 Mickey Mantle bats with two outs in the bottom of the ninth inning, the Yankees trailing the Twins, 4-3, and the tying run on second. He smashes the ball to deep shortstop, where Zoilo Versalles snares it, fumbles it, and makes the long throw to first. As Mantle describes it, "I thought I had a shot at it. I noticed that he fumbled the ball and I tried to give it a little extra. All of a sudden, I heard something pop in my [right] thigh. Then I toppled over." Minnesota's Bernie Allen hears the pop from his position at second base. Mantle goes down in a heap less than ten feet from first base, the easy final out of the game. "I thought I broke this leg then," Mantle told Jane Leavy, author of *The Last Boy*, years later. "It wouldn't come back down. It just stuck up, and when I fell, I tore this [left] knee up." Teammates help him off the field, and he leaves Yankee Stadium on crutches for a night at Lenox Hospital. The verdict is a torn adductor muscle in his right hip and strained ligaments behind his left knee. This latest devastating leg injury sidelines him for five weeks.

May 19, 1998 Yankee Stadium, host to dozens of boxing title matches over the years, hosts one of baseball's nastiest brawls. When Orioles reliever Armando Benitez nails Tino Martinez in the back following a home run in the eighth inning, Martinez, plunked earlier by Doug Johns, takes it personally and charges the mound, igniting the action. The teams square off for ten minutes; George Steinbrenner calls it "the worst brawl I've seen in 25 years," and he ought to know. Yankees reliever Graeme Lloyd, racing in from the bullpen, is somehow the first to punch Benitez, who retreats in front of his dugout. In succession, he is charged by Scott Brosius, Jeff Nelson, and Darryl Strawberry, who succeeds in punching Benitez in the face, launching Round 2 of the fight. The mess sprawls across the field and spills into the Orioles dugout while the bloodthirsty Yankee Stadium crowd of 31,311 roars with delight. Says Strawberry, "I took a couple of knocks. It was like a hockey game." Five players are ejected.

May 20, 1976 In their first meeting of the season, the Yankees lead the Red Sox, 1-0, in the sixth inning when all hell breaks loose. Lou Piniella tries to score from second on a single but is out by a mile, so he crashes into Carlton Fisk, who tags him between the eyes with the ball. As they tangle in the dirt, the benches empty and the battle begins, with skirmishes all over the place. You know it's a nasty fight when Thurman Munson is the peacemaker. Graig Nettles body-slams pitcher Bill Lee, resulting in a shoulder injury which keeps Lee out of the rotation until August. When Lee screams at him, Nettles punctuates the festivities by punching him in the eye. The enraged Red Sox pound three late home runs to win, 8-2. Addressing the press, Nettles insists, "I could have hurt him a lot worse if I wanted to when he was on the ground, but I'm not like that." Kudos for drawing the line at kicking the man when he was down.

Over the years, Bill Lee became the most celebrated Yankees-hater among active players. On **March 17, 1977**, still recovering from the shoulder injury, Lee summed up the experience: "Last year I was assaulted by George Steinbrenner's Nazis, his Brown Shirts. He brainwashes those kids over there and they're led by Billy Martin—Herman Goering 2nd. They've got a convicted felon running the club. What else do you expect?" Indeed.

May 21, 1930 Isn't it bizarre that even though Babe Ruth hit three homers in a game twice in the World Series, he did it only twice in the regular season? This is one of them, and they're all wonderfully wasted. At Shibe Park, Ruth homers off George Earnshaw his first time up, and in his second trip, he hits one out of the ballpark and into the backyard across the street, helping the Yankees to a 6-0 lead. The third one doesn't come until the eighth inning, off Lefty Grove, and by then the Athletics lead, 13-6, thanks to a nine-run seventh inning.

May 22, 1992 Steve Howe, midway through his journey toward the major league record for drug suspensions, makes Yankees fans wonder what he's on after an ugly relief appearance at Yankee Stadium against the Brewers. They applaud when he enters with a 9-4 lead in the eighth inning, the bases loaded, and nobody out. Just like that, there's a two-run single, and the next guy hits a sacrifice fly. The Yankees want Howe to appeal the runner leaving third base too soon, and he tries to oblige. But his ho-hum toss sails into the box seats behind third base, and a wild pitch makes it 9-8. After a single, Howe is replaced, and he trudges off the mound, greeted by the kind of raucous booing that comes after seven innings of guzzling beer. The runner he leaves behind scores, the Yankees lose in 14 innings, and two weeks later, Howe's season is over. Commissioner Fay Vincent suspends him after he pleads guilty to a cocaine possession charge in Montana.

May 23, 2010 CC Sabathia will soon go on a nine-game winning streak, but not before he gets this embarrassing loss out of the way. At Citi Field, Sabathia faces fellow lefty Johan Santana, who gives up just one run before leaving in the eighth inning. The Mets drill Sabathia for four runs in the second inning, and Jason Bay's two homers give them a 6-1 lead. The Yankees rally in the ninth inning, make it 6-4, and put the tying runs on base, but K-Rod fans A-Rod to end it. . .

May 23, 2015 CC Sabathia's stars are again out of alignment against the visiting Rangers. In the third inning, he gives up six runs while getting just one out, and the man who relieves him pours gasoline on the fire. That's Esmil Rogers, and it's 10-0 by the time he gets the third out. He gives up three more runs before concluding his contribution to a 15-4 pasting. Three appearances later, Rogers' career is done, when the Yankees release him and his 5.59 career ERA.

May 24, 1918 In the longest game ever at the Polo Grounds, the Indians beat the Yankees, 3-2, in 19 innings. The hero is Smoky Joe Wood, a 34-game winner in 1912 who blew out his arm and is now a left fielder. In the seventh inning, he "lines the ball like a rifle shot into the left field open bleacher," as the *New York Times* describes it, breaking a scoreless tie. The Yankees tie it in the bottom of the ninth, and reliever George Mogridge battles the Indians through a bunch of extra innings. For the Indians, future Hall of Famer Stan Coveleski permits eighteen Yankees to reach base, but nobody scores after Ping Bodie's ninth-inning sacrifice fly. In the top of the 19th, Wood does it again. According to the *Times*, "it travels with the same wicked velocity, in the very same direction and lands in almost the same spot." Coveleski pitches all nineteen innings for the victory.

May 25, 1922   The 1922 season has been awful for Babe Ruth so far. Suspended for unauthorized barn-storming after the 1921 season, he has been back for just five games and is batting .095, not even half his weight. This is also his sixth game as the Yankees' captain, the most responsibility he's had in his life. He shrugs it off like so many hotdog wrappers, taking his frustration out on umpire George Hildebrand, who calls him out trying to stretch a single into a double. Ruth comes up with a handful of dirt he throws at Hildebrand, who ejects him. Taunted by the Polo Grounds crowd, Ruth hears the magic words from a fan described as "particularly lungful." He climbs over the dugout and into the crowd, charging after his tormentor, who quickly escapes. For his adventure, Ruth is suspended one game and gets a going-over in the press. "Babe Ruth Still Trying To Prove He Is Bigger Than Organized Baseball," reads a typical headline. Ruth can't help defending himself: "They can boo and hoot me all they want. That doesn't matter to me. But when a fan calls insulting names from the grandstand and becomes abusive I don't intend to stand for it. . .I would go into the stands again if I had to." You betcha, but not as captain, as the Yankees relieve him of that burden.

May 26, 1907   It's a miserable day at South Side Park in Chicago, just right for bringing out the bush-league instincts of the Highlanders. Ed Walsh of the White Sox gives them an early run without a hit, but the White Sox counter with four runs off Al Orth. It's raining the whole time, and it gets worse in the fourth inning, bringing a delay. New York manager Clark Griffith makes his first pitching appearance of the year after play resumes, with a goal of stalling so that they can't finish 4½ innings to make the game official. He takes all the time he can, making endless tosses to first base until the runner refuses to step off the bag. Forced to pitch, he gives up easy hits and more runs. The rain gets harder, but the White Sox and the umpires don't coop-erate, and finally the game is official. One more storm in the bottom of the fifth inning brings rain, hail, and lightning, and it goes in the books as an 8-1 victory and a no-hitter for Ed Walsh.

May 27, 1995 The Yankees' offense consists solely of a sixth-inning single by Luis Polonia, a high hopper which just eludes pitcher Steve Ontiveros and rolls into center field. Ontiveros, who tossed a two-hitter at the Yankees in 1994, walks two men and strikes out seven. "Ontiveros pitched well," admits manager Buck Showalter, "but put it this way: we're not swinging the bat well." Nice understatement by Buck, who can't just admit that his offense sucks. That's nine losses in eleven games, with just six runs scored during the current five-game losing streak. It isn't getting better soon, either. After salvaging one win at Oakland, they lose ten of their next twelve, plunging to last place. Hard to believe they're so helpless with a lineup that includes Don Mattingly, Wade Boggs, Paul O'Neill, Bernie Williams, and Danny Tartabull, but that's too bad.

May 28, 1996 Kenny Rogers pitches seven innings of no-hit ball in Anaheim before Garret Anderson leads off the eighth with a soft line drive to center for a single. Rogers takes a one-hitter to the bottom of the ninth, but not a lead, because the Yankees come up empty against Ross Grimsley, who's safely in the dugout with a five-hit shutout. Rogers is quickly sabotaged by rookie utility man Andy Fox, giving Derek Jeter a rare day off at shortstop. Fox makes his second throwing error of the game, putting Rex Hudler on base with one out. Randy Velarde doubles Hudler to third, and after Rogers intentionally walks the next guy, he unintentionally walks Chili Davis to force in the winning run. A disgusted Rogers says, "I kind of wish someone would have just hit a home run. It wouldn't have felt good, but it would have been easier to digest." Says Fox, "It stinks. . .I'm not going to sleep too well." The important thing is that Jeter gets his day of rest so he can be back in the lineup tomorrow when they get shut out again.

May 29, 1987 The Oakland A's come to town and waste no time teeing off on Dennis Rasmussen, as the team hits for the cycle in the top of the first inning. Tony Phillips singles, Jose Canseco homers, Ron Cey doubles, and, after an intentional walk, Mike Davis triples to make it 4-0. Rasmussen doesn't make it through the second inning, and the A's cruise to a 13-5 win. In a masterpiece of understatement after the game, manager Lou Piniella concedes, "He's laying the ball in there and they're teeing off. He might be in a little bit of a rut." Despite an 18-6 record in 1986, Rasmussen's neck is in a New York noose. He hangs on until August, when he is traded to Cincinnati along with his 9-7 record and 4.75 ERA.

May 30 Way back when, Memorial Day was May 30 and baseball celebrated with nothing but doubleheaders. Here are some memorable sweeps:

- **1947:** Spud Chandler loses a three-hitter in the opener at Philadelphia, 1-0, and the Yankees lose the nightcap, 4-0. The shutouts are authored by Dick Fowler—later Billy Martin's longtime drinking buddy and pitching coach—and Joe Coleman.
- **1951:** The Yankees waste a seven-run inning at Fenway Park as the Red Sox rally and win on a Vern Stephens homer in the 15th inning. In the nightcap, a five-run seventh erases a 4-2 Yankees lead. Ted Williams honors Memorial Day by going 7-for-12 on the day, with three doubles, a triple, a home run, and five RBI.
- **1958:** The last-place Senators stun the Yankees twice, 13-8 and 7-2. Three-run home runs by Roy Sievers and Ken Aspromonte in the eighth inning key the first victory. In the nightcap, Sievers and Jim Lemon both hit a pair of home runs.

May 31, 1995 The Yankees conclude a disastrous 1-8 trip to the West Coast with a disturbing 11-9 loss in Seattle. Lots of things upset them:

- In the sixth inning, Jim Leyritz is beaned by the scariest pitcher in baseball, Randy Johnson, whose fastball deflects off Leyritz's shoulder and nails him in the cheek. He survives.

- When Johnson isn't ejected, manager Buck Showalter wags his finger in umpire Tim Tschida's face and is kicked out of the game.
- The Yankees blow two-run leads in consecutive innings, and Tino Martinez's three-run home run off Bob MacDonald gives the Mariners the lead for good.
- The loss is the Yankees' twelfth in their last fifteen games, part of a dismal 5-19 stretch between May 13 and June 10.

June

The Yankees demonstrate the wrong way to handle adversity after blowing an 8-3 lead at Milwaukee. Yankees reliever Jim Roland pitches four strong innings before blowing sky-high in the 12th inning. He walks ex-Yankee Mike Ferraro and, after a sacrifice, he walks Bill Voss. After the second out, he walks Ron Theobald. Up comes Rick Auerbach. Who are these guys? Voss, Theobald, Auerbach—sounds like a Swiss bobsled squad, yet they're too much for Roland. He walks Auerbach and forces in the winning run. When home plate umpire Jim Kunkel—who pitched for the Yankees in 1963—calls the 3-2 pitch ball four, the Yankees go nuts. Roland charges Kunkel, shakes a baseball in his face, and heaves the ball into the outfield. Thurman Munson invades the umpires' locker room to berate the startled arbiters, and Ralph Houk goes off on a reporter who asks why he didn't replace Roland. "What do you want me to do, ruin the guy [relief ace Sparky Lyle] who's been winning every ball game for us? Should I pitch him 180 games a week? What if he comes up with a sore arm? What do I do then? Who do you think I was going to bring in, the damn center-field post?" Before long, Roland is pitching for the Rangers.

From the "Managing Is Fun" department: Yogi Berra uses twenty players in a ten-inning game at Toronto, losing 9-8, and it takes a team effort to blow the game in the tenth inning. Clay Christiansen (2-4, 6.05 ERA for the Yankees in his only season in the majors) hits a batter, and catcher Butch Wynegar picks him off but throws the ball away, sending the runner to second base. After another walk, Yogi brings in Bob Shirley, who walks the next batter to load the bases. Yogi twitches again, bringing in Curt Brown, but Ernie Whitt smacks his first pitch for a game-winning hit. That is Brown's last pitch as a Yankee. Wynegar says—before this ugly loss, the Yankees' tenth in fourteen games: "How much of this can we take? How much of this can George [Steinbrenner] take? I could not sleep last night. This is torture." No wonder he can't throw straight.

June 3-8   **Draft disasters:** The amateur draft was created to prevent wealthier teams like the Yankees from stockpiling prized prospects. The first one was held on June 8, 1965, with the Yankees getting one pick per round just like everybody else, forcing them to use judgment in addition to their checkbook. We'll celebrate some of the worst judgments and wastes of money here, listed by calendar date.

June 3, 1975   The Yankees take high school first baseman Jim McDonald with the 19th pick, ahead of Andre Dawson, Lee Smith, Lou Whitaker, and Dave Stewart. McDonald never makes it past AAA.

June 3, 1991   With the first overall pick, the Yankees take can't-miss phenom Brien Taylor, who pitched 84 innings in high school this spring, allowing just 18 hits while striking out 203 batters. After two seasons in the minors, he wrecks his arm in a bar fight and never makes it to the majors.

June 4, 1970   With the twelfth overall pick, the Yankees grab 19-year-old lefty Dave Cheadle, who once struck out 49 batters (!) in a Babe Ruth League game (suspended for three days and lasting 23 innings, but hey, they didn't coddle pitchers in those days). As a pro, he can't find home plate; in 1973-1974, he issues 209 walks in 230 innings. His major league career consists of two innings—with Atlanta in 1973. Still, that's two more innings than the Yankees' second draft choice, Rick Earle. Who'd they miss? Just Goose Gossage and Dave Parker.

June 5, 1969   You could make an all-star team from the players drafted after the Yankees tab Charlie Spikes with the eleventh overall pick. Spikes hits .147 in 34 at-bats as a Yankee. Here's that all-star team: Dave Winfield, Bert Blyleven, Ken Griffey, Sr., Dwight Evans, Buddy Bell, Bob Boone, Bill Madlock, and Rick Burleson.

June 5, 1963   On another note, Mickey Mantle suffers the latest of several grotesque leg injuries. Leaping for a home run ball at Memorial Stadium in Baltimore, he somehow gets his left foot caught in the wire-mesh fence, breaking it. This sidelines him for two months, and pretty soon he has to get wrapped in bandages befitting a mummy just to make it onto the field.

June 6, 1967   Here's another all-star team—of players the Yankees bypassed while squandering the first overall pick on Ron Blomberg, a nice guy but a first baseman with only 52 career home runs. We have Vida Blue, Jerry Reuss, Ted Simmons, Don Baylor, Bobby Grich, John Mayberry (a first baseman who hit 255 homers), Dusty Baker, Darrell Evans, Davey Lopes, and Al Hrabosky. GM Lee MacPhail gushes, "I feel Ronnie is the best prep prospect to come along in several years. We had six of our scouts watch Ronnie and they unanimously agreed that he was the one we should sign." No wonder it takes them another decade to win a title.

June 6, 1978   With three first-round picks, the Yankees load up on Rex Hudler, Matt Winters, and Brian Ryder, somehow missing out on Cal Ripken, Jr., Ryne Sandberg, Kent Hrbek, Kirk Gibson, Bob Horner, and Dave Stieb.

June 7, 1985   Back in these pre-wild card days, losing the division race meant going home to dwell on the wins you turned into losses. This is one such game, one reason the Yankees lose the division to Toronto by two games. "Walks, too many damn walks," moans Billy Martin, and he isn't kidding. The Yankees come back five times from deficits in this complicated affair at Milwaukee, but when it counts, walks kill them. Their only lead is 7-6 in the eighth inning, but a pair of one-out walks precede a Paul Molitor triple, and it's 9-7 Brewers after eight innings. Just as in the 1960 World Series, the Yankees tie it in the top of the ninth before losing, 10-9, though they don't give it away until the tenth inning. Dave Righetti walks leadoff man Jim Gantner, and when Don Mattingly fields a bunt and throws too late to second base, both runners are safe. This time Molitor bunts them over, and Charlie Moore cashes in the winning run with a hard smash to third baseman Andre Robertson, who falls to his knees in snaring it and throws late to the plate. "You can't win games coming back like we did and giving it right back with walks," says Martin sagely. "You can't defense against the walk."

June 8, 1965   For our final, fond look at the Yankees' worst picks in the amateur draft, we go back to the first one, when they select Bill Burbach with the 19th overall pick. Which is worse: what they get or what they miss? They get a 6'4", 215-pound right-hander from Wisconsin who posts records of 2-9 and 3-14 in his first two minor league seasons. He climbs up the ladder anyway to a parent club that has recently gone down the tubes. His major league career consists of 37 appearances for the Yankees from 1969-1971, with a 6-11 record. Meanwhile, they miss out on Nolan Ryan, Johnny Bench, Hal McRae, Sal Bando, Amos Otis, and Ken Holtzman. Good call, Ralph Houk!

June 9, 2000   In a dream game for Mets fans, Mike Piazza's third-inning grand slam off Roger Clemens ignites a 12-2 Mets romp in front of 55,822 paying customers at Yankee Stadium. Clemens allows nine runs in five-plus innings and now sports an ugly 13.17 ERA in three career starts against the Mets, which begins to explain his sudden urge to throw a broken bat at Piazza in the World Series later this year. Clemens now sports a 4-6 record and a 4.82 ERA, and after exiting to a cacophony of boos, he tells reporters, "I was as hacked off as anybody. About the situation, about the way things were turning out."

A few months later, Clemens got his payback in Game 2 of the World Series. When Piazza dribbled a ball foul near the plate and took a few steps up the line, Clemens took the barrel of Piazza's sheared-off bat and threw it at him. The bat sailed just in front of the startled Piazza. Joe Torre, in *The Yankee Years*, described coach Mel Stottlemyre following Clemens into the clubhouse after the inning and finding him in tears, horrified by his own burst of roid rage.

June 10, 1908 A routine extra-inning loss drops the High-landers' record to 23-21, nothing to fret over. New York blows three leads against the Tigers at Bennett Field in Detroit, and Ty Cobb drives in the winning run in the 12th inning. This launches the worst prolonged stretch in franchise history; in the next 10 weeks, they will win exactly 10 games while losing 52, featuring distinct losing streaks of 7, 6, 6, 7, 12, and 7 games. While losing 19 of 20, they score more than three runs only twice, and once their offense goes in the tank, it never emerges. Shut out 20 times in setting a franchise record with 103 losses, the horrid offense averages 2.9 runs per game for the season! Outfielder Charlie Hemphill leads the team with 44 RBI, thanks to a *team* OPS of .575. In a true team effort, their pitching staff also has the majors' worst ERA.

June 11, 1948 The 67,924 fans at Yankee Stadium enjoy a pre-game exhibition of obedience skills and drills by 24 dogs, then turn rabid themselves in the fourth inning. Yogi Berra forgets himself after hitting a three-run homer, thinks he rules the world, and throws multiple tantrums over umpire Cal Hubbard's judgment of balls and strikes. Hubbard ejects Berra, and the outraged Yankees faithful pelt him with everything they can find. Joe Trimble of the *New York Daily News* provides this inventory: beer cans, vendor cartons, a tennis ball, and one especially Yankee-ish fellow who races onto the field and heaves a cardboard container from thirty feet away that just misses Hubbard. The dogs behaved much better. Once special police restore order and eject the invader, the Yankees proceed with losing to the Indians, 10-8.

June 12   Attention, Indians fans! Here's how they swept the Yankees three times on this date, all in front of enormous crowds totaling 215,661:

- **1948:** In front of 68,586 witnesses at Yankee Stadium, ex-Yankee Joe Gordon drives in six runs with three homers, including the go-ahead blast in each game, as the Indians sweep, 7-5 and 9-4.
- **1949:** Bob Lemon and Mike Garcia stifle the Yankees with a pair of complete games, winning 6-1 and 3-1 while allowing a combined nine hits all day. The biggest crowd of the season at Cleveland's Municipal Stadium, 77,543, relishes every minute of it.
- **1955:** It's another throng of 69,532 at Municipal Stadium as Early Wynn and Bob Lemon nearly pull off the same double-complete game trick. Wynn cruises in the opener on a five-hitter, winning 10-2, while Lemon needs ninth-inning relief from Mike Garcia in a 7-3 nightcap victory.

June 13, 2013   After Robinson Cano hits a two-run homer in the top of the first inning at Oakland, the Yankees are shut out for the next 17 innings before the A's beat them, 3-2. The heart of the Yankees' order—Mark Teixeira, Travis Hafner, Kevin Youkilis, and Vernon Wells—go a combined 0-for-28, each professional hitter fanning three times. In the A's 18th, Mariano Rivera relieves Preston Claiborne after a one-out single and quickly sends the Oakland fans home happy. Seth Smith singles the runner to third, and another household name, Nate Freiman, singles home the winning run.

June 14, 2000 More than 54,000 fans pile into Yankee Stadium to see the big duel between Roger Clemens and Boston's Pedro Martinez. The game is ready to start, but where is Roger? He's in the clubhouse getting his groin tended to. Well, he does hold the record for most strained groins. Perhaps he's also engaged in his favorite pre-game practice of slathering Texas hot sauce on his testicles to ratchet up his anger to the fever pitch of a major league warrior. Or perhaps not. Clemens struggles through the first inning, walking two batters and allowing one hit, and calls it a night after 28 painful pitches. It's another record-setting strain. As the expert himself puts it, "They were afraid I really hurt it. It's not torn, but it's frayed." He lets Pedro go on without him, missing his next three starts.

June 15, 1912 Bobby Wallace singles in the winning run against Russ Ford in the bottom of the ninth inning to defeat the Highlanders, 2-1, at Sportsman's Park, igniting the worst stretch of baseball in franchise history. They lose seven games in a row, win one, lose seven more, win again, and finish with eight more losses. That adds up to a 2-22 skid, including scores of 15-8, 13-2, 11-1, 13-6, 10-2, 12-5, 12-1, and 11-3 (twice). They play six doubleheaders and are swept in five of them—four in one week! When the plunge ends on July 12, they're in last place with a record of 19-52, with 50 more losses ahead of them.

June 16, 1997 Facing each other for the first time in the regular season, the Mets defeat the Yankees, 6-0, silencing the Yankees fans among the 56,188 spectators at Yankee Stadium. The Mets score three runs off Andy Pettitte in the top of the first, the last a steal of home by catcher Todd Hundley on a double steal. John Olerud drives in three runs, and Dave Mlicki pitches a slick nine-hit shutout. . .

June 16, 2015 Dealt by the Miami Marlins to the Yankees after the 2014 season, Nate Eovaldi gets what every traded pitcher craves: a chance to show his old team and their home crowd what a mistake they made in getting rid of him. Instead, he lives every starting pitcher's recurring nightmare, suffering an eight-run battering without getting out of the first inning at Miami. After retiring the leadoff hitter, he is rocked for six straight singles, a triple, (an out,) a single, and a double. That's when Joe Girardi shows some mercy and yanks him, already most of the way toward a 12-2 loss.

June 17, 1925 The Marlins' assault on Nate Eovaldi was fun, but not like the fun the Tigers enjoy at Yankee Stadium while annihilating the Yankees, 19-1. James Harrison breaks the *New York Times'* rule against hyperbole by calling it "the greatest slaughter the world has seen since the days of old King Herod." Really! The Tigers lead, 4-0, when Alex Ferguson begins the sixth inning by loading the bases with nobody out, then commits an error and allows a triple by Tigers pitcher Hooks Dauss that makes it 8-0. In comes Alex Beall, who walks three straight Tigers and leaves with a 9-0 deficit. Next into the arena of this Coliseum-like mismatch against hungry Tigers comes Hank Johnson, who can't get anybody out either. Ty Cobb greets him with a grand slam, Harry Heilmann triples, and it goes downhill from there until one of the Yankees' starters, Sad Sam Jones, enters and concludes the one-inning slaughter with 13 runs on six hits, seven walks, and two errors.

June 18, 1977 In a celebrated blow-up that still shows up on baseball telecasts when they need a little spice, Billy Martin I and Reggie Jackson try to attack each other during a nationally televised game at Fenway Park. With the Red Sox leading, 7-4 in the sixth inning, Jackson cautiously plays a Jim Rice hit into a double, and Martin waves his $2.9 million free agent acquisition in to the dugout, replacing him. Reaching the dugout, Jackson confronts Martin, who is already livid, and two coaches have to keep them from acting out an episode of *Celebrity Deathmatch*. "I only ask one thing of my players— hustle," Martin claims. "When a player shows the club up, I show him up." Jackson responds, "I'm just a black man to them who doesn't know how to be subservient. I'm a big black man with an IQ of 160 making $700,000 a year and they treat me like dirt."

June 19, 1995   Under suspension for repeated drug abuse and under house arrest for tax evasion, Darryl Strawberry signs a one-year deal as George Steinbrenner's latest reclamation project. He can't even play until August, and by then there are doubts about how he'll fit in. Reliever Steve Howe, eventually the record-holder for drug suspensions, says of his new teammate, "If he's a distraction in the clubhouse, it'll show. If he doesn't make it to a game, you'll know about it." In 1996, they add Dwight Gooden to the mix, turning Yankee Stadium into a halfway house. Strawberry plays a grand total of 231 games for the Yankees, his last five seasons in the majors, hitting a modest .255 with 41 home runs. Slowed further by colon cancer, he retires from baseball in 1999 but has continuing careers in drug abuse and other illegalities.

June 20, 1922   Before the game at Cleveland, Babe Ruth learns that he has been suspended three days for yesterday's fracas with umpire Bill Dinneen. Apparently Ruth had a better view from left field of a tag play at second base than Dinneen, who was standing a few feet away, and his ravings earned him an ejection and this suspension. Outraged, Ruth confronts Dinneen and tells him, "If you ever put me out of a game again I'll fix you so will never umpire again, even if they put me out of baseball for life." Ruth wants to tangle with Dinneen but is restrained. AL President Ban Johnson tacks on a few days to Ruth's suspension and tells the press, "My reports show that Ruth used vulgar and vicious language, calling Umpire Dinneen one of the vilest names known." Say what?

June 21, 1916   George "Rube" Foster, the #5 pitcher on a staff headed by George "Babe" Ruth, no-hits the Yankees at Fenway Park, walking three in a 2-0 victory. . .

It's fun at the ballpark, old-style. Already trailing 4-0 in the second inning at the Stadium, Yankees right-hander Thad Tillotson nails Red Sox third baseman Joe Foy on the helmet. Jim Lonborg retaliates by drilling Tillotson between the shoulder blades in the home half of the second. In the ensuing brawl, which police have to break up, Joe Pepitone strains his wrist and has to leave the game. Amazingly, neither pitcher is ejected, so the fun continues. Tillotson doesn't miss a chance to low-bridge Reggie Smith in the third inning and Lonborg in the fourth before he is sent to the corner. Manager Ralph Houk joins him, ejected later that inning as the Red Sox take an 8-0 lead. Lonborg starts the fifth inning with a pitch that somehow finds Dick Howser's helmet, knocking him out of the game. In a true sign of the times, after all that headhunting, with an 8-1 lead, and despite facing 42 batters—a fifth time through the lineup!—Lonborg pitches a complete game.

June 21, 1967

Maybe it's the summer solstice, but Yankees pitchers have endured many drubbings on this calendar date:

June 22

- **1912:** After losing to the Red Sox 15-8 and 11-3 in their previous two games, the last-place Yankees are demolished twice more, losing 13-2 and 10-3 as the Red Sox complete a five-game sweep. Starting pitchers George McConnell and Jack Warhop are drilled for eight runs apiece.
- **1932:** Lou Gehrig homers in his last two at-bats, but the fans in St. Louis don't mind. The Browns have already ripped Danny MacFayden and Jumbo Brown for a ten-run sixth inning and win easily, 17-10. The next day brings another football score as Goose Goslin's three homers help the Browns win, 14-10.
- **1986:** Joe Niekro actually gets to the fifth inning of a 1-1 tie in Toronto before the floodgates open. He is joined by Bob Shirley and Ed Whitson in the international incident. By the time the Yankees are allowed to leave the country and continue on to Boston, the final score is Toronto 15, New York 1.

Manager Lou Piniella sings a sad chorus of "June 22 Blues," telling reporters, "It's embarrassing. Embarrassing, that's what it is. It's embarrassing with a capital 'E'. Is everybody clear on that?"

June 23, 1988 If a manager with a 40-28 record is ever enti- tled to feel that his neck is on the line, it is Billy Martin V. "I'm not looking for no vote of confidence," he insisted last night after an ugly series in Detroit in which they lost twice in extra innings and once when they led 6-1 to the bottom of the ninth and gave up six runs. "It's George's ball club. If he wants to fire me, O.K." George does want to fire him, and today's the day. Maybe it was the erratic use of his pitching staff that did Martin in. Or the suspension for throwing dirt at an umpire. Or the fight in the topless bar in Texas in May after getting kicked out of a game. Or badmouthing George Steinbrenner and GM Bob Quinn a few days ago over a roster move he didn't like. In the end, it's just Billy being Billy, but this time his managing career is over.

June 24, 1908 Clark Griffith, the only manager the young franchise has known, resigns in the wake of twelve losses in the last thirteen games, dropping them into seventh place. "It was simply useless for me to continue as manager," he says. "I have tried everything, but... finally I grew disheartened. It was fighting against fate, and I knew when I had enough." It might seem panicky with a 24-32 record, but it was 23-20 two weeks ago, and the sharp-eyed "Old Fox" can't be fooled. Shortstop Norman "Kid" Elberfeld takes over, and the team somehow plays even worse for him, losing fifteen of their first eighteen games. Things don't get better, and they finish last by seventeen games.

June 26, 1978 With the Yankees trailing the Red Sox by 9½ games, the Yankees hold a 2½-hour meeting involving George Steinbrenner, manager Billy Martin I, his agent, and team president Al Rosen, who later issues a statement saying, "This should end the speculation that has been developing of late concerning

Billy's job. . . .I think this commitment to him is warranted in view of his cooperative attitude at the meeting." Rosen adds, "We felt that getting Billy away from a feeling of anxiety might precipitate an emotional uplift for our ball club." As if anything could tug Billy Martin away from a "feeling of anxiety." What a delusion! But Billy buys it, proclaiming, "I'm the manager." His agent falls for it, too, declaring, "They wanted to make it very clear to Billy Martin that they weren't going to make any managerial moves on him at any time this year." It's like giving themselves the kiss of death. Billy isn't fired. Four weeks later, he resigns under fire (see July 24), and the club's "emotional uplift" begins almost the minute that he departs.

June 27, 1971   Washington manager Ted Williams gets a jolt of *deja vu* when Gerry Janeski walks the first two Yankees in the bottom of the first inning of a doubleheader. That's how Teddy Ballgame used to make a living, he'll tell you, cleaning up easy RBI after dumb pitchers walk two men in front of him. He'll be damned if—he gives Janeski the quick hook and brings in Joe Grzenda. One runner scores, but that's it for the Yankees. Williams sits back and watches his own dumb pitchers mow down the Yankees in front of a stupefied crowd of 41,173 at Yankee Stadium. Grzenda pitches into the seventh inning, winning 2-1 on a Del Unser home run. In the nightcap, Jim Shellenback spins a neat six-hitter as the Senators sweep, 8-0.

June 28, 1907   Washington beats the Highlanders 16-5, humiliating their catcher by stealing thirteen bases. That nightmare, plus a season's batting average of .182, persuades the catcher to seek a new line of work. He goes to law school, coaches baseball on the side, and makes it back to the majors as a manager and executive known as Branch Rickey. . .

June 28, 1976   In a performance that solidifies his status as baseball's new darling, Detroit's Mark Fidrych pitches a slick seven-hitter to beat the Yankees, 5-1. That makes eight straight wins for the rookie who talks to the baseball, compulsively plays with the dirt on the mound, and cheers on his teammates like a Little Leaguer. It's his sixth complete game, and a national television audience (for Monday's ABC "Game of the Week") joins 47,855 fans at Tiger Stadium in witnessing the talent and charisma of the man they dub "The Bird."

June 29, 1934   Playing an exhibition game at the packed ballpark of their Norfolk farm club, the Yankees are stunned to see Lou Gehrig beaned in his second at-bat after hitting a home run his first time up, knocking him unconscious for five minutes. The Norfolk team physician says it's a moderate concussion, and Gehrig might miss tomorrow's game at Washington and end his streak at 1,414 consecutive games played. "I have a slight headache," Gehrig says, "but I feel all right otherwise, and will be in there tomorrow." He is, but it brings a different kind of pain. Gehrig slugs three triples in the first five innings, but heavy rain and wind force a postponement before the game is official, wiping out his quick recovery and remarkable performance. He doesn't even get credit for a game played.

June 30, 1908   Cy Young has as much fun as a 41-year-old can have at a ballpark. He no-hits the Highlanders at the Hilltop, winning 8-0, allowing only a walk to Harry Niles, and pounds out three hits himself, including a pair of two-run singles. This season, he completes 30 of 33 starts and posts a 21-11 record and a 1.26 ERA. . .

June 30, 2018   As proof that this is Boston's season, the Red Sox trample the Yankees, 11-0, in front of 47,125 fans at Yankee Stadium. Rafael Devers smashes a grand slam off Sonny Gray in the top of the first inning, and the Yankees manage just one hit in seven innings, a first-inning single by Giancarlo Stanton, off Chris Sale, who strikes out 11 Yankees. Devers goes 5-for-5 as the Red Sox outhit the Bronx Bombers, 17-2.

July

July 1, 1990 — Occasionally, a major league pitcher will lose a 1-0 game despite giving up no hits, but nobody gets reamed worse than Andy Hawkins, who loses this no-hitter, 4-0. It takes a lot of help from his Yankees teammates. The game is scoreless until the bottom of the eighth inning at Comiskey Park. Hawkins gets the first two outs before a Mike Blowers error gives the White Sox a runner. Two walks load the bases, and then things get truly ugly. Robin Ventura lifts a fly ball to left field, where rookie Jim Leyritz drops it, letting all three runners score. The next batter hits a lazy fly to right field, but Jesse Barfield loses the ball in the sun and can't catch it, allowing Ventura to score. "I'm stunned. I really am," Hawkins says afterwards. "This is not even close to the way I envisioned a no-hitter would be." Hawkins suffered a further indignity years later when a committee wiped his no-hitter off the record books because he didn't pitch nine innings, posting a line of 8 0 4 0 5 3.

July 2, 1975 — I'm tickled by the Yankees letting two of the worst hitters in baseball beat them. At Cleveland, it's 3-3 to the bottom of the ninth. Dick Tidrow retires the first two Indians but gives up a single to Duane Kuiper (with his .313 career slugging percentage and one home run in 3,379 at-bats). Ed Crosby, a reserve infielder with a .220 career batting average, also singles to center, and Kuiper heads for third. Center fielder Bobby Bonds fires a strong throw that clanks off Kuiper's helmet. When the ball rolls away, Kuiper races home with the winning run. . .**July 2, 2014**: The Yankees lose to Tampa Bay at Yankee Stadium, 6-3, and fall below .500 (41-42) on the latest calendar date since 1992. Sean Rodriguez hits the game-winning home run off Joe Kelley.

July 3, 1914 Philadelphia fans have the pleasure of watching the Yankees fail to score in 18 innings. After Charles Bender five-hits them to win the opener, 2-0, they scratch out a paltry three hits off future Yankees manager Bob Shawkey and lose, 1-0. All three runs are unearned courtesy of a trio of errors by Fritz Maisel, a horrible third baseman who leads the league with 35 errors. . .

July 3, 2004 The Mets come back from three deficits and win, 10-9, in the ninth inning, part of a three-game sweep at Shea Stadium. With Mariano Rivera resting comfortably in the bullpen, Tanyon Sturtze coughs up the game. He loads the bases on two walks and a hit batter, then gets flummoxed by Shane Spencer's squibber. He lunges for it but rushes his throw, which sails over Jorge Posada's head. "It just kind of rolled up my glove a little bit," Sturtze explains. "I had to hurry up because [Kaz] Matsui was running. I was kind of forcing it a little bit." Unlike those two walks and the HBP, when he's perfectly relaxed.

July 4, 1973 On George Steinbrenner's first birthday as the owner, Bobby Murcer's home run is the only run the Yankees get all day at Yankee Stadium as the Red Sox sweep them, 2-1 and 1-0. Thurman Munson's ninth-inning error keys the winning rally in the opener, and Carl Yastrzemski singles in the only run Roger Moret needs in the nightcap. . . . .

July 4, 2006 In 2006 (with birthday-boy Steinbrenner in attendance in his hometown), the Indians shred six Yankees pitchers for 21 hits in a 19-1 rout. Reliever T. J. Beam is drilled for six of the nine runs scored by the Indians in the fifth inning.

July 5, 1912 The Highlanders finish off a 2-13 road trip by losing their fifth straight game in Washington. The good news is that the Senators, after sweeping them in back-to-back holiday doubleheaders, beat them only once today. It still takes

16 innings, with Walter Johnson and Jack Warhop duking it out from the fourth inning on, both in relief. The Senators finally win it on three singles.

July 6, 1966 They don't write like this any more—the opening of Red Foley's New York Daily News coverage from Yankee Stadium: "No one will ever confuse him with Nero, but it's going to be hard to convince the 14,211 who sat in the steamy Stadium yesterday that Ralph Houk didn't burn as he watched his Yankees fiddle away a 5-3, 5-4 doubleheader to the Red Sox." Dalton Jones' pinch-hit homer in the ninth inning off Pedro Ramos wins the opener, and Carl Yastrzemski drives in three runs in the second game as the Yankees drop ten games below .500 and remain locked in a fierce battle for seventh place with the Athletics and Senators.

July 7, 1995 The Yankees activate pitcher Dave Pavlas, a former "replacement player" before the players' union strike ended, and the players aren't happy. "I'm going to look at him basically as a scab, to tell you the truth," first baseman Don Mattingly, the team's captain, tells Jack Curry of the New York Times. "But he's a scab that's on our team. He's on our team. To a point, he's out there with us on the field. But after that. . ." In Arlington, Texas, Andy Pettitte gives up five runs in the second inning as the Yankees lose, 10-0. Pavlas, a 32-year-old baseball nomad who has played in Mexico, Taiwan, Chicago, and Italy, makes his Yankees debut, pitching a scoreless inning. He pitches 20 times for the Yankees in 1995-1996, ending his career with a 2-0 record.

July 8, 1969 It's "Babe Ruth Day" in Baltimore, and his widow, Claire, takes part in the pre-game ceremony. She's a Mets fan, so she enjoys the afternoon of baseball as the Orioles sweep the Yankees, 10-3 and 4-1. In the opener, the Orioles set a franchise record by scoring ten runs in the fourth inning, mashing buddies Fritz Peterson and Mike Kekich. In the nightcap, Ralph Houk gets ejected for, of all things, stalling before making a pitching change—while losing 3-0 in the second inning—as if maybe he'll get beamed up somewhere instead of having to watch his awful team. By the end of July, they seize fifth place, 24 games behind the first-place Orioles.

"I never thought I'd be called upon to beg for Yankee Stadium to get a facelifting," says the other long-standing Yankees widow, Eleanor Gehrig, on **December 7, 1971**. The Yankees, coveting a chance to get New York City to pay for renovations to Yankee Stadium, use today's hearing before the Board of Estimate to go straight for the sentimental jugular. They trot out 67-year-old Eleanor, who tells the panel, "I beg you really to remember the great traditions. It's a landmark. Remember the Colosseum in Rome—people go there and nasty people played in that place, but it's a great money-maker." What an apt epitaph for Yankee Stadium, too: nasty people played there, but it made money.

July 9, 1921   The Yankees lead, 8-0, in the seventh inning at Comiskey Park, but Carl Mays can't hold it. Leading 9-6 in the bottom of the ninth, he loads the bases and is replaced by future Hall of Famer Waite Hoyt, who lets the White Sox tie it. In extra innings, Hoyt misses a suicide squeeze bunt, making the runner breaking from third, Wally Pipp, an easy out. Hoyt and Chicago's Shovel Hodge put up goose-eggs until the 16th inning, when Earl Sheely's RBI single beats him. . . .

July 9, 1999   Mike Piazza breaks a 2-2 tie with a sixth-inning, three-run homer off Roger Clemens at Shea Stadium. Al Leiter holds the Yankees to two hits in eight innings to pick up the 5-2 win, one of six losses for Clemens in nine regular-season decisions against the Mets.

July 10   It's always extra satisfying when the American League's have-nots beat up Yankees pitching, as in these twin-bill trouncings: **1925**: The Browns trail the Yankees, 8-4, going to the bottom of the ninth of the first game at Sportsman's Park and shock them with five runs to win it, then pile up 20 hits in winning the second game, 13-3. . .**1932**: The sixth-place Browns do it again, amass-ing 33 hits in the doubleheader while winning, 10-9 and 8-7, at Yankee Stadium. Goose Goslin goes 5-for-5 off Lefty Gomez in the opener, and the Yankees blow a 7-2 lead to get swept . . . **1966**: A Senators sweep, 3-2 and 9-2, drops the Yankees into ninth place. They're a disaster: Whitey Ford pitches in relief, Roger Maris can only pinch-hit, and Mickey Mantle is too battered to play at all. No wonder the 16,471 suffering supporters at Yankee Stadium serenade the helpless under-studies with boos.

July 11, 1992 About the same time that Don Mattingly admits that he doesn't know who Lou Gehrig was, "Old-Timers' Day" at Yankee Stadium proves that Mattingly's igno-rance is about average among current pinstripers. Phil Rizzuto laments, "A lot of them hardly remember Mickey Mantle and they barely know Joe DiMaggio. They don't know about what happens when you put on a Yan-kee uniform." Current third baseman Charlie Hayes serves up Exhibit A, chirping, "I don't know any of these old-timers. I don't know one. Phil Rizzuto? I hear he announces games, but I don't even know what he looks like." A crowd of 39,533 enjoys the old-timers' game much more than the actual game, which the Mariners win, 5-3, in twelve innings. The key play is a potential double play ball that clanks off Mattingly's wrist. Just how Gehrig would've played it.

July 12, 1952 Billy Martin and Browns catcher Clint Court-ney engage in a battle that starts a long-last-ing feud. Courtney spikes Martin at second base to break up a double play, then knocks the ball out of Yogi Berra's glove to score. From the dugout, Casey Stengel hollers, "Hey, how long you guys gonna take that?" Not long. When Courtney tries to steal second later in the game and is out by so much that he doesn't bother to slide, Martin seizes the oppor-tunity and tags him hard, right between the eyes, breaking Courtney's glasses. A fight ensues in which umpire Bill Summers is knocked down, all part of Ladies' Day festivities at Yankee Stadium.

July 13, 2001 "Torre Never Told Jeter There'd Be Games Like This," reads the headline over Buster Olney's coverage in the *New York Times* as Derek Jeter plays a game that would embarrass a Little Leaguer. He kicks two grounders, makes a bad throw home, misses a pickoff throw, grounds into a bases-loaded double play, and goes o-for-4 as the Yankees are humbled by the Marlins, 11-1. When he manages to catch a popup in the fifth inning, Olney writes, "The fans roared facetiously, an unsubtle reminder of all the mistakes he had made. Jeter touched the bill of his cap in acknowledgment and grinned at his own expense." Jeter, explaining his problems with the relatively dark lighting in Miami, claims, "I don't pick up the ball here at all. That didn't have anything to do with the errors, but even the plays I made, I don't pick up the ball at all." He gets revenge in 2017 by buying the Marlins and trading away all the players worth squinting at to see, neatly cutting attendance in half.

July 14, 1934 Lou Gehrig slides through a loophole to extend his streak to 1,427 games. He left yesterday's game in the second inning after wrenching his back, and the diagnosis is lumbago, 1930s lingo for lower back pain. He can hardly move, but he gets a break because the Yankees are playing at Detroit, and he insists on being in the lineup. Manager Joe McCarthy lists Gehrig as the leadoff batter and shortstop, and it adds to the Gehrig mystique that he singles to start the game. Red Rolfe pinch-runs for Gehrig, who goes back to the hotel to rest. Gehrig, his lumbagone the next day, goes 4-for-4 with three doubles.

On **January 30, 1937**, Gehrig, with 1,808 straight games under his belt, states his intention of breaking all the records he can, with the exception of Babe Ruth's home run mark. "I only put my goal at 2,500 games tentatively. If it develops that I am hurting the team by trying to stay in, why, I'll get out and the record will end right there. But I feel right now as if I could go through with the idea and certainly there's no harm in trying." A dissenting view is presented on April 29 by Everett Scott, whose record of 1,307 Gehrig broke years ago. Says Scott, "Gehrig is shortening his life and career. I ought to know." Unfortunately, he was half-right; Gehrig died a few years later, while Scott lived to 67.

July 15, 1963 How does a pennant-bound team blow five leads in one game? First, your future Hall of Famer squanders three of them. Gino Cimoli's RBI triple erases Whitey Ford's first lead, Jerry Lumpe's sacrifice fly makes it 4-4, and Ed Charles' second homer of the game ends Ford's struggles with a 6-6 tie through six innings. The Yankees go up again in the top of the ninth, but two relievers combine to wreck that win. A three-run 11th inning seems to give the Yankees a lead they can't blow, but right-hander Hal Reniff crushes that hope, and Doc Edwards' two-run single ties it, 10-10. In the bottom of the 12th, Bill Stafford hits one Athletic and walks three more, with the pass to Jerry Lumpe bringing in the winning run.

July 16, 1910 The recent sign-stealing fiasco is just part of a long tradition of cheating in baseball. Today, five Chicago White Sox accuse the Highlanders of "signal tipping" at their home field, Hilltop Park. Suspicious after a 13-run New York outburst, the White Sox spot something fishy on a center field signboard, moving from side to side. When Lee Tannehill leaves the White Sox bench to see what it is, New York pitcher Tom Hughes races ahead of him, gets there first, and hides the evidence. One player tells the *New York Times*, "Ed Walsh with the aid of a pair of strong field glasses could plainly see the slides in the signboard move to and fro as each rival batter came to bat." Maybe that's why the Highlanders scored 21 percent more runs at home that season.

July 17, 1923 Few players caused as many difficulties as Carl Mays did with the Yankees, even though he went 80-39 for them from 1919-1923. In 1920, his submarine delivery froze shortstop Ray Chapman of the Indians, and his fastball killed him. After going 27-9 in 1921, he lost two of his three starts in the World Series, and he lost his only start in the 1922 Series as the Yankees lost again to the Giants. Manager Miller Huggins suspects that Mays wasn't trying his hardest in the Series, and today he punishes him. After relegating Mays to long relief and mop-up work for three months, he gives him a start at Cleveland, facing Chapman's old teammates. A five-run fourth inning gives the Indians a 7-0 lead, but Huggins leaves Mays in. The carnage spills over in the seventh inning, when five more runs push the lead to 13-0. Huggins makes Mays finish the game, and he is pounded for 13 runs on 20 hits. Huggins explains, "He told me he needed lots of work, so I gave it to him." Indeed.

July 18, 1934 "This was a melancholy day in the life of the Yankees," reports James Dawson in the *New York Times*. It certainly sucks for Babe Ruth and his teammates. Ruth is leading off first base in the third inning when Lou Gehrig's wicked line drive nails him on the right shin. He's carted off on a stretcher and taken by ambulance to the hospital, where they find no break but a picturesque purple contusion that sidelines him for ten days. Meanwhile, the Yankees score five runs in the ninth inning to erase a 12-9 deficit, and after a lead-off double in the bottom of the ninth, manager Joe McCarthy, taking no chances, brings in ace Lefty Gomez (with a 14-2 record) for only his third relief appearance of the season. Gomez promptly gives up a triple, a game-tying double, and a game-winning single by Earl Averill as the Yankees lose, 15-14.

July 19 It's hard to choose between these two games 62 years apart, in which the Yankees allowed a combined 38 runs. **1925**: The Tigers drill 22 hits, including nine doubles, and beat the Yankees, 18-12, in Detroit. The Tigers lead 12-3 before the Yankees waste a bunch of runs in the late innings. **1987**: While Don Mattingly's streak of eight straight games with a home run ends, the Yankees get annihilated, 20-3, in Texas. In a team effort, Steve Trout, Rich Bordi, Tim Stoddard, and Pat Clements allow five runs apiece, while catcher Rick Cerone shows them up by retiring three straight Rangers to end the mayhem. What a performance!

July 20, 1998   First the bad news: the Yankees lead 3-0 by the third inning, turn five double plays, pound out 13 hits, draw 14 walks, and steal three bases. Now the good news: they lose anyway! In a 17-inning, 350-minute nightmare, the Yankees leave 22 runners on base, 18 of them while being shut out over the final 14 innings. It kills them that Chuck Knoblauch, Tino Martinez, Scott Brosius, and Jorge Posada combine to go hitless in 27 at-bats. The Yankees load the bases in the eighth, tenth, 12th, and 15th innings, twice with just one out, without scoring. Picture the squirming and anguish of the 36,285 fans at Yankee Stadium. In the 17th inning, Darren Holmes gives up a run on three singles to lose, 4-3.

July 21, 2019   The Yankees begin the most dreadful pitching week in franchise history, allowing 73 runs in seven games. It starts modestly enough with an 8-4 loss to the Rockies in the final game of a home stand, with James Paxton knocked out in the fourth inning after allowing seven runs. Then:

- **July 22:** In the opener at Minnesota, CC Sabathia serves up four home runs as the Yankees lose, 8-6.
- **July 23:** Domingo German gives up eight runs in less than four innings, but the Yankees rally late and take a 12-11 lead to the bottom of the ninth. Aroldis Chapman blows the save but scavenges the win, 14-12 in ten innings.
- **July 24:** The Yankees give J. A. Happ a 9-3 lead in the fourth inning but he still gets kayoed before he can pick up the win. That goes to Nestor Cortes as the Yankees hold on, 10-7.
- **July 25:** Moving to Fenway Park, Masahiro Tanaka runs into a seven-run first inning by the Red Sox, but Aaron Boone leaves him in long enough to give up five more runs in the fourth. Backup catcher Austin Romine hurls the eighth inning, giving up two homers and three runs to make the final score 19-3.
- **July 26:** James Paxton nearly duplicates his previous start, roughed up for seven runs in the first four innings. Mookie Betts hits three homers off Paxton in the 10-5 romp.

- **July 27:** The horrible pitching week concludes with another bad outing by CC Sabathia, who can't get through the fifth inning in a 9-5 defeat. For the week, Yankees starting pitchers combine for an 0-5 record with a 16.62 ERA on 26 innings pitched, 56 hits, 52 runs, 48 earned, 12 walks , 30 strikeouts, and 18 home runs allowed.

July 21, 1988 In a trade they'll long regret, the Yankees send Jay Buhner to Seattle for Ken Phelps. The Yankees give up on the 23-year-old outfielder because he has one hit in his last 29 at-bats with 15 strikeouts, overlooking his 13 RBI in his first 40 at-bats. Buhner blossoms in Seattle, hits over 300 home runs, and becomes one of the team's most popular players. Phelps hits .240 with 17 homers as a Yankee before a 1989 trade to Oakland for Scott Holcomb, who never reaches the majors.

July 22, 1962 One of the joys of being a baseball fan is that on any given day, the Yankees might play like bums. Today they are helpless against the last-place Washington Senators, treating 26,842 fans at Yankee Stadium to a pair of losses. In the opener, Dave Stenhouse (16 career wins) pitches a complete-game four-hitter to win, 3-2. In the second game, Bennie Daniels (7-16 in 1962) also goes the distance, conquering the Yankees with a slick ten-hitter. Jim Bouton takes the loss, leaving in the eighth inning with a 4-1 deficit. Luis Arroyo's first pitch results in a three-run, inside-the-park home run by Chuck Hinton. Daniels adds the cherry on top of the Sunday sundae by homering off Tex Clevenger in the ninth inning, making the final score 8-3.

July 24, 1983 Ah, the Pine Tar Game! After George Brett's homer off Goose Gossage puts the Royals ahead in the ninth inning, Billy Martin III launches a sore-loser protest that Brett's bat had pine tar too far up the barrel. The umpires agree and call Brett out, prompting Brett to go berserk. But the last laugh is on the Yankees when American League President Lee MacPhail (a former Yankees GM) upholds the Royals' protest. He says that Brett's blast counts, and the game is concluded several weeks later. "It's a terrible rule," says Martin, "but if it happened to me I would have accepted it." Yeah, right.

> "That's the maddest I have ever seen a human being in my life," Gossage told a 2013 gathering at the Hall of Fame, adding, "I hated George Brett." He had thrown the pitch *at* Brett. "If he hadn't hit a home run, it would have hit him in the neck. I don't know how he did it."

July 24, 2004 The Red Sox win, 11-10, on a ninth-inning Bill Mueller home run, but the real fireworks explode earlier, when Alex Rodriguez and Jason Varitek start a benches-clearing brawl. Drilled in the arm by a Bronson Arroyo pitch, A-Rod screams curses at Arroyo until Varitek advises him to shut up and take his base. "Come on!" screams A-Rod, so Varitek comes on and punches him in the face, launching the usual fracas.

July 25, 1977 Addressing Billy Martin I's fears that he's about to be fired, George Steinbrenner says, "Martin should forget trying to make a martyr out of himself. We've been through this three times already. He seems to love being a martyr. We've come to a time when we must demand an accountability of what Martin does and says." Steinbrenner and GM Gabe Paul list seven criteria for judging Martin's performance:

- Is the won-lost record O.K.?
- Does he work hard enough?
- Is he emotionally equipped to lead men?
- Is he organized?
- Is he prepared for each game?
- Does he understand human nature?
- Is he honorable?

Over the years, Steinbrenner remained consistently ambivalent about the shifting answers to these questions. He hired Martin as his manager in 1975, 1979, 1983, 1985, and 1988. It took Martin until 1978 to blow the first job, but after that he was gone within a year every time.

July 26, 1959

All hail Frank Lary, the celebrated "Yankee Killer" of the Detroit Tigers from 1955-1964. Today is one of the games that cements that reputation, a ten-inning, 1-0 victory at Briggs Stadium. He has already won three starts against them this season, making his career record 20-5 against them. No kidding. In 1958, he went 7-1 against them with a 1.86 ERA. The popular right-hander had no explanation for his success, saying simply, "I just throw them that breaking stuff of mine." He gives up eight hits today and escapes in the eighth inning when Bobby Richardson is thrown out at home trying to score on Mickey Mantle's single. In the tenth inning, Tigers manager Jimmie Dykes sends Neil Chrisley and his .089 average up to hit for Lary, and he comes through with the game-winning single. Lary winds up 28-13 in his career against the Yankees.

July 27, 1991

Meet Bettie Taylor, the mother of the Yankees' first-round draft choice, Brien Taylor. Bettie is airing her doubts about GM Gene Michael. When he traveled to North Carolina to scout the high school pitching prospect, she says, "He didn't even give me a hello. If you ask me, that was downright disrespectful." Not only that, the Yankees have offered her son a measly $500,000 to sign, less than half what the previous year's top draft choice, Todd Van Poppel, was offered. "As things go along, I'm beginning to wonder," she says. "Is it because we're back here, we're poor and we're black?" She delivers an ultimatum to the Yankees: "Once Brien goes to college, the Yankees will have no chance at him. They have the opportunity now. If they want him, now is the time to sign him." Eventually, aided by "advisor" Scott Boras, Taylor negotiates a $1.55 million signing bonus. Good thing, because Brien never makes it to the major leagues. He gets involved in a fight after the 1993 season, injures his pitching shoulder, loses his 98mph fastball, and fades away a few years later. Way to throw Momma from the gravy train, Brien!

July 28, 1997

Four starts into his Yankees career, Hideki Irabu is exiled to the minor leagues. The $12.8 million the Yankees shelled out for Irabu is apparently a big mistake. The only thing bothering him more than the swarming Japanese press is

American League hitters, and a 2-2 record can't disguise a 7.97 ERA plus six home runs allowed in his last dozen innings. He comes back and has a few bright moments as a Yankee, but mostly he gets booed at Yankee Stadium, his owner calls him a "fat toad," and after three seasons of anguish, he escapes to Canada. Fittingly, in his final appearance as a Yankee, he gets ripped for eight runs in relief in a blowout at Fenway Park in the 1999 LCS.

(July 29, 1978) It's Old-Timers' Day at Yankee Stadium, and Bob Lemon's fifth day as manager following the ouster of Billy Martin I. Lemon hears public address announcer Bob Sheppard introduce him, and he's applauded as he trots out to join the old-timers. He hears Sheppard's next introduction: "Managing the Yankees in the 1980 season and hopefully for many seasons after that will be. . .No. 1. . ." That's as far as Sheppard gets with the surprise announcement. The crowd of 46,711 goes nuts and gives Martin a seven-minute ovation. How about a moment of silence for Lemon? All he does in 1978 is manage them to a 48-20 record and a World Series title. He gets into mid-June of 1979 with a 34-31 record and whomp! Here comes Billy Martin II. That's how it goes in the upper cages of the Bronx Zoo in the late 1970s, which helps explain the absence of titles until 1996.

(July 31) I wish I had seen these July 31 games. . .**1908**: A 16-3 shellacking in Cleveland concludes the worst month in franchise history. Seven straight losses leave them with a 6-24 record in July and a solid grip on last place. . .**1911**: During a week when they allow 67 runs, the Yankees get a complete game from Jack Warhop—who loses, 13-0, giving up 17 hits. . .**1992**: In a 13-2 blowout at Toronto, starter Shawn Hillegas and reliever Tim Leary give up six runs apiece, making such a strong impression that a month later, neither one is a Yankee. . .**2002**: Mike Mussina and three relievers are pounded for 21 hits in Texas as the Rangers win, 17-6. The Rangers tie an AL record with seven extra-base hits in one inning, six doubles plus a homer by Alex Rodriguez.

August

In a ninth inning packed with delicious ironies, the Red Sox get the best of the Yankees for a 3-2 win at Fenway Park. With one out, a 2-2 tie, and Thurman Munson on third base, Gene Michael misses a suicide squeeze attempt, and Munson is a dead duck, so he runs into Fisk, precipitating a 15-minute fight. Joseph Durso of the *New York Times* details the action: Fisk "was royally flattened in the collision by Munson. Somehow Fisk held onto the ball for the out, then flipped Munson over to get rid of him. Munson threw a punch, they clinched, and then Michael. . .jumped over Munson to throw a few for the visitors." Munson's intriguing appraisal is that "There's no question I threw the first punch, but he started it." Soon there are 50 players on the field, and eventually the umpires eject Fisk and Munson—but not Michael, who makes the third out. Sparky Lyle gets the first two outs in the bottom of the ninth but is done in by irony. Bob Montgomery, Fisk's replacement, singles and moves to second on a walk. Up steps Mario Guerrero, a rookie utility infielder, whose eighth career RBI turns Lyle into a loser.

A Yankee Stadium crowd of 43,304 greets the visiting Toronto Blue Jays with chants of "U.S.A., U.S.A." during batting practice, boos the Canadian national anthem, and later throws bottles and a bat at their right fielder. "That's New York," says Toronto center fielder Devon White, a Manhattan native. "I wouldn't expect anything else.". . .

August 2, 2018 The Yankees travel to Fenway Park to start a four-game series, trailing the Red Sox by 5½ games. They get clobbered, 15-7, in the opener, as Mookie Betts goes 4-for-4 and Steve Pearce smacks three home runs.

August 3, 1982 In the liveliest game of managerial musical chairs in baseball history, Gene Michael is fired as Yankees manager—for the second time in eleven months! (Follow the bouncing manager. . .) In September 1981, Michael was fired and replaced by Bob Lemon, who was canned only 14 games into the 1982 season. Michael took over again, but with the team languishing around the .500 mark, and after losing a doubleheader to the White Sox, 1-0 and 14-2, Michael is gone. He is replaced by Clyde King, who has already served as advance scout, pitching coach, and advisor to George Steinbrenner this season. King finishes this season and is replaced by—of course—Billy Martin III, who begets Yogi Berra II, who begets Billy Martin IV. You beget the idea. . .

August 3, 2018 Steve Pearce kills the Yankees again, a two-run homer in the first inning as Rick Porcello one-hits the Yankees, 4-1, allowing only a homer by Miguel Andujar.

August 4, 1985 Making his only start this season in New York, Tom Seaver earns career victory #300 with a complete-game six-hitter as the White Sox beat the Yankees, 4-1, at Yankee Stadium. Seaver raises his record to 12-8 and lowers his ERA to 2.92, not bad for a 40-year-old. The ever-gracious Rickey Henderson complains after the game about taking a called third strike from Seaver: "It was a bad call. If they wanted to give him the win that way, they should've told me and I wouldn't have played." In his other three at-bats, Henderson fails to get the ball out of the infield. . .

August 4, 2018 For the second straight day, the Yankees lose, 4-1, at Fenway Park as their pennant hopes dim. This time it's a Keith Moreland two-run homer in the first inning that stands up, and Nate Eovaldi holds the Yankees to three hits in eight innings.

August 5, 2018 The Red Sox complete their sweep at Fenway Park after spotting the Yankees a 4-1 lead going to the bottom of the ninth. Then comes the Aroldis Chapman roller-coaster ride: strikeout, walk, walk, strikeout, walk, putting the tying runs on base. J. D. Martinez singles home two of them, and the tying run scores on Miguel Andujar's error. In the tenth inning, manager Aaron Boone, desperate to avoid the sweep, turns to. . .Jonathan Holder, fresh off a seven-run flogging in the series opener. He can't match that here, only because the first run, driven in by Andrew Benintendi's single, ends the game.

August 6, 1991 The Yankees open a three-game series at Comiskey Park with a five-run first inning, which becomes a distant memory as the White Sox pummel the Yankees, 14-5. The White Sox take an 8-5 lead to the eighth inning. In comes former phenom Wade Taylor, now a struggling rookie with a 5-6 record and 6.48 ERA. This performance accelerates his demise as a major leaguer. The first three runs are generated by future Hall of Famers; Tim Raines leads off with a double and scores on a Frank Thomas single, followed by a Carlton Fisk homer. But Taylor puts the next three mortals on base and they score too. This win starts an embarrassing sweep during which the Yankees are outscored, 28-8.

August 7, 2000 "Yanks Get Canseco, but the Question Is Why" is the headline over Buster Olney's column in the *New York Times*, and everybody is stumped. The injury-riddled, 36-year-old Canseco has been idling away the summer with the Tampa Bay Rays, only occasionally flexing his muscles at the plate, and his only viable "position" these days is designated hitter, which he confirms by making four errors in five games in the outfield for the Yankees. Joe Torre declares, "I'm a little stunned" about the waiver claim. The Yankees already have David Justice and Glenallen Hill to DH, and Canseco plays 37 games over the final two months, 26 as the DH, batting .243 with 19 RBI. The Yankees have the same winning percentage with and without him.

August 8, 1953   Scoreless in the sixth inning at Yankee Stadium, Mickey Mantle makes a hustling play to keep Bob Boyd's hit from going to the fence, plants his right foot to throw to second, and feels the knee buckle. It's the same knee he wrecked in the 1951 World Series. "Yankee Stadium must be a jinx to me," he moans while his knee is treated with ice. "I've never been hurt in a baseball game until I joined the Yankees." Declining surgery for the torn ligaments, he stubbornly returns to the lineup ten days later, wearing a brace, and his production buckles, too. His average drops from .309 to .295 over the rest of the season, and his slugging percentage dips under .500, which doesn't happen again until 1965.

August 9, 1968   Normally easy-going Mickey Mantle gets himself kicked out of a game for the eighth and last time in his career. In the ninth inning of a tied game, Mantle picks a fight with umpire Hank Soar, who rules that a Mantle bouncer near the third base bag is fair, resulting in a force play. After the inning, Mantle goes after Soar, curses him, and gets the thumb. In the 11th inning, trailing 4-3 with two outs and a runner on second, Mantle's spot in the batting order arrives. Without Mantle, it's lifetime .236 hitter Andy Kosco instead, and his weak fly ball ends the game. Soar explains, "Mantle asked me, 'If the ball had gone past third base, would you have called it fair?' I said yes. Then he cussed me out." What's with Mickey? Perhaps he's touchy because a week ago, his career batting average officially fell below .300, and he knows he'll never get it up there again.

August 10, 1982   Doyle Alexander, a disaster as a Yankee, sees his record fall to 0-6 after a 10-0 drilling by the Tigers in Detroit. After losing a start for the Yankees in the 1976 World Series, he left as a free agent, but they got him back in a trade from the Giants on the eve of this season. Today he allows a home run to the first batter, Lou Whitaker, and two-run homers by Glenn Wilson and Richie Hebner before leaving in the fourth inning. George Steinbrenner orders Alexander back to New York for a physical, slamming him thusly: "I am afraid some of our players might get hurt playing defense behind him." With that encouragement, Alexander goes 1-7 for the 1982 Yankees and 0-2 the next year before they release him. It must be them, since he manages to win 73 games elsewhere in the next five years.

August 11, 1908 Ed Walsh of the White Sox picks up his eighth win of the season against the Highlanders, raising his record to 26-8. Yesterday he beat them, 2-1, with a complete-game five-hitter, and today he relieves Doc White, pitches four shutout innings, and contributes an RBI double to their 6-1 win. Walsh is enjoying the ironman season of the century: 66 games, 49 starts, 42 complete games, 11 shutouts, 464 2/3 innings, 269 strikeouts, a 1.42 ERA, and a 40-15 record. His favorite patsies are the last-place Highlanders, giving them just 11 earned runs in 86 innings for a 1.15 ERA to go with his 9-1 record.

August 12, 1973 Following this loss to Oakland at Yankee Stadium, manager Ralph Houk admits, "We really played bad. Probably the worst I've ever seen us play." That's quite a testimonial from the man who has watched them stink since 1966; how bad could they be? They lead, 11-5, going to the seventh inning, with starter Sam McDowell still on the mound. With two outs and two men on, Reggie Jackson's single makes it 11-6, and that's when Ralph Houk lifts McDowell in favor of Sparky Lyle. He faces four batters, giving up a walk, a double, and two singles, and in comes Tom Buskey. Errors by Horace Clarke and Graig Nettles leave the game tied 11-11. In the eighth, another Nettles errors fuels the winning rally, and Roy White flies out with two men on base to end Ralph Houk's waking nightmare.

August 13, 1945 For the second straight day, the pennant-bound Detroit Tigers stick it to the Yankees, sweeping a doubleheader, 15-4 and 11-9, at Briggs Stadium. Yesterday it was 9-6 and 8-2, all part of a nine-game losing streak, all on the road, dropping the Yankees from third place to sixth place in a week. The key to the second game is a bunt which Yankees pitcher Ken Holcombe throws wildly to second base, and George Stirnweiss' hurried relay to the plate also sails away, letting three runners score. As Joe Trimble puts it in the *New York Daily News*, "If the Yankees didn't actually curl up and die here this afternoon, they certainly took a couple of staggering strides toward perdition."

August 14, 1960   The Yankees suffer a double loss to the Senators that exasperates a Yankee Stadium crowd of 29,970. The nightcap lasts fifteen innings thanks to the Yankees blowing a lead in the ninth inning. But the most horrifying thing for the fans is seeing Mickey Mantle get benched in the sixth inning by Casey Stengel for not running out a double play ball. Stengel explains, "I took him out because he didn't run and I'm tired of seeing him not run. If he can't run, he should tell me." The move helps Stengel run out of players in the bottom of the 15th, and pitcher Art Ditmar, representing the tying run at the plate, makes the final out of the game.

August 15, 1991   Captain Don Mattingly, hardly a long-haired hippie, is benched and fined by manager Stump Merrill for refusing to get his hair cut as ordered by GM Gene Michael. "I'm overwhelmed by the pettiness of it all," complains Mattingly, whose extra hair is evidently the reason the Yankees are in fifth place. Merrill says, "If someone from management tells you you need a haircut, you get a haircut." Michael adds, "He's the captain and he's got a big contract. If we asked the captain to get his haircut, he should get it cut." Mattingly puts it in perspective: "If Stick wants the players to do exactly what he says, then he should be the pitching coach, batting coach, and fielding coach. Then come down here and be a part of it. But take part of the blame, too."

August 16, 1920   Carl Mays, who has a wicked submarine delivery and a reputation for throwing at batters, nails Cleveland shortstop Ray Chapman in the head with a fastball. Chapman lies motionless for several minutes, starts to walk it off, but collapses again and never regains consciousness, dying the next morning. Mays turns himself in to the New York District Attorney, who doesn't press charges. Debate rages around the league about whether Mays deliberately beaned Chapman; he had also thrown at the head of the previous batter. Other teams threaten to boycott Mays, but eventually the cloud disperses, and the Yankees keep him for three more years.

August 17, 1935 Tony Lazzeri thinks that Tigers third baseman Marv Owen tagged him too hard, so he jumps up and starts a fight. Once that dies down, the Detroit crowd gets into it, pelting Yankees outfielders with apples, oranges, and lemons. After a five-minute barrage and a forfeit threat by the umpires, the crowd settles down to savor the exquisite way the Yankees lose. Tied in the tenth inning, the Tigers load the bases with one out. Mickey Cochrane slaps a double-play ball right at second baseman Jack Saltzgaver. The utility infielder freezes, unable to decide whether to throw to the catcher or the shortstop, and when he finally realizes he has to do something, he actually throws the ball to first base, letting the winning run score unchallenged.

August 18, 1983 In a morning hearing in the Appellate Division of the New York State Supreme Court, a judge tells the Yankees and Royals to complete the "Pine Tar Game" (see July 24). Only 1,245 spectators witness the ten minutes of "action" at Yankee Stadium, consisting mostly of Billy Martin III still trying to get George Brett called out. The Yankees appeal that Brett missed a base while running out his home run on July 24, but the umpires are forewarned and prepared. This is a different quartet from the July 24 crew, who provide affidavits informing Martin that they saw Brett touch all the bases. Forced to play baseball, the Yankees mercifully go out in order in the ninth inning. The Royals win, 5-4. Yankees outfielder Don Baylor sums it up, "If I wanted to watch a soap opera, I'd stay at home."

August 19, 1995   There's plenty of frustration for the Yankees in this 5-3 loss at Anaheim. They blow two early leads, thanks to a pre-replay rarity, a call reversed by the umpires. Third base ump Larry Barnett calls an out on a line drive to center with two runners on base, then yields to second base ump Al Clark, who overrules him, calling it a trap by Bernie Williams that allows the tying run to score. After the game comes the word that replays showed Williams making a clean catch. David Cone puts it in perspective, saying, "I don't think the umps cost us the game. I think it was the six walks I permitted that came back to kill us." This launches an eight-game losing streak that drops the Yankees from second to sixth place in the inaugural wild card race.

August 20, 1964   John Buzhardt holds the Yankees to seven useless singles, winning 5-0 to complete a four-game sweep in Chicago in which the Yankees total six runs. On the bus after the game, Phil Linz is playing the harmonica, and manager Yogi Berra yells from the front that he'd better cease his off-key rendition of "Mary Had a Little Lamb." Linz doesn't hear him, asks what's up, and a helpful Mickey Mantle tells him, "Yogi wants you to play louder." So the Linz plays on. Pretty soon, Yogi charges back there, ready to pummel Linz, telling him, "You lose four straight and you act like you won the pennant." Yogi settles for fining him $200. This lack of discipline is cited as one reason the Yankees decide before the season is over to fire Yogi no matter what. As proof that the whole thing is a joke, Ralph Houk, the GM who fires Yogi in October, gives Linz a raise on **February 16, 1965** and tells him, "I want it clearly understood that this extra $200 is not in any sense repayment of your fine—you have to use it specifically for music lessons so that you can play that thing better." And Yogi is gone.

August 21, 1964   After fining Phil Linz, Yogi says, "Maybe it'll wake us up." It doesn't. For the second straight day, the Yankees can't get an extra-base hit, much less a run. This time it's a 7-0 loss at Boston, held to six singles by Bob Heffner, a pitcher with a career record of 11-21. They're in third place, five games behind the White Sox, and primed for Yogi's wasted comeback. . .

August 21, 1989 Luis Polonia, a proud Yankee for exactly two months, pleads no-contest in Milwaukee to charges of having sex with a 15-year-old girl at Milwaukee's Pfister Hotel the week before. In October, he is sentenced to 60 days in jail plus a $1,500 fine. The Yankees, bless their hearts, hold his job, and in 1990, he gets in 22 at-bats before they trade him.

August 22, 1976 Catfish Hunter and Ron Guidry get ripped for eight runs, and it's 8-0 Angels in the bottom of the ninth inning. Somehow, the Yankees wake up and get three straight hits, a walk, and four more hits, capped by Roy White's game-tying home run. They can't lose after that, can they? Watch this. In the 11th inning, Sparky Lyle fails to get an out on a bunt, White's throw from left field hits a runner and bounces away, Lyle's hurried throw back to the plate eludes the catcher for another error, and shortstop Jim Mason's throwing error helps a third run score. The Bat Day crowd of 52,864 at Yankee Stadium could've gone home an hour earlier instead of witnessing the 11-8 horror-show that completes a weekend sweep by the sixth-place Angels.

August 24, 1929 The two-time defending champion Yankees trailed the Athletics by a dozen games when they arrived in St. Louis for a four-game series. This is the third game, and they haven't scored a run yet! Future Hall of Famer Waite Hoyt lost the opener, 10-0, to Sam Gray. Yesterday, future Hall of Famer Herb Pennock lost, 5-0, to George Blaeholder, with Babe Ruth and Lou Gehrig going hitless. Today, Alvin "General" Crowder is even better, holding the Yankees to a pair of hits by Gene Robertson and winning, 4-0. Crowder even doubles in two of the runs off Roy Sherid. In the series finale, Babe Ruth smacks a pair of solo homers, enough for them to lose, 3-2, and complete the sweep that buries them even further.

August 25, 1952 Detroit's Virgil Trucks becomes only the third pitcher to throw two no-hitters in one season, smothering the Yankees, 1-0. For four innings, however, it's a one-hitter. In the third inning, Johnny Pesky fields Rizzuto's grounder but has trouble getting the ball out of his glove and throws late to first base. Official scorer John Drebinger calls it an error, but press-box colleagues pressure him into changing it to a hit because the ball stuck in the webbing of Pesky's glove. After consulting with Pesky in the seventh inning, Drebinger changes the call back to an error, drawing cheers from the Yankee Stadium crowd. Trucks retires the final twenty batters to earn his niche in history.

August 26, 2003   "Roger Clemens's mother, Bess, threw out the ceremonial first pitch at Yankee Stadium last night," begins Tyler Kepner's account in the *New York Times*. "Then she kissed her son before he warmed up to face the Chicago White Sox. It was a pitching change the Yankees never should have made." Clemens is jolted for four homers in less than five innings, capped by Frank Thomas' grand slam. The Yankees yield six homers and lose, 13-2. After allowing nine runs in a game for the sixth time, Clemens echoes Kepner, saying, "They should have let her stay on the mound. It's a bad night when your mother has better stuff than you do. She'll let me know about it, too."

August 27, 1981   In a typical expression of Yankees empathy, George Steinbrenner orders Reggie Jackson to undergo a day-long physical examination. As Reggie's owner explains, "I ordered the examination for Reggie's good and for my edification, but mostly for Reggie's good. The eye exam and the reflex test were especially important." Steinbrenner's need for edification is prompted by Reggie's .212 average with just six homers in 61 games. Reggie regards the command as "obvious harassment" in the wake of Steinbrenner's refusal to discuss a new contract during the final year of the 35-year-old "straw that stirs the drink"'s contract. "George has mentally defeated him," a source tells the *New York Times*' Murray Chass. "George has won the battle with Reggie, but he lost the war." After the Yankees lose the World Series, Reggie becomes a free agent and gets as far as he can from Steinbrenner, signing with the California Angels.

August 28, 1924   The Yankees lead the Senators by a half-game as they open a four-game series at the Stadium. The Yankees, behind two Babe Ruth home runs, lead 6-3 after seven innings when it all blows up. Herb Pennock, Milt Gaston, and Sam Jones can't retire the Senators, who explode for eight runs. The key blow is a bases-loaded drive by Goose Goslin that goes for a triple after center fielder Whitey Witt loses it in the sun and hears it clank off his shoulder. The Senators romp, 11-6, and take over first place. Senators skipper Bucky Harris crows, "Watch us from now on. The Yankees will have Walter Johnson to beat tomorrow." Johnson wins, 5-1, and the Senators never look back, dethroning the Yankees and winning again in 1925.

August 29, 1925   Miller Huggins, the 5'6" Yankees manager dubbed "Mighty Mite," finally stands up to (6'2") Babe Ruth, fining him $5,000 and suspending him indefinitely for "general misconduct" off the field. Asked if that means Ruth has been drinking, Huggins says, "Of course it means drinking, and it means a lot of other things besides." There isn't room in this book to print *that* list. Huggins insists, "Patience has ceased to be a virtue. I have tried to overlook Ruth's behavior for a while, but I have decided to take summary action to bring the big fellow to his senses." Naturally, Ruth tries going over Huggins' head to escape discipline, and he is shocked when the owner backs the manager. The suspension is lifted after nine days but the fine stands, costing Ruth roughly 10 percent of that season's salary.

August 30, 1922   Enjoy this *New York Times* description of Babe Ruth's reaction to taking a called third strike: "The Babe's fiery Peruvian blood boiled in his veins with an audible hissing sound. He took his stand by the plate, and gave two or three gruff Peruvian barks to clear his throat. Then he launched on the air a crisp, unflattering oration directed at the arbiter. [Tommy] Connolly had the last word, however, and the Babe was banished from the grounds." Hundreds of kids in the right field upper deck at the Polo Grounds spend the rest of the day screaming at Connolly. Ruth gets suspended, too.

August 31, 2004   Yankee Stadium is sold out, and George Steinbrenner is there, too, as the Yankees suffer the worst defeat in franchise history. The carnage begins with Travis Hafner's bases-loaded triple in the first inning. Javier Vazquez is knocked out in the second inning, but three relievers don't do any better. The Indians are already routing the Yankees before they score six runs in the fifth inning and six more in the ninth. Vazquez takes the loss after giving up six runs, matched by Esteban Loaiza but outdone by Tanyon Sturtze's seven. The final score (fanfare!): 22-0. It's the biggest margin of defeat in Yankees history and the largest shutout margin in the majors since 1900. Steinbrenner is so angry he can't even bark at reporters, slamming the door to his limo without looking back.

September

September 1, 1925 In the most humiliating episode of his playing career, Babe Ruth is sent to the corner by the Yankees. Three days after being suspended by Miller Huggins, Ruth makes his appeal to Jacob Ruppert. He's sorry for those nasty things he said about Huggins but still doesn't understand why Huggins suspended him. Ruppert backs Huggins, who says the suspension will continue because "Ruth will have to realize that the club is bigger than he is." Meeting in the clubhouse, Ruth asks Huggins, "Can I put on a uniform and practice?" Huggins tells him, "I will let you know when I am ready to see you." Ruth goes home and sulks like a bad little boy stuck indoors while the other kids are choosing up sides. He doesn't return to action until September 7.

September 2 Gather around, Red Sox fans, for five great games on this date. 1912: The Red Sox sweep a doubleheader at the Polo Grounds, 2-1 and 1-0. Russ Ford balks in the winning run in the first game, and Joe Wood wins his 30th game of the season in the second, and his fourteenth straight. 1946: The largest Yankee Stadium crowd of the season, 73,551, see the pennant-bound Sox sweep two games. Boo Ferriss wins his 24th game in the opener, 5-2, and Mickey Harris stifles them to win the nightcap, 3-1. 1990: The Sox win, 7-1, at Fenway Park to polish off a three-game sweep in which they outscore the Yankees, 29-5. Ellis Burks and Mike Greenwell drive in all the runs as the Red Sox win all the season's home games against the Yankees for the first time.

September 3, 1906   Perhaps only an umpire called "Silk" O'Loughlin could handle a ballplayer as frenzied as
Highlanders shortstop Norman "Kid" Elberfeld, dubbed "The Tabasco
Kid" for his fiery temper. Objecting to a call at second base, Elberfeld
charges at O'Loughlin, who waves him aside. Not so soon. Elberfeld
makes six attempts to kick O'Loughlin, tries to stomp O'Loughlin's feet
with his spikes, jerks his arm, pushes him, is led back to the bench by
policemen, charges onto the field again, punches a teammate who tries
to stop him, makes another run at O'Loughlin, and is finally subdued by
police while his home-town fans hiss and boo him nonstop. He's suspended for a week.

September 4, 1908   Twenty-year-old Walter Johnson of Washington shuts out the Highlanders, 3-0, holding
them to six scattered singles and a walk. He's just getting started. He'll
shut them out again tomorrow at the Hilltop on a four-hitter. After blue
laws force them to take Sunday off, he comes back on Monday to throttle
them with his third shutout in four days. This time they get just two hits
off him, while he scores two runs in a 4-0 victory. The kid, who now has
15 wins in the majors, gets a lot of attention for this feat, overwhelming
the New Yorkers with a blazing sidearm fastball and not much more.
These are three of his untouchable record of 110 shutouts—21 against the
Yankees, part of his 61-38 career record against them.

September 5, 2013   The Red Sox arrive at Yankee Stadium, eight
games up in the pennant race with the
Yankees hoping to snag a wild card berth in the postseason tournament.
The Red Sox lead, 7-2, in the seventh inning when the Yankees erupt with
six runs to take the lead. But Mariano Rivera blows the save after getting
the first two outs in the ninth inning. Mike Napoli's broken-bat hit starts
it, a pinch-runner steals a base, and another single ties it, the favored
Boston strategy against Rivera. In the tenth, they try it against Joba
Chamberlain. Jacoby Ellsbury singles and steals second, and Shane Vic-
torino, a switch-hitter, elects to hit right-handed against Chamberlain.
This becomes pivotal on a two-strike check-swing; first base umpire Joe
West rules it a no-swing, and after Victorino's single scores Ellsbury,

Chamberlain is removed from the game by Joe Girardi and removed much further by West, who ejects him for screaming obscenities from the dugout. The Red Sox win, 9-8.

September 6, 2013   This time the Yankees blow a five-run lead in the seventh inning, as Mike Napoli's grand slam off Boone Logan ties it, 8-8. Logan later admits, "My mind wasn't there. My elbow was distracting me," a twinge that became a home run. Preston Claiborne is almost as bad. Shane Victorino's two-run homer (he also homered off Claiborne yesterday) gives Boston the lead, and pretty soon it's 12-8 Boston, the final score. The Yankees drop to fourth place, where they finish the season. . .

September 6, 1981   Forget that Gene "Stick" Michael just managed the Yankees to the first-half title in the 1981 split season, guaranteeing them a playoff spot. George Steinbrenner forgets it quickly enough when Michael complains publicly about repeated threats to fire him. He wants Michael to apologize for feeling threatened, i.e. bullies Michael to apologize for being bullied. Michael refuses, so Steinbrenner fires him, replacing him with Bob Lemon.

September 7, 2013   There's no suspense this time as the Red Sox crush the Yankees for the third straight game at Yankee Stadium. They drill starter Phil Huff for nine runs in the first four innings, including the first of Mike Napoli's two homers. Jim Miller, making one of three career appearances as a Yankee, contributes three more runs to the fun, two on Xander Bogaerts' homer. The Yankees score some late runs to make the final score 13-9, completing a three-game stretch in which the Yankees score 25 runs while allowing 34 runs and 45 hits.

September 7, 1965   For the second straight day, the Yankees drop two games to the Orioles at Yankee Stadium. The Orioles never trail all day, winning 4-2 behind Dave McNally and 9-5 behind a 16-hit attack. The Yankees have lost seven games in a row and are heading for their first second-division finish since Calvin Coolidge was President. Happy days ahead!

September 8, 1919   The Red Sox sweep a doubleheader at the Polo
Grounds, 3-1 and 3-0. In the opener, Boston
left fielder Babe Ruth socks a home run deep into the right field stands,
his 26th of the season, breaking the "modern" record set by Buck Freeman
in 1899; he'll finish with 29. The *New York Times* describes it: Ruth "took
a mighty swing and the ball sailed on a line to the right field grandstand.
It was not one of those fluke affairs which just manage to tumble into the
stands. The ball kept rising as it traveled and when it banged into the
seats in the farthest corner it was still going upward." This is Ruth's most
versatile season. He leads the American League in runs, home runs,
on-base percentage, and slugging percentage while posting a 9-5 record
and a 2.97 ERA in 17 games. Then they trade him to the Yankees, who take
away half his fun by limiting him to the outfield.

September 9, 1962   Rookie pitcher Dick Radatz of the Red Sox
earns his nickname of "The Monster" with
this *nine-inning* relief outing at Yankee Stadium. The 6'7", 260-pound
right-hander with the overpowering submarine delivery enters in the
seventh inning of the second game of a doubleheader, after the Red Sox
won the opener, 9-3. After surrendering a quick run that ties the game,
4-4, Radatz settles down and gives up almost nothing over the next eight
innings—five hits, no walks, and seven strikeouts. Marshall Bridges
matches him until the 16th inning, when Bob Tillman scores on Billy
Gardner's squeeze-bunt single. Radatz gets his first win against the Yankees; in his career, he'll go 6-1 against them.

September 10, 1999   David Cone, author of a recent perfect game,
calls this the best pitching effort he's ever
seen, and nobody argues, especially not the 55,239 paying witnesses at
Yankee Stadium. Pedro Martinez of the Red Sox gives up a second-inning
homer to Chili Davis, and that's it, the Yankees' only baserunner apart
from Chuck Knoblauch, hit by a Martinez pitch to start the game. Pedro
fans 17 of the 28 batters he faces in the one-hitter that raises his record to
21-4. Mike Stanley's two-run homer off Andy Pettitte is the difference in
the 3-1 win. "I had no clue," admits Darryl Strawberry, who pinch-hit and

struck out, one of five straight Yankees to whiff as Martinez concludes his gem in style.

September 11, 1961   The New York metropolitan area hummed all summer with the Mantle-Maris assault on Babe Ruth's record of 60 home runs. Everybody is rooting for Mantle, whose chances are butchered today thanks to a medical mishap. He gets a "flu shot" that goes very wrong, causing a hip abscess and other gross complications. It turns out that the shot, administered by a quack, was actually amphetamines that didn't sit well with The Mick. Trailing Maris, 56-53, before today, Mantle hits just one more homer the rest of the season, fizzling out of the quest. Maris, a guy who wants the spotlight even less than Mantle does, breaks the record without getting the glory.

September 12, 1954   The largest crowd in American League history (84,874 paid, 86,563 total) jams Cleveland's Municipal Stadium to see the hometown Indians sweep the Yankees and virtually knock them out of the pennant race. Bob Lemon twirls a six-hitter to win the opener, 4-1, his 22nd victory. In the nightcap, Early Wynn wins #21, striking out a dozen Yankees and giving up just one hit after the first inning. He also singles to start a two-out, three-run rally in the fifth inning that is all he needs to win, 3-2. The sweep leaves the Yankees eight games out of first place with only ten games to play. Despite a record of 103-51, the Yankees finish eight games behind the Indians and get to spend all of October playing golf.

September 13, 2010   After CC Sabathia and David Price duel through eight innings, the Yankees lose, 1-0, in ten innings at Tampa Bay. Reid Brignac's homer off Sergio Mitre sends the Yankees to their seventh loss in eight games. It's part of a picturesque collapse down the stretch, as the Yankees lose 17 of their final 26 games. That's exactly what it takes—losing their last two games at Fenway Park, to boot—to lose the division by one game, setting up a postseason loss on the road.

September 14, 1985 The Blue Jays break open a 2-2 tie with a five-run fifth inning, a disastrous outing by Dave Righetti which drops the Yankees 3½ games behind the division-leading Blue Jays. This is the second of eight straight losses for the Yankees, knocking them out of the pennant race. . .

September 14, 2011 Wouldn't you know it—a Seattle shortstop named Rodriguez hits a 12th-inning, walkoff homer to pin the 2-1 defeat on Cory Wade, his only loss of the season. Oh, that would be Luis Rodriguez, belting the last of his ten career home runs. Rodriguez, who began the day with a .176 average, earlier belted a pair of doubles off Ivan Nova, matching the extra-base output of the Yankees.

September 15, 1940 The Yankees start the day 2½ games behind first-place Detroit and end it four games behind first-place Cleveland, thanks to a dismal performance at Sportsman's Park. The Browns sock it to them twice, 10-5 and 2-1. In the opener, Johnny Niggling pitches a slick 12-hitter to defeat Red Ruffing, and Eldon Auker completes the sweep. The Yankees, four-time defending champions, never lead the pack again and finish third.

September 15, 1964 Dean Chance of the Los Angeles Angels two-hits the Yankees, completing the most dominating season any pitcher ever has against them. In five starts, he allows exactly one run, a Mickey Mantle homer, and his worst performance is a four-hitter! The only time he doesn't beat them, he gives up just three hits in 14 innings but leaves with a scoreless tie. In 50 innings, he gives the Yankees 14 hits and 9 walks, striking out 36 with a 0.18 ERA.

September 16, 1955 Unless you saw Mickey Mantle play a lot, you wouldn't suspect how terrific a drag bunter he was. This is one time when he regrets beating out a bunt. He tears a hamstring against the Red Sox, and over the rest of the season, he pinch-hits twice and that's it. In the World Series, his performance is futile. After missing the first two games, he homers in his first at-bat in Game 3, off Johnny Podres. But he goes 1-for-9 the rest of the Series and can only pinch-hit in Game 7, when the Yankees are shut out by Podres to give the Dodgers their only Brooklyn championship. But did I mention that I never saw a better drag bunter?

September 17, 1982 There's nothing like getting eliminated from a pennant race in style, as the Yankees do with this 14-0 drubbing in Milwaukee. German-born Stefan Wever makes his major league debut, allows nine runs in less than three innings, and is never heard from again. Gorman Thomas' three-run homer caps a five-run first inning, while Robin Yount and Paul Molitor combine for seven hits and six runs scored. This is the sixth of nine straight losses for the Yankees, who go 6-15 down the stretch and drop to fifth place. . . **1991**: Milwaukee's Chris Bosio gives up a hit on his first pitch of the game but allows the Yankees only one more as he beats them, 2-0, their eleventh loss in twelve games. Manager Stump Merrill sums the whole thing up nicely: "Same crud, different verse."

September 18, 1920 The White Sox pummel Bob Shawkey and three relievers, piling up 21 hits in a 15-9 win. Buck Weaver and Happy Felsch have the most fun with four hits apiece, just ten days before their professional careers end with the revelation of their part in the "Black Sox" scandal.

September 18, 1979 Paul Mirabella is knocked out in the first inning of a 16-3 loss at Cleveland, but Bob Kammeyer's demise is truly epic. Entering with a 4-0 deficit, he serves up a gopher ball to the first hitter, Ted Cox. It goes downhill from there— double, single, single, Toby Harrah's three-run homer, double, hit batter, and another single before Billy Martin II sends relief. The eight-run bludgeoning, Kammeyer's only appearance this season, concludes his career.

September 19, 1968 Talk about tainted home runs! Mickey Mantle blasts career home run #535, passing Jimmie Foxx to grab second place in American League history. Too bad the achievement is spoiled by the gopher pitcher, Denny McLain of the Tigers. McLain wins his 31st game of the season today, so he knows what he's doing. He salutes Mantle as The Mick circles the bases at Tiger Stadium, and he later admits telling Mantle he'll groove an easy fastball to let him hit the home run. "McLain has made a fan of me for life," says Mantle, without saying why. He needs all the help he can get, limping into retirement with a .237 batting average and .398 slugging percentage in his final season.

September 20, 1958   It's easy to think of Hall of Famer Hoyt Wilhelm as merely a relief pitcher; when he shattered the record by pitching 1,070 games in the majors, only 52 were starts. Like Dennis Eckersley, Wilhelm also tossed a no-hitter in the majors, making monkeys of the Yankees today at Memorial Stadium in Baltimore. The 36-year-old knuckleball artist, picked up by the Orioles on waivers four weeks earlier, walks two and retires the final 17 Yankees. He strikes out eight batters, including Hank Bauer and Elston Howard twice each. The Orioles win, 1-0, on a seventh-inning homer by catcher Gus Triandos off Bobby Shantz. The no-hitter is no fluke, as Wilhelm wins 15 games and an ERA title in 1959 as a starter before becoming a bullpen star in his forties.

September 21, 1985   After giving up 38 runs in his last 37 innings, embattled Yankees right-hander Ed Whitson takes on an easier opponent, a 160-pound lawyer in a Baltimore bar. Whitson grabs the man by the throat, and suddenly, like a moth drawn to a flame, there's Billy Martin IV. Whitson gladly transfers his hostility toward Martin, and they engage in a 45-minute battle. Murray Chass described it in the *New York Times*: "Witnesses said it began in the bar, moved to the hotel lobby, where Whitson kicked Martin in the groin, then moved outside the hotel, where Whitson broke away from people restraining him, rushed at Martin and knocked him down, winding up on top of him." After they're sent to their rooms, Martin calls Whitson to invite him to the parking lot for more, but Whitson resists the temptation. Martin suffers the worst defeat of his long pugilistic career, losing points for a broken arm and two cracked ribs. He also loses his job.

September 23, 1970   Four years after the franchise's demise, here's how thoroughly the losing mentality has pervaded the Yankees clubhouse since the departure of Yogi Berra, Whitey Ford, and Mickey Mantle. Champagne flows and spills tonight in the Yankees clubhouse in a post-game celebration after a 6-4 victory over the Senators—which clinches second place! That's what passes for glory these days at Yankee Stadium, where the paid crowd for this momentous event is a skeptical 5,082. After finishing tenth, ninth, fifth and fifth the previous four seasons, they finish second! Manager Ralph Houk is all smiles in his office, flanked by equally gleeful GM Lee MacPhail and club president Mike Burke, when players douse them with three buckets of cold water. Who can blame them—we're talking second place, folks! Oh boy! Joe DiMaggio must have puked when he heard about it.

September 24, 1934   Babe Ruth plays his final game at Yankee Stadium, and nobody seems to care. Only a couple of thousand people show up, and there isn't much to see as the Yankees lose 5-0 to the Red Sox and lefty Spike Merena, who records his only victory in the majors. The loss eliminates them as the Tigers clinch the pennant. Hobbled by a leg injury, Ruth walks in the first inning, calls for pinch-runner Myril Hoag, and vanishes into the sunset.

September 24, 1974   Shea Stadium is crowded with 46,448 rowdy fans as the first-place Yankees are swept by the Red Sox in a twi-night doubleheader, 4-2 and 4-0. The *New York Times'* Joseph Durso surveys the angry crowd, "many of whom spent the evening in pitched battles with one another and with the Shea Stadium guards. . . They threw fists, whisky bottles, beer, rubber balls and firecrackers in outbreaks of fighting and hooligan behavior that kept the crowd howling."

September 25, 1968   Luis Tiant of the Indians beats the Yankees, 3-0, with a one-hitter, a first-inning single by Mickey Mantle in his final game at Yankee Stadium. In four starts against the Yankees, Tiant pitches three shutouts, allowing only 14 hits and striking out 36.

September 25, 2011   The Yankees lose, 7-4, in 14 innings to the Red Sox at Yankee Stadium. Scott Proctor, approaching the end of his career faster than he knows, gives up the game-winning three-run homer by Jacoby Ellsbury.

September 25, 2016   Tyler Clippard comes in to save a 3-2 lead at Toronto and becomes the losing pitcher instead. On a squeeze bunt, he tries to scoop the ball with his glove to the catcher but fails miserably, letting the winning run get to second. A moment later, the Yankees have lost their eleventh game in the last fourteen, sending them from wild card contention to fourth place in their own division.

September 26, 1940   Facing a $1 million lawsuit filed by Lou Gehrig, *New York Daily News* reporter Jimmy Powers retracts his **August 18** column, one of the most ill-advised in journalism history. Trying to explain why the four-time defending champion Yankees were languishing in fifth place, Powers suggested that the players were victims of a "polio germ" contracted from Gehrig, diagnosed in 1939 with a form of infantile paralysis. "The Yankees were exposed to it at its most acute stage," wrote Powers. "They played ball with the afflicted Gehrig, dressed and undressed in the locker with him, traveled, played cards and ate with him." The half-dead Gehrig is outraged and wastes time and energy getting Powers to admit that he knows little about medicine and that "Gehrig has no communicable disease that supposedly played havoc with the Yankee ball club." His readers knew less than he did, and his assertion caused a germ-panic around New York City. The *News*' public apology calms the public, and the suit is settled out of court for $17,500.

September 27, 1940   In their final 13 games, the Philadelphia Athletics are swept in six doubleheaders. This is their only single game, a 6-2 victory that eliminates the Yankees from the pennant race. The Yankees finish two games behind the Tigers and can blame it on their inability to solve Johnny Babich, a National League reject who beats them five times this season. You'd think Joe DiMaggio, Bill Dickey, and the boys would solve a guy with a 30-45 career record in his sixth start against them, but he holds them to two hits until the ninth inning.

September 28, 2011   A gruesome, 8-7 loss in 12 innings over almost five hours at Tampa Bay gives the Yankees a four-game losing streak going to the postseason. They take a 7-0 lead by the fifth inning, but Joe Girardi is playing musical chairs on the mound, giving eleven pitchers a little tune-up for the October haul. Several of them suck, notably Boone Logan and Luis Ayala, who give up three runs apiece in the eighth inning. The Rays win it off Scott Proctor, making the final appearance of his career, walking off into baseball oblivion after Evan Longoria's 12th-inning homer. Sure enough, the momentum-less Yankees, despite the best record in the AL, bomb out in the Division Series against Detroit.

September 29, 1916   Boston's 21-year-old southpaw phenom, George "Babe" Ruth, shuts out the Yankees, 3-0, on a five-hitter to finish the best pitching season of his career. How good is he? His 23-12 record features a league-leading nine shutouts. He leads the AL in that new stat, ERA, at 1.75. For good measure, he wins a 14-inning 2-1 decision in the World Series. The Yankees finish fourth. Maybe the Yankees turned him loose in the outfield because they were tired of seeing him pitch. In 23 starts against the Yankees, he went 17-5 with a 2.21 ERA and 21 complete games. If the AL had a designated hitter back then like the one Connie Mack had proposed, nobody ever would have known (or cared) whether this kid could hit.

September 30, 1973   After losing 8-5 to the Tigers, it's farewell to Yankee Stadium for two years of exile in Flushing while Yankee Stadium gets a bad facelift. But that isn't far enough for manager Ralph Houk, who is fed up with the interference of new owner George Steinbrenner. A Yankee since 1939 as a player, coach, manager, and general manager, Houk resigns. "A man has to go with his convictions. I blame no one but myself. .. It's been a little rough since 1966." After pennants in his first three seasons as manager, Houk became the GM who wrecked the managing careers of Yogi Berra and Johnny Keane. He paid his penance by kicking himself back down to the dugout, presiding over eight floundering campaigns. Ultimately, this ex-Marine who earned a battlefield promotion to major at the Battle of the Bulge when he was 25, needed just five months under Steinbrenner's command to resign with two years left on his contract. He managed nine more years with the Tigers and Red Sox.

October 10, 1904 Jack Chesbro wins 41 games, tops in the 20th century, but his amazing season goes up in smoke in the ninth inning on the season's final day. With the score tied, he throws a wild pitch that allows the winning run to score, giving Boston the winning run that clinches the pennant. Chesbro, a spitball pitcher, may have crossed up catcher Red Kleinow, who should have been charged with a passed ball according to some historians. It doesn't matter—the biggest winner in franchise history lost the pennant on one pitch.

Part II

The Postseason

World Series Era (1903-1968)

In today's version of major league baseball, where one-third of the teams make it to the postseason, it's easy to forget what it was like before there *was* a postseason. It always jars me to read about "Babe Ruth's postseason record," since two decades after Ruth's death, there was still only the World Series following the regular season. Only two teams out of sixteen got to keep playing. Thus the delightful frustration of Casey Stengel's 1954 Yankees, who won more games (103) than any other squad during Stengel's tenure in the Bronx but still finished eight games behind the Cleveland Indians and were toast before September ended.

It took eighteen years for New York's American League franchise to play in its first World Series. That is, it took until their acquisition of Ruth in the biggest New York swindle since Peter Minuet hit town. Ruth's Yankees won three of six World Series they reached in the 1920s, but the real Yankees dynasty didn't begin until 1936, when they won the first of four straight Series. From 1936-1964, the Yankees played in 22 of the 29 World Series, losing only six of them. That means we get to celebrate nine World Series in this section, in all their inept glory.

1921 World Series

The final best-5-of-9-game World Series—and the Yankees' first—was unusual because all eight games were played at the Polo Grounds, which the Giants rented to the Yankees for a decade, with alternating home teams. After spotting the Yankees the first two games, the Giants took five of the next six to give John McGraw his first title since 1905. The Giants' lineup was anchored by four future Hall of Famers: third baseman Frankie Frisch, first baseman George "Highpockets" Kelly, right fielder Ross Youngs, and shortstop Dave Bancroft. Art Nehf was their lone 20-game winner on a deep staff that held opponents to 203 fewer runs than the Giants scored.

October 7

Game 3: Down 2-0 in games and 4-0 in the third inning, the Giants come alive and trounce the Yankees, 13-5. It's 4-4 to the seventh inning, when Yankees reliever Jack Quinn gives up a single to Frisch and a double to Youngs to start the inning. Two pitchers later, it's 12-4, with Youngs' bases-loaded triple capping the eight-run rally.

October 9

Game 4: Carl Mays holds the Giants hitless until two outs in the sixth inning and takes a 1-0 lead to the eighth before his bubble bursts. Johnny Rawlings' RBI single ties it. After a bunt single and a sacrifice, George Burns doubles to put the Giants up, 3-1. The Yankees waste a late Babe Ruth homer and lose, 4-2.

October 11

Game 6: The Giants get good news: Babe Ruth is done for the Series. He has a sprained knee, sprained wrist, pulled leg tendon, and infected arm, and he tweaked the last two of those in the Game 5 victory. The arm wound reopened again, and the doctors' warning is heeded; his only remaining action is a futile pinch-hitting attempt. Today, the Yankees score three runs in the first inning but the Giants quickly tie it on homers by Irish Meusel and Frank Snyder off surprise starter Harry Harper, just 4-3 in his only season with the Yankees. The Yankees lead, 5-3, before a bad error by third baseman Mike McNally sets up a four-run rally as the Giants win, 8-5.

October 12 **Game 7:** Giants right-hander "Shufflin' Phil" Douglas shocks the Yankees with his second complete-game win of the Series, beating Carl Mays again, 2-1. The winning run comes in the seventh inning when Johnny Rawlings reaches on a two-out error by second baseman Aaron Ward and scores on Frank Snyder's double.

October 13 **Game 8:** Waite Hoyt pitches his third complete game of the Series without allowing an earned run—and loses! Two walks in the top of the first inning give the Giants an opening, and Roger Peckinpaugh's error at shortstop allows a run to score. The Yankees can't believe that this Art Nehf guy, the southpaw they beat twice last week, is suddenly unhittable today. Only twice do they get a runner as far as third base, where Babe Ruth spends the day coaching, limping, and yelling at his teammates to say hello on their way home. His plea for company is unheeded. In the ninth inning, still trailing 1-0, Ruth grounds out weakly and, after a walk, Johnny Rawlings makes a great stop on a smash by Home Run Baker to start a Series-ending double play.

Yankees Goats: First baseman Wally Pipp, shortstop Roger Peckinpaugh, and center fielder Elmer Miller all bat below .180 while the Yankees score 22 runs in eight games. Bob Shawkey, 18-12 during the season, has a terrible time with the Giants, immediately blowing the four-run lead in Game 3 and taking the loss in Game 6 after giving up five runs in relief of Harper.

1922 World Series

For the second straight year, baseball fans could camp on Coogan's Bluff to catch all the World Series action at the Polo Grounds. For the second straight year, they saw Babe Ruth's Yankees crushed by the Giants, who treated their tenants roughly. Game 2 was a ten-inning tie called by darkness, and that was the Yankees' high point in this final comeuppance from their decade-long landlords before they slinked across the Harlem River to their own ballpark in 1923.

October 4

Game 1: Leslie "Bullet Joe" Bush, after posting a 26-7 record in his first year as a Yankee, escapes three jams in the first seven innings, enjoying a 2-0 lead. It all falls apart in the eighth when the first four Giants single—Dave Bancroft, Heinie Groh, Frank Frisch, and Irish Meusel—before Waite Hoyt comes in to give up the game-winning sacrifice fly by Ross Youngs.

October 6

Game 3: After the Game 2 tie, John McGraw hands the ball to knuckleball pitcher Jack Scott, who went 8-2 after the Giants signed him in August. McGraw knows something, because Scott limits the Yankees to four puny hits, beating Waite Hoyt, 3-0.

October 7

Game 4: This is the game that makes Miller Huggins suspect that Carl Mays is up to no good, probably because it resembles the way Black Sox pitchers lost games in the 1919 Series. Mays takes a 2-0 lead to the fifth inning and gives up four quick runs, with key hits including a double by opposing pitcher Hugh McQuillan and a cheap single on a ball Mays fails to handle. That's all the Giants need to win, 4-3, and get within one win of a sweep.

October 8 **Game 5:** A sweep it is with a 5-3 victory in which Art Nehf gets the Series-clinching victory for the second straight year. Just as in Game 1, Joe Bush takes a lead to the eighth inning, this time 3-2, and blows up when it matters most. He gives up four hits and three runs, with George Kelly's bases-loaded single the game-winner.

Yankees Goats: The Yankees hit a feeble .203 as a team, scoring 11 runs in five games. Babe Ruth is the biggest disappointment, batting a weak .118 with just a single and a double in five games. Three other Yankees can't crack .200: catcher Wally Schang, second baseman Aaron Ward, and shortstop Everett Scott.

1926 World Series

This Series is famous for 39-year-old Grover Cleveland Alexander, legendarily either drunk or hung over after winning Game 6 the day before, coming out of the bullpen to strike out Tony Lazzeri with the bases loaded in Game 7 and save the Series for the St. Louis Cardinals. Aficionados also know that it had the most embarrassing ending to a World Series ever, with Babe Ruth getting thrown out trying to steal second for the final out as Alexander finished off his heroics. But there was plenty of agony for Yankees fans in this Series before Ruth's ill-advised dash for the cash. The Cardinals were led by player-manager Rogers Hornsby, with first baseman Jim Bottomley and third baseman Les Bell the most productive hitters.

October 3

Game 2: This was a tough year for "Pete" Alexander. After eight years with the Cubs, he got off to a sluggish start and found himself put on waivers, a fading alcoholic with his future much in doubt. After going 9-7 for the Cardinals, he's in vintage form in this start at Yankee Stadium, a complete-game four-hitter, winning 6-2. He strikes out ten Yankees, holding Babe Ruth and Lou Gehrig hitless, and right fielder Billy Southworth breaks up the game with a three-run homer off Urban Shocker.

October 5

Game 3: Fans of Jesse Haines figure he deserved Hall of Fame election just for this effort, a 4-0 joyride in front of 37,708 fans at Sportsman's Park, a record in that ballpark. Haines, 20-8 during the season, limits the Yankees to five harmless singles, and his two-run homer off Dutch Ruether is the icing on the cake.

October 9 **Game 6:** After the Yankees go ahead in the Series, Alexander ruins their triumphant return to Yankee Stadium with another complete-game gem, a nearly carefree 10-2 victory. The Cardinals hammer Bob Shawkey for three runs in the top of the first inning, and he bites the dust during a five-run seventh that is facilitated when left fielder Bob Meusel loses a fly ball in the sun, not realizing how early it gets late out there.

October 10 **Game 7:** For the second time, Waite Hoyt loses the deciding game of a World Series without giving up an earned run. All it takes is a three-run fourth inning. After a one-out single, shortstop Mark Koenig kicks a ground ball. On a fly ball between Koenig and Meusel, neither one catches it, loading the bases. Bob O'Farrell lifts a fly to center on which Meusel, having a stronger throwing arm, cuts in front of center fielder Earle Combs to catch the ball—and drops it. Tommy Thevenow's single finishes off the scoring at 3-2, setting up Alexander's heroics and Ruth's blunder on the bases, the only boner of his career that he didn't enjoy.

In *My Greatest Day in Baseball*, Alexander told Francis J. Powers about baseball's most notorious failure to steal: "I caught the blur of Ruth starting for second as I pitched and then came the whistle of the ball as [Bob] O'Farrell rifled it to second. I wheeled around and there was one of the grandest sights of my life. [Rogers] Hornsby, his foot anchored on the bag and his gloved hand outstretched, was waiting for Ruth to come in."

Yankees Goats: Besides Ruth and Meusel in the crucial game, the spectacular disaster in this Series is rookie Mark Koenig. He goes 4-for-32 (.125), strikes out six times, grounds into three double plays, and commits four errors. Meusel, the #3 RBI guy on "Murderers' Row," doesn't drive in a run in the whole Series.

1942 World Series

In 1942, the Yankees won over 100 games for the fifth time in seven years, and they have won their last eight World Series. That streak ends here against the St. Louis Cardinals, whose manager, Billy Southworth, played on the 1926 championship team. The Cardinals won 106 games during the season, three more than the Yankees, and they will win four of the next five National League pennants. Though World War II affects many teams starting this season, the Yankees and Cardinals remain largely intact, and the Yankees have four future Hall of Famers up the middle: Joe DiMaggio, Joe Gordon, Phil Rizzuto, and Bill Dickey. The Cardinals are led by Enos Slaughter and rookie Stan Musial. This looks like an even match on paper, but not so much on the field.

October 1

Game 2: The Cardinals even the Series on a complete-game, 4-3 win by rookie right-hander Johnny Beazley, 21-6 during the season. After the Yankees rally to tie the game in the eighth inning, the Cardinals construct the winning run the way you're supposed to, with two future Hall of Famers coming through with two outs. Slaughter doubles, goes to third when Rizzuto fumbles the relay throw, and scores on a single by 21-year-old Stan Musial.

October 3

Game 3: Neither team manages an extra-base hit in this duel at Yankee Stadium between the Yankees' Spud Chandler and southpaw Ernie White, who will win only five more games in the majors after this year. He's a humdinger today. The Yankees never get more than one runner in an inning, and Joe DiMaggio, who has two of the Yankees' six hits, strikes out the only time it matters, with a runner on third base. Bunts and slippery fielding help the Cardinals to the 2-0 win.

October 4

Game 4: After yesterday's sedate game, this is a wild one. The Cardinals batter Hank Borowy in a six-run fourth inning, but the Yankees manage to tie it, 6-6. Atlee Donald is the culprit this time, walking Enos Slaughter and Stan Musial to start the seventh inning. Both come around to score, and the Cardinals win, 9-6.

October 5

Game 5: The 1942 Cardinals become the only team to sweep three games at Yankee Stadium and win the Series going away. Johnny Beazley rides again, defeating Red Ruffing, 4-2. It's a 2-2 tie in the ninth when third baseman Whitey Kurowski's two-run homer off Ruffing puts the Cardinals on the brink of the title. The Yankees get the first two men on in the home ninth, but Joe Gordon caps an awful Series by getting picked off second base by catcher Walker Cooper, killing the Yankees' last hope.

Yankees Goats: Joe Gordon is the man, batting .095 (2-for-21) and making the brain-cramp mistake that ends the Series on an embarrassing note. First baseman Jerry Priddy just edges him out with a .100 average, while Gordon, Bill Dickey, and third baseman Red Rolfe all get through the Series without driving in a run.

1955 World Series

The 1955 season becomes the proverbial "next year" that Brooklyn fans have been awaiting forever. They haven't gotten to celebrate a title all century, with the Dodgers' cumulative record in World Series action 13-31 after losing the first two games at Yankee Stadium. The Bums come alive back at Ebbets Field in another all-New York Series with no days off, and the home team wins the first six games before Johnny Podres breaks the string and gives Brooklyn its only World Series title. The Dodgers are anchored by their own quartet of future Hall of Famers: MVP Roy Campanella, Jackie Robinson, Duke Snider, and Pee Wee Reese.

September 30

Game 3: The climb back begins with a Podres complete game, an 8-3 win in which the Dodgers knock Bob Turley out in the second inning. Campanella homers and drives in three runs, delighting a cozy Ebbets Field crowd of 34,209 which happily celebrates Podres' 23rd birthday.

October 1

Game 4: Trailing 3-1 in the fourth inning, the Dodgers take the lead on homers by Campanella and Gil Hodges off Don Larsen, and Duke Snider's three-run blast in the next inning off Johnny Kucks enables the Dodgers to coast to an 8-5 win that squares the Series.

October 2

Game 5: The Dodgers belt three homers off Bob Grim, two by Snider (giving him four in the Series) and one by Sandy Amoros, and lead all the way, winning 5-3 to get within one win of their first title.

Game 7: After Whitey Ford wins Game 6, Podres, a nine-game winner during the regular season, blanks the Yankees on an eight-hitter, with Gil Hodges driving in both runs in the 2-0 finale. Podres is saved by a miraculous sixth-inning catch by left fielder Sandy Amoros, just put in the game as a defensive replacement. Amoros runs down a Yogi Berra drive in the corner, and his relay via Pee Wee Reese doubles Gil McDougald off first base to squelch the Yankees' best threat.

Yankees Goats: While an injured Mickey Mantle sees limited action, Bob Cerv and Irv Noren, who relieve him in center field, combine to go 3-for-32, driving in one run apiece. That RBI futility is matched by three other regulars: right fielder Hank Bauer, shortstop Phil Rizzuto, and third baseman Gil McDougald.

1957 World Series

In 1953, the Braves abandoned Boston and, in the first franchise shift in a half-century, became the Milwaukee Braves. They set attendance records in their first few seasons and reaped the reward with a World Series title in 1957. Big underdogs against the perpetual Yankees, they prevailed in seven games thanks largely to two men. Lew Burdette's exploits earned him recognition as the Series MVP. It could just as easily have been Hank Aaron, fresh off his first home run title with 44, who led all players in this Series with a .393 average, 11 hits, 3 homers, and 7 RBI.

October 3

Game 2: Lew Burdette, 17-9 during the regular season, earns a complete-game victory at Yankee Stadium, 4-2. It's 2-2 in the fourth inning when Yankees starter Bobby Shantz surrenders two runs on three singles plus Tony Kubek's error. From there, it's just Burdette and his surreptitious spitball, threatened only in the bottom of the ninth, when the Yankees get the tying runs on base before Burdette retires Hank Bauer to end it.

October 6

Game 4: In one of the most dramatic Series games of the decade, the Braves prevail in ten innings, 7-5. Warren Spahn has two outs in the ninth inning when Elston Howard's three-run homer ties it, 4-4. In the top of the tenth, the Yankees take the lead on Hank Bauer's RBI triple off Spahn, but the Yankees are helpless in the home half. When Tommy Byrne hits the leadoff batter, Casey Stengel yanks him and puts in Bob Grim. After a sacrifice, Johnny Logan doubles in the tying run, and Eddie Mathews blasts a homer to win it and square the Series.

Game 5: The key game of this Series is a terrific pitching duel between Burdette and

Whitey Ford at County Stadium. It's scoreless in the bottom of the sixth inning when consecutive two-out singles by Eddie Mathews, Hank Aaron, and Joe Adcock give Burdette a 1-0 lead. That's enough as Burdette polishes off a seven-hitter in which the Yankees never get a runner past second base.

Game 7: There isn't much suspense for the 61,207 fans at Yankee Stadium as Burdette

wins his third game of the Series, 5-0. The Braves knock starter Don Larsen out in the third inning, scoring four runs, and Burdette takes a four-hitter to the bottom of the ninth. Three singles load the bases before he retires Moose Skowron to bring the title to Milwaukee. For Burdette, it's a huge redemption. Originally signed by the Yankees in 1947, he spent five years in their minor league system, pitching exactly twice for the parent club before a trade to the Braves liberated him.

Yankees Goats: Second baseman Jerry Coleman takes the blame for the key Game 5 defeat. Mathews' hit is a high bounder which Coleman plays nonchalantly, and Mathews beats Coleman's soft throw. Credit also goes to Mickey Mantle, out of the lineup with a sore shoulder, who gets the call from Casey Stengel as a pinch-runner in the eighth inning of Game 5, and is thrown out trying to steal second in the 1-0 loss.

1960 World Series

This Series is a particular favorite with Yankees-haters because the Yankees managed to blow it despite outscoring the Pittsburgh Pirates, 55-27. How could that happen? The Yankees squandered their offensive explosions in support of Whitey Ford, who didn't need that much help, winning 10-0 and 12-0. Their other win was a 16-3 blowout in Game 2 behind Bob Turley. In the other games, the close ones where every little play mattered, the Pirates won every time, including twice at Yankee Stadium.

October 5

Game 1: It's a sign of things to come when Bill Virdon leads off for the Pirates with a walk, steals second, and races to third when nobody covers second! The Pirates knock out Art Ditmar in the first inning, take a 3-1 lead, and Vern Law and Roy Face hold off a couple of late rallies to win, 6-4.

October 9

Game 4: After getting blown out twice, the Pirates win another close one, 3-2, to even the Series. Vern Law is the two-way star of this one, winning his second game with 6 1/3 solid innings and contributing a big hit to the winning rally. Trailing 1-0 in the top of the fifth inning at Yankee Stadium, with two outs and two runners on base, Law doubles to tie the game, and Virdon follows with a two-run single that wins it. Roy Face saves the game for Law by retiring the final eight Yankees.

October 10

Game 5: In the key game, 62,753 fans crowd Yankee Stadium to see the Pirates lead all the way in the 5-2 victory. Art Ditmar gets roughed up in the second inning, and third baseman Don Hoak and second baseman Bill Mazeroski drive in two runs apiece for the Bucs. Harvey Haddix gets the win, and Face nearly duplicates his feat from yesterday. Again he gets the final eight outs, this time interrupted only by a walk to Mickey Mantle.

October 13

Game 7: Imagine a major league game where nobody strikes out! It sounds like T-ball, not the major leagues, yet it happens in this 10-9 classic that brings Pittsburgh its first title since 1925. In this grand seesaw battle, the Pirates lead early, 4-0, but the Yankees take a 7-4 lead to the bottom of the eighth inning. You know the wildness that follows: a five-run eighth, capped by Hal Smith's three-run homer, unfairly forgotten now because the Yankees tie it in the ninth inning to set up Bill Mazeroski's famous smash over the left field wall at Forbes Field, a section of wall still preserved a half-century after Forbes' abandonment by the Pirates. Among the Yankees who screw this one up are starting pitcher Bob Turley; Bobby Shantz and Jim Coates, both bombed in the five-run eighth; Ralph Terry, who serves up Maz's ticket to the Hall of Fame, and Roger Maris, 0-for-5 including two foul-outs with two runners on base.

Yankees Goats: The Yankees hit .338 and average eight runs a game in this Series, so the finger points at Art Ditmar and Ralph Terry, each responsible for two of the close losses. Ditmar is especially awful, knocked out in the first inning of Game 1 and the second inning of Game 5, retiring five Pirates while allowing six runs. Terry is the loser as the Game 4 starter and gains a perverse immortality as Mazeroski's victim, trudging toward the dugout after the first series-ending "walk-off" homer in Series history.

1963 World Series

The opening of Dodger Stadium in 1962 and the enlargement of the strike zone started a trend toward great pitching that increased over the rest of the decade. In 1963, the Dodgers and White Sox posted *team* ERAs under 3, and several teams were just over that mark, including the Yankees, who won 104 games. The Yankees continued their fine pitching in the World Series with a 2.91 team ERA—and they didn't have a chance. Sandy Koufax emasculated them in Game 1, and they never recovered, scoring a puny two runs in the next three games as the Dodgers became the first team since 1922 to sweep them.

October 2

Game 1: On a bright afternoon at Yankee Stadium, Sandy Koufax shows New Yorkers that he has become an unstoppable force. He retires the first 14 Yankees on ten strikeouts, three foul popups, and one dribbler to third base. By then, the Dodgers have staked him to a 5-0 lead, three of them on catcher Johnny Roseboro's homer off Whitey Ford and the other two on a single by ex-Yankee Moose Skowron. Koufax loses his shutout in the eighth inning but wins, 5-2, setting a Series record with 15 strikeouts.

October 3

Game 2: Johnny Podres is a 31-year-old veteran now, and this is his last good season, 14 wins giving him a total of 129 in a decade as a Dodger. He makes the most of his final World Series start and takes a five-hit shutout to the ninth before needing relief help to finish off a 4-1 win. Moose Skowron homers off Al Downing, making the Yankees regret trading him after he drove in 80 runs for them in 1962.

Game 3: The 55,912 fans at Dodger Stadium enjoy a terrific pitching duel lasting two hours and five minutes, leaving plenty of time to hit the beach. Don Drysdale shows the Yankees no mercy after their only scoring chance in the second inning. Mickey Mantle leads off with a bunt single, Drysdale nails Joe Pepitone, New York's hairdryer-toting first baseman, with a pitch, and after an intentional walk, Drysdale fans Jim Bouton to end the threat. Bouton doesn't know it, but he has already lost this game which features exactly seven singles and no extra-base hits. Two tricky hops in the first inning cost Bouton. His two-out pitch just eludes Elston Howard for a wild pitch, sending Jim Gilliam to second. Tommy Davis' hard grounder to second takes a bad hop off Bobby Richardson's shin into the outfield, scoring Gilliam with the game's only run. Drysdale gives up just three hits, and the 1-0 classic leaves the Dodgers one win away from a sweep. In a textbook case of baseball denial, Ralph Houk tells the *New York Times*, "It isn't the Dodger pitching. It's a Yankee batting letdown."

> October 5

Game 4: When Sandy Koufax takes the mound at Dodger Stadium against Whitey Ford, even Ralph Houk knows the Yankees have no chance. Their only runner in the first four innings comes from Willie Davis losing a fly ball in the sun. The Dodgers have just one hit off Ford, a Frank Howard single, when Howard strikes in the fifth inning with a home run. Mickey Mantle matches that in the seventh inning, and in the home seventh, Whitey Ford finds an ugly way to lose a two-hitter. Jim Gilliam bounces a ball to third base, and Clete Boyer makes the routine throw to first—where Pepitone never sees the ball. The white-shirted crowd combines with the glare of a sunny SoCal Sunday to blind him. The ball bounces off his wrist and caroms into foul territory, while Gilliam races all the way to

> October 6

third. Willie Davis' fly ball scores Gilliam easily, and Koufax does the rest, finishing off the New Yorkers, 2-1, with a six-hitter and eight strikeouts.

Yankees Goats: This is a team effort, especially by the offense, which averages one run per game while batting .174. Only Elston Howard hits over .250. Give an extra gold star to Boyer, 1-for-13 with six whiffs, and for failing to throw a ball that can stick in Pepitone's glove whether he sees it coming or not.

1964 World Series

This season could be called "The Rise and Demise of Manager Yogi," who overcame many obstacles to get within one win of the World Series title that *might* have saved his job. About the time he lost his grip on the team, an 8-14 stretch in August dropped them into third place, before a late-September, 11-game winning streak got them to the Series. The Cardinals played sub-.500 ball until mid-July and also got hot late, going 26-10 at one point. Led by future Hall of Famers Bob Gibson and Lou Brock, they featured an array of significant baseball figures, including Curt Flood, Tim McCarver, Bill White, and Ken Boyer.

October 7

Game 1: Whitey Ford loses his fourth straight World Series start and never gets another one. Mike Shannon's homer highlights a four-run sixth inning that knocks Ford out, while Brock and Flood each drive in two runs in the 9-5 victory at Busch Stadium. Trailing 6-5 in the eighth inning with two runners on, Mickey Mantle fans on a Barney Schultz knuckler to end the threat, and the Cardinals get three unearned insurance runs courtesy of a Clete Boyer error.

October 11

Game 4: The Cardinals even the Series at Yankee Stadium with one swing of the bat. After the Yankees jump to a 3-0 lead in the first inning, Al Downing cruises through five innings of one-hit ball, but the narcoleptic southpaw has a waking nightmare in the sixth. Pinch-hitter Carl Warwick singles, as does Curt Flood. After an out, Bobby Richardson's error loads the bases. Up steps third baseman Ken Boyer, the brother of Yankees third baseman Clete Boyer, who gets a good view of the baseball's trajectory as it sails high and past him for a grand slam. That's all there is. In comes Ron Taylor, a right-hander from Canada who later excels in the bullpen of the 1969 Miracle Mets. All he does is mow down the Yankees over the final four innings, with a two-out walk to Mickey Mantle the only runner.

October 12

Game 5: The Cardinals win two of three games at Yankee Stadium thanks to the first of seven straight Series victories by Bob Gibson. What he does to the Yankees today is more impressive than his 17-strikeout showpiece against the Tigers in 1968. Through eight innings, he scatters four singles, strikes out 11, and leads, 2-0, starting the scoring rally with a single. But the Yankees tie it on two unearned runs in the bottom of the ninth. In the tenth inning, Tim McCarver's three-run homer off Pete Mikkelsen makes for a 5-2 final score as Gibson goes the distance and fans 13.

October 15

Game 7: After Jim Bouton's second win of the Series forces Game 7 at Busch Stadium, it's Bob Gibson against rookie Mel Stottlemyre, the Game 2 winner. Stottlemyre cracks first, giving up three runs in the fourth inning, and Al Downing gives up three more in the fifth. The Yankees fight back on Mickey Mantle's home run, but Gibson takes a 7-3 lead to the ninth inning. With one out, Clete Boyer homers. With two outs, Phil Linz, of all people, homers, and St. Louis manager Johnny Keane almost takes Gibson out. He decides, as he puts it, to make "a commitment to [Gibson's] heart." Gibson rewards that commitment by getting Bobby Richardson to pop to second to bring the Cardinals their first title since 1946.

Yankees Goats: Joe Pepitone hits a lead-padding grand slam in Game 6, but otherwise goes 3-for-25 and drives in one run. That's how many Roger Maris drives in with his .200 average in seven games. You've seen the woes of Whitey Ford and Al Downing, who both posted ERAs over 8.

Playoff Era (1969-1993)

As dedicated despisers of the Yankees know, this era was the least successful in franchise history. It began in the doldrums, with CBS leaving a legacy as the only Yankees owners who didn't make a killing on the team. They sold out at a loss to a dozen investors led by George Steinbrenner, and from 1976-1981, the Yankees did reach the newfangled "postseason" five times. But they drifted for a dozen seasons after that, finishing as high as second only three times as Steinbrenner's incessant interference, unpredictable spending, and fickle firings of management personnel took their toll. The Yankees won a modest two titles during this quarter-century, so we'll focus on the three series they lost, each a thing of beauty in its own way.

1976 World Series

After squeezing into the World Series when Chris Chambliss' home run won the AL Championship Series from the Kansas City Royals, the Yankees run up against the Cincinnati Reds, who just swept the Phillies in the NLCS. During the season, the Reds scored 87 more runs than any team in the majors, with a lineup including Pete Rose, Joe Morgan, Johnny Bench, Tony Perez, George Foster, and Ken Griffey Sr. The Yankees' only future Hall of Famer is Catfish Hunter, but Billy Martin I was once a Cincinnati Red who broke the jaw of an opposing pitcher, punched him right on the infield (cost, $10,000 in an out-of-court settlement; reputation, priceless), and he is not afraid of the defending champions even if other people want to ballyhoo them as the "Big Red Machine". Even after they outscore the Yankees, 22-8, in a sweep, he won't buy into it!

October 16

Game 1: It begins at Riverfront Stadium with an easy 5-1 victory. Joe Morgan homers off Doyle Alexander in the first inning, Tony Perez has three hits, and the Yankees manage just five hits off Don Gullett and Pedro Borbon. After the game, Martin I scoffs, "Do I think they're awesome? Hardly. We hit more line drives for outs than they did for hits."

October 17

Game 2: Catfish Hunter seems like the man for the occasion, but the Reds rock him for three runs in the second inning. It takes until the seventh for the Yankees to tie it, and Hunter is still in there in a 3-3 tie in the bottom of the ninth. He gets the first two outs, but shortstop Fred Stanley, a weak hitter who sticks around because of his fielding, charges Ken Griffey's slow chopper, hurries the throw, and heaves the ball into the dugout, sending Griffey to second. After an intentional walk, Tony Perez lines a single to left, where Roy White has no chance to throw Griffey out at the plate. "Blooper power, blooper power," Martin I moans later. "Except for that last ball, which was hit good, the blooper's been killing us."

October 19

Game 3: Dan Driessen, the first National League ballplayer to take a day off as a designated hitter, goes 3-for-3 as the Reds kayo Dock Ellis in the fourth inning and coast to a 6-2 win at Yankee Stadium. Though the Reds led the majors in home runs during the season, in the Series they chiefly show off their speed, stealing seven bases and running wild on the weak throwing arms of the Yankees' outfield. Here they use two stolen bases in a three-run rally off Ellis in the second inning, and they never look back. "It was bloop hits again," Martin I explains. "Their bloop hits are falling in and ours aren't. That's the only difference. Every time we hit the ball hard, it seems to go right at someone." The Yankees are out-hit in this game, 13-8.

October 21

Game 4: The Reds finish off the sweep with a 7-2 victory in front of 56,700 fans at Yankee Stadium. Gary Nolan goes 6 2/3 innings and gives up eight hits, half of them by Thurman Munson, but holds a 3-2 lead thanks to Johnny Bench's two-run homer off Ed Figueroa. The Reds pad the lead in the ninth inning on another homer by Bench, a three-run shot off Dick Tidrow that sews up the title. Moments later, Martin I is ejected by Bruce Froemming after riding the umpires all night and throwing a ball on the field. Martin's grace after defeat is predictable: "We're a better ballclub. We just didn't prove it. I still think we're as good as the Reds." Oh yeah, he assures us, the umpires were brutal, too. Go figure.

Yankees Goats: There's plenty of blame to go around, with awful batting averages and two starters torched for five runs each. But Mickey Rivers loses the most style points. From his first at-bat, he's flummoxed by third baseman Pete Rose, who plays so shallow he dares Rivers to hit the ball past him. Rivers can't do it, and when he does get on base, he gets picked off once and doubled off in a key spot. And the Reds make him look like an eighth grader in the field as they take advantage of his eighth grader's arm.

1980 AL Championship Series

After the Yankees spent the late 1970s knocking out the Kansas City Royals in the LCS, the Royals' day finally came in 1980. The core of the 1976 Royals is still there—George Brett, Hal McRae, Amos Otis, Frank White, and Dennis Leonard—with the key additions of speedy center fielder Willie Wilson and relief stalwart Dan Quisenberry. The Yankees have had almost a complete turnover, Steinbrenner-style. The Yankees, who won 103 games to the Royals' 97, have a big power advantage and expect to stomp on them for the fourth time in five years. Instead, the Yankees put runs on the board in only three innings in the whole Series.

October 8   **Game 1:** The Yankees flash their power early at Royals Stadium on back-to-back homers by Rick Cerone and Lou Piniella in the second inning, but ex-Yankee Larry Gura shuts them out the rest of the way. Ron Guidry struggles, surrendering the lead for good in the third inning on Willie Aikens' two-run single. Brett, the talk of baseball after flirting with a .400 average down the stretch, settles for a double off Guidry and a home run off Ron Davis in the 7-2 win.

October 9   **Game 2:** A crowd of 42,633 at Royals Stadium sees the Royals take their second straight game behind Dennis Leonard. Willie Wilson has the big hit, a two-run triple in the third inning off Rudy May. Shortstop U. L. Washington's single knocks in Wilson with the eventual winning run. The Yankees make it 3-2 in the fifth inning but can't tie it, coming close in the eighth, when a stumbling Willie Randolph is gunned down by Brett's relay throw while trying to score from first on Bob Watson's double. Quisenberry relieves Leonard after a leadoff single in the ninth inning and gets Graig Nettles to ground into a game-ending double play.

October 10

Game 3: It's a duel between southpaws Tommy John and Paul Splittorff in front of 56,588 unhappy fans at Yankee Stadium, scoreless until Frank White's homer off John in the top of the fifth inning, following a 32-minute rain delay. In the sixth, Quisenberry relieves after a one-out double, and the Yankees score twice to take the lead. Then comes a fateful moment for Dick Howser. John, a 22-game winner during the season, gets the first two outs in the seventh inning and gives up a double to Wilson. Howser decides it's time to bring in Goose Gossage, the flame-throwing beast. But U. L. Washington beats out an infield hit, bringing up Brett. Mike Lupica writes in the *Daily News*: "What did the Stadium sound like? What will Judgment Day sound like?" For Gossage, it sounds like stunned silence after his first-pitch, 99-mph fastball is crushed by Brett into the upper deck. The Yankees are done; they load the bases with nobody out in the eighth inning, but Quisenberry escapes, and the final score is right where Brett left it, 4-2.

Yankees Goats: Six runs in three games won't get it, so we'll salute the entire offense. Remember Bobby Brown? Here's why you don't—he went 0-for-10 against the Royals. Reggie Jackson, Bob Watson, and Bucky Dent all failed to drive in a run. Gossage gave up the Brett blast for which this LCS is largely remembered, and he's still pissed about it, even more than about Brett's 1983 "Pine Tar" home run.

1981 World Series

After the two-month-long players' strike screwed things up so thoroughly that the team with the best record in the National League didn't even qualify for the postseason, the Yankees—with the third-best record in their own division—landed in the World Series against the Los Angeles Dodgers. As they did with the Royals the year before, the Yankees felt cocky against the franchise they defeated in the 1977-1978 Series, especially after winning the first two games at Yankee Stadium. The Dodgers had pretty much the same lineup, centered around their long-tenured infield of Steve Garvey, Davey Lopes, Bill Russell, and Ron Cey. Things turned in Los Angeles thanks to a remarkable pitcher concluding an amazing season.

October 23

Game 3: "Fernandomania" gripped Southern California throughout the 1981 season. Fernando Valenzuela, a 20-year-old left-hander from Mexico whose eyes search the sky during his windup and whose screwball dips to the ground, paralyzes the National League by allowing just two earned runs in his first 83 innings, tossing five shutouts in his first seven starts in 1981. He comes back to earth after the strike but his 13-7 record and 2.48 ERA earn him a Cy Young Award plus Rookie of the Year honors. Today he lacks his best stuff but fools enough Yankees in key spots to prevail. Early homers by Bob Watson and Rick Cerone give the Yankees a 4-3 lead, but after the Dodgers go ahead against George Frazier in the fifth inning, it's all up to Fernando. He guts it out despite handing out nine hits and seven walks, getting two key double plays and making the Yankees go 1-for-10 with runners in scoring position. It's a 145-pitch, 5-4 gem that dissolves the Yankees' momentum.

October 24 **Game 4:** This time the Yankees go up 4-0 early but it isn't enough. Starter Rick Reuschel is gone by the fourth inning, and it's 6-6 in the seventh inning when the Dodgers load the bases with nobody out against Ron Davis. Manager Bob Lemon brings in Tommy John, who lets two runs score. Reggie Jackson's home run gets one run back but that's it. Steve Howe pitches three innings to win it for the Dodgers, and George Frazier loses for the second day in a row, 8-7.

October 25 **Game 5:** For the third day in a row, the Dodgers win a one-run decision from the Yankees. Jerry Reuss pitches a complete-game five-hitter, allowing only a second-inning run. Ron Guidry pitches better, taking a two-hit shutout to the seventh inning. That's when he gets rocked by the one-two punch of Pedro Guerrero and Steve Yeager, back-to-back homers that make Guidry a 2-1 loser.

After this game, George Steinbrenner gets in a scuffle in the Los Angeles hotel elevator with two drunken Dodgers fans. Though his adversaries aren't identified or found, Steinbrenner claims that one broke a bottle over his head before he knocked both of them down. For his part, he sports a cast on his left hand, a swollen lip, and a bruise on his head.

October 28 **Game 6:** After a rainout, the Series resumes at Yankee Stadium, where it's a calm 1-1 game in the fourth inning when the key move occurs. With no designated hitter in this Series, Tommy John is due up with two outs and two men on base. Bob Lemon has Bobby Murcer pinch-hit, he makes the third out, and here comes George Frazier, primed to lose again. Ron Cey, beaned in Game 5 by Goose Gossage, singles in the go-ahead run, and Pedro Guerrero's triple knocks in two more runs. A four-run outburst in the sixth inning makes it 8-1, and the Dodgers coast from there, winning 9-2.

Yankees Goats: Frazier becomes the first pitcher to lose three games in one World Series while trying to win, matching the three losses of "Black Sox" hurler Lefty Williams. He and fellow reliever Ron Davis combine to give up 15 runs in six innings. In the long run, a more significant failure is the performance of Dave Winfield. The high-priced free agent lays an egg in the first season of a ten-year deal, going 1-for-22 in the Series, a harmless single, and drives in one run with a bases-loaded walk. By the time the Yankees reach the postseason again in 1995, it will be more like a tournament involving various combinations of teams from six new divisions.

After the loss, George Steinbrenner issues this statement: "I want to sincerely apologize to the people of New York and to the fans of the New York Yankees everywhere for the performance of the Yankee team in the World Series." This pisses off the players on both teams, but the Yankees spend the rest of the 1980s limiting Steinbrenner's equally unnecessary tirades and apologies to the regular season.

Wild Card Era (1995-2019)

The labor fiasco of 1994-1995 launched a series of experimental structures during both the regular season and the postseason. First we got 14 teams and three divisions in each league, with a wild card team and a new playoff round called the Division Series. Next came 16 teams in the NL and 14 in the AL, with the addition of interleague play during the season. After that, Bud Selig made the Houston Astros move to the AL, leaving 15 teams in each league and the necessity of interleague series every day of the season. The All-Star Game's attraction was wrecked, leaving it playing second fiddle to a home run contest, and eventually we got a second wild card spot. It became more important to get *into* the postseason than to get through it, because the extra round made it that much tougher to survive. Since the Yankees ended their last run of success in 2000, they have made the postseason 15 times—and they lost all but once. This gives us plenty of demises and disasters to celebrate, and for an appetizer, here's one of the most shocking postseason endings in Yankees history.

1995 Division Series

Does anybody remember why the Yankees—yes, the first AL team to squirm into the postseason without winning their own division—got to play the Seattle Mariners (79-66) instead of the Cleveland Indians (100-44), as the wild card team would today? No matter, since another now-discarded format helped the Mariners. After the Yankees won the first two games in the Bronx—the second one in 15 innings—they played the last three games in Seattle.

October 6

Game 3: The Yankees' luck runs out when they face Randy Johnson, winner of the Cy Young Award with an 18-2 record. He pitched the one-game playoff with the Angels that won the division title; rested now, he pitches seven innings, striking out ten Yankees and leaving with a 7-2 lead. Most of the damage is inflicted on Jack McDowell, beginning the Worst Weekend of his life. Tino Martinez's homer gives the Mariners the lead, and McDowell leaves after loading the bases in the sixth inning. Steve Howe comes in to give up an RBI hit by Martinez, and Bob Wickman gives up three more quick runs that contribute to a 7-4 final score.

October 7

Game 4: You'd think the Yankees are playing the Red Sox when it takes 4:08 for this nine-inning struggle to unfold. It's worth the wait for the 57,180 fans at the Kingdome, who get to see the Yankees cough up an early 5-0 lead and blow sky-high in the eighth inning. Edgar Martinez's three-run homer starts the comeback, and Scott Kamieniecki gives the whole lead back before exiting after five innings. It's tied in the eighth when Buck Showalter brings in John Wetteland, his stud reliever who saved 31 games during the season but also had a 1-5 record. It's the latter pitcher who shows up today. Wetteland walks the leadoff batter, gives up a bunt single, and hits Ken Griffey Jr. with a pitch, loading the bases. There's Edgar Martinez again, and his grand slam settles things as the Mariners tie the series with an 11-8 win.

October 8 **Game 5:** Edgar Martinez isn't done after driving in seven runs in yesterday's win-or-die game, but it takes awhile to get around to him. First, Buck Showalter has to earn his upcoming exit as Yankees manager. David Cone leads, 4-2, in the eighth inning when he gets into trouble. In 2020, Showalter wouldn't consider sending him out there, since he's already thrown 118 pitches and is heading through the Seattle lineup for the (gulp!) *fourth* time. Ken Griffey homers with one out, and after Cone retires Edgar, he can't make that last good pitch. He walks Tino Martinez. Jay Buhner singles, and Cone walks Alex Diaz, a part-time outfielder, to load the bases. That brings him up to 141 pitches. Where's Buck? Reserve infielder Doug Strange pinch-hits, and Cone pitches to him. The count goes full—ball four—the 147th pitch for Cone. That one gets Showalter out of the dugout, but it's too late. The game goes to extra innings. In the 11th, Randy Johnson, who had come in in the 9th inning on one day's rest, gives up a run. No problem. Jack McDowell, who fanned Edgar Martinez in a key spot in the ninth inning, is still in the game. Joey Cora beats out a bunt to resume McDowell's nightmare. Griffey singles him to third, and up steps Edgar. He takes a hanging slider and hooks it into the left field corner. Cora scores easily, and Griffey just beats the relay throw to score the winning run. Johnson strikes out six Yankees in three innings to earn the 6-5 victory.

Yankees Goats: The obvious choice is McDowell, loser of two games in three days before fleeing New York as a free agent a few weeks later. But we can't leave out Randy Velarde, who goes 3-for-17, all singles, and makes multiple gaffes in the field and on the bases, one described by a reporter as "an atrocity" when he fails to turn an easy double play and allows the tying run to score.

> Take a moment to savor the greatest postseason series a batter ever had against the Yankees. Edgar Martinez, born in New York City, made himself at home by going 12-for-21 (.571) with 6 walks, driving in 10 runs in five games, scoring six runs, and posting a gaudy OPS of 1.667. He had four three-hit games. In Game 3, he went hitless because they were afraid to pitch to him, walking him three times, twice intentionally; both times, Tino Martinez drove in a run behind him. Pitching to Martinez in Game 4 did not work any better, as he drove in seven runs.

1997 Division Series

Let's linger in the 20th Century for a moment to see how the Yankees managed to lose their second Division Series in the middle of their last dynasty. Their 96 wins were second in the American League—to the Baltimore Orioles, making the Yankees the wild card team again. That sent them to Cleveland to face an Indians squad that scored almost as many runs as the Yankees did, led by Jim Thome, Matt Williams, David Justice, and Manny Ramirez. Once again, the format put the first two games at Yankee Stadium and the rest at Jacobs Field in Cleveland.

October 2

Game 2: After the Indians blow a 5-0, first-inning lead and lose the first game, it's the Yankees' turn today. They score three runs in the first inning, but Andy Pettitte takes his lumps. He gives up four straight two-out hits in the fourth inning, and Joe Torre lets him give up a fifth-inning homer to Matt Williams that puts the Indians ahead, 7-2, before getting him out of there. It's too late, and the Indians win, 7-5, to even the series.

October 5

Game 4: After David Wells wins easily, the Yankees have a great chance to wrap it up when they take a 2-1 lead to the bottom of the eighth inning at Jacobs Field. Starter Dwight Gooden is long gone, and it's Mariano Rivera blowing another save when he serves up a fat 2-0 pitch to catcher Sandy Alomar Jr., who homers to the opposite field to tie it. Still, Rivera throws just nine pitches, making it surprising that Torre hands the ball to Ramiro Mendoza in the bottom of the ninth. It takes Mendoza just five pitches to lose it. Marquis Grissom singles, advances on a sacrifice bunt, and scores when Omar Vizquel smacks the ball off Mendoza's glove and it gets past a diving Derek Jeter and into left field. "Hell, it wasn't meant to be," Torre decides, forgetting how he helped it along.

October 6   **Game 5:** Ultimately, Andy Pettitte had a 19-11 record in postseason play, but this is one of his worst losses. It gets away from him early. Manny Ramirez's double in the third inning drives in two runs, and Williams' RBI single makes it 3-0. They score again in the fourth inning when Alomar doubles, goes to third on Thome's sacrifice bunt (!), and scores on a sacrifice fly by Tony Fernandez. That's the game-winner right there. Paul Assenmacher and Jose Mesa combine to shut the Yankees out over the final three innings, and the 4-3 victory puts the Yankees in the corner for the big dance.

Yankees Goats: Pettitte is the main culprit with two losses and an ERA of 8.49, and David Cone gives up six runs in his only start. Though the Yankees average five runs a game, the offense is hurt by the cold bats of Bernie Williams (.118) and Joe Girardi (.133), who combine for four hits and one RBI while grounding into four double plays.

2001 World Series

The late-1990s run of the Yankees was largely the effort of home-grown talent as an aging George Steinbrenner, burned by the ten-year Dave Winfield fiasco, felt less inclined to throw money at free agents. On the 2001 Yankees, even big imports like Roger Clemens, Paul O'Neill, and Tino Martinez arrived via trades. They coasted through a weak division, upset the 102-win Oakland A's in the Division Series, and greatly upset the 116-win Seattle Mariners in the ALCS. Their World Series opponent seemed like a letdown: the Arizona Diamondbacks, in just their fourth season of existence. Still, the upstarts had Luis Gonzalez and his 57 home runs, and there was some concern about their 1-2 punch on the mound, Curt Schilling (22-6) and—that 6'10" buzzkill again—Randy Johnson (21-6). But Clemens went 20-3, and they have Jeter and they're the Yankees. Well. . .

October 27

Game 1: Schilling gives up a run in the top of the first inning when he hits Jeter and Bernie Williams drives him in with a double. That's the last fun the Yankees have all day. Craig Counsell's homer in the home first ties it, and the Diamondbacks score four runs in both the third and fourth innings. Luis Gonzalez gives them the lead with a two-run homer off Mike Mussina, and the 9-1 final makes the Yankees blink.

October 28

Game 2: Randy Johnson had a "career" record against the Yankees of 6-8, but that was with the Mariners in the 1990s, and it counted only the regular season. It's a different story in October, and today the 38-year-old shows the Yankees no mercy. He strikes out seven of the first nine Yankees he faces and doesn't let them get a runner to second base until the eighth inning. By then, he leads, 4-0, mainly on Matt Williams' three-run homer off Andy Pettitte. That's the final score, an emphatic three-hitter with 11 strikeouts.

Game 6: After the Yankees win all three games at home, two in extra innings, it's back to Phoenix and another meeting with Randy Johnson. His seven solid innings aren't as special as the 22-hit attack that administers the Yankees' worst Series defeat, 15-2. Andy Pettitte is knocked out in the third inning, replaced by Jay Witasick, who writes his ticket out of the Bronx with a horrible effort. The first four Diamondbacks single, and after an out, four more consecutive hits, and voila! It's 12-0 Arizona. Danny Bautista paves the way with five runs batted in, and even Johnson contributes a bases-loaded RBI single.

November 3

Game 7: The Roger Clemens-Curt Schilling duel in Game 7 of the World Series lives up to its billing, as the two aces combine to strike out 19 batters in 14 innings of work. Leading 2-1 in the eighth inning, the Yankees turn to Mariano Rivera, the best reliever in postseason history. Rivera strikes out the side in the eighth but records only one out in the bottom of the ninth. Mark Grace starts with a broken-bat single. On a bunt, Rivera throws wildly to second base, and both runners are safe. Jay Bell also bunts, and Rivera makes the force at third base this time, but Scott Brosius holds the ball instead of throwing to first base. Tony Womack's broken-bat double scores the tying run and sends Jay Bell to third. Rivera hits Craig Counsell, loading the bases and forcing Joe Torre to bring the infield in. That's the key move, because when Rivera jams Luis Gonzalez with his patented cut fastball, Gonzalez's broken-bat flare just eludes Derek Jeter, scoring the winning run. The four-year-old Diamondbacks upset the mighty Yankees, one season away from completing their first century, to win the World Series. Before the game, Rivera said, "We're going to win. But no matter what happens, it's in God's hands." That means it was God who

November 4

decided not to try for the likely double play on Bell's bunt, even though Rivera later blames the lapse on Brosius.

Randy Johnson relieved in the eighth inning the night after winning Game 6 and retired all four Yankees he faced, picking up his third victory of the Series. Nobody got more bang for his buck against the Yankees in the postseason: 5-0 in five appearances, a 1.63 ERA, and 35 strikeouts in 27 1/3 innings. As a Yankee, he was winless in three postseason starts with a 6.92 ERA. Nice work all around, Big Unit.

Yankees Goats: Though the Series goes seven games, the Yankees are outscored, 22-12, not including the 15-2 romp. Most of the pitchers struggle, the awful defense creates seven unearned runs, and the whole offense is helpless against Johnson and Schilling. They combine for 38 2/3 innings, 21 hits, 6 runs, 5 walks, and 45 strikeouts; the only Yankee who bats over .240, Paul O'Neill, doesn't drive in a run. Derek Jeter (.148) and Chuck Knoblauch (.056) barely hit .200 added together.

2002 Division Series

The Yankees tied the Oakland A's with 103 wins, pitting them against the wild card Anaheim Angels in the ALDS. A jinxed franchise, the Angels are in their 42nd season and have never even *reached* the World Series. They won 99 games and outscored opponents by more than 200 runs, a potent offense led by Tim Salmon, Garret Anderson, Troy Glaus, and Darin Erstad. After winning a seesaw series opener, 8-5, on Bernie Williams' eighth-inning homer, the Yankees like their chances heading to the second game at Yankee Stadium.

October 2

Game 2: Andy Pettitte is knocked out again after three innings, but the Yankees come back and take a 5-4 lead to the eighth. Yankees favorite Orlando "El Duque" Hernandez, just a four-game winner during the season, has already pitched four innings in relief. Now he runs out of gas. Anderson ties it with a home run. Glaus follows with another blast, and the Angels square the series with an 8-6 win.

October 4

Game 3, October 4: The Yankees give future Hall of Famer Mike Mussina a 6-1 lead in the third inning, but he doesn't know what to do with it. He's gone after the fourth inning, and it's 6-6 into the bottom of the eighth. Lefty reliever Mike Stanton gives up doubles to two lefty hitters, so Joe Torre brings in righty Steve Karsay to face righty batter Tim Salmon. He belts a homer that makes the final score 9-6.

Game 4: The pummeling of Yankees pitchers continues, with the Angels focusing the fun on the fifth inning. The Yankees lead, 2-1, when Shawn Wooten homers off David Wells to tie it. Before Joe Torre can rouse the bullpen, Wells gives up five more hits, and Ramiro Mendoza lasts long enough to put the finishing touches on an eight-run rally that kills the suspense. Jarrod Washburn (18-6 during the season) gets the 9-5 win as the Angels complete the first step toward their first title.

Yankees Goats: The Angels score 34 runs, a robust team ERA of 8.21 for the Yankees. Special mention goes to Wells, Pettitte, Karsay, and Mendoza, all posting ERAs over 10. The offense scores 25 runs, but one guy whose awful series costs them is Alfonso Soriano, who goes 2-for-17 (.118).

2003 World Series

The Yankees, after leading the AL with 101 wins, defeated the Twins in four games in the opening round of the postseason tournament, then came from behind against the Red Sox in the ALCS. Their reward was a World Series rendezvous with the Florida Marlins. The Marlins took a different path to the Series, going 21-8 down the stretch to secure the wild card spot, beating the 100-win Giants and the Cubs. Their offense was led by catcher Ivan Rodriguez, third baseman Mike Lowell, first baseman Derrek Lee, and center fielder Juan Pierre, plus a rookie named Miguel Cabrera who just had a big series against the Cubs.

October 18

Game 1: The first shock comes at Yankee Stadium when the Marlins beat David Wells, 3-2. Pierre, after leading the majors with 65 stolen bases, flashes his speed right away, beating out a bunt and scoring on Rodriguez's sacrifice fly. It's 1-1 in the fifth inning when Pierre drives in two runs with a single, and that's all the Marlins need. Brad Penny gets in trouble in the sixth, but Jack McKeon brings in starter Dontrelle Willis and then closer Ugueth Urbina, who hold down the fort.

2003 ALCS: The Yankees' Game 3 win at Fenway Park on **October 21** was upstaged by the unforgettable sight of 72-year-old Yankees coach Don Zimmer making a bullheaded rush at torreador Pedro Martinez, whose casual swipe sent Zimmer face-first into the turf. That was the feeble finale to a brawl initiated by testosterone-fueled showdowns involving Pedro, Roger Clemens, and Manny Ramirez.

Game 4: After the Yankees win a pair of 6-1 games, we have the key game of the Series at Pro Player Park. The Marlins jump on Roger Clemens for three runs in the first inning, two on a Miguel Cabrera homer, and Carl Pavano holds the Yankees down, leaving after eight innings with a 3-1 lead. But the Yankees tie it against Urbina, and we go to extras. It ends abruptly in the 12th on a leadoff homer by shortstop Alex Gonzalez off Jeff Weaver, who never pitches again for the Yankees.

October 22

Game 5: When David Wells leaves in the second inning after wrenching his back, he throws out the Series as well. Jose Contreras, idle for eight days, is rushed into the game, gives up a pair of two-out walks, and is burned by Alex Gonzalez's double and a two-run single by Brad Penny. That's all Penny needs, with the Yankees managing just two runs off him in seven innings. The 6-4 final puts the Marlins one win away from a huge upset.

October 23

Game 6: Red Sox fans revere Josh Beckett for winning four games during the 2007 title run, but for Beckett, this is the game of his life. The 55,733 fans at Yankee Stadium watch him duel with Andy Pettitte, who bends first in the fifth inning when Luis Castillo singles in a run. In the next inning, the Marlins cash in a Derek Jeter error for an unearned run. Then Jack McKeon kicks back and watches Beckett mow down the Yankees with precision and terrific stuff. The Yankees never get a runner past second base, strike out nine times, and ground into two double plays. It adds up to a five-hitter for Beckett, a 2-0 victory, and two frustrating World Series losses in three years for Yankees fans.

October 25

Yankees Goats: Weaver and Contreras are the obvious goats on the mound, and the biggest bust in the lineup is Aaron Boone. In a letdown after his series-winning homer against the Red Sox, he goes 3-for-21 (.143), commits three errors, and blows his big chance to be a hero by striking out with the bases loaded and one out in the 11th inning of Game 4.

2004 League Championship Series

Look where we are! The Yankees won 101 games and took the division title for the eighth straight season, then had to win twice in extra innings to survive the Twins in the ALDS. They're happy to face their cousins, the Red Sox, who haven't won a title since Ted Williams was a dozen *days* old. It's business as usual while the Yankees take the first three games, capped by a 19-8 drubbing at Fenway Park. You know the situation. No team had ever come back from 3-0 down to win a series except in hockey. The Yankees led Game 4 in the ninth inning with Mariano Rivera on the mound. What could go wrong? The following:

Game 4: In the past four seasons, one-third of Rivera's blown saves have come against the Red Sox. The Yankees take a 4-3 lead in the sixth inning although Derek Jeter grounds out with the bases loaded, a key out. Rivera's big mistake is a leadoff walk to Kevin Millar. Dave Roberts pinch-runs, steals second, and scores on Bill Mueller's season-saving hit. In the top of the 11th inning, Bernie Williams makes the disastrous final out with the bases loaded. Well past midnight, five hours after the game's start was delayed so the FOX Network could slobber over a football game, the game arrives at the bottom of the 12th. Come on in, Paul Quantrill! Serve one up to David Ortiz and let's get the hell out of here! Drive home safely, folks. Final score, 6-4. See you tomorrow night.

October 17

Game 5: Over 35,000 fans wedge themselves into Fenway Park to see Pedro Martinez and

October 18

Mike Mussina duke it out. Mussina gets the best of it, and they both exit in the seventh inning with the Yankees up, 4-2. Against the ropes again, the Red Sox tie it in the eighth inning. Ortiz leads off with another big homer off Tom Gordon, and Jason Varitek's sacrifice fly saddles Rivera with another blown save. The game drifts into extra innings, and it's after 2:00 AM in Boston when Ortiz ends it again, this time in the 14th inning, with a two-out RBI single off Esteban Loaiza. Let's go back to Yankee Stadium!

October 19

Game 6: Fun at the ballpark! Tonight's hero is Curt Schilling, who holds the Yankees to one run and four hits in seven innings despite pitching with a dislocated ankle tendon that has to be sutured before the game, leaving him with a bloody sock that winds up in the Hall of Fame. A stranger story is Alex Rodriguez almost getting away with a cheap shot in the eighth inning. Trailing 4-2, Rodriguez grounds weakly to pitcher Bronson Arroyo, who moves toward the first-base line to tag him. As they meet, Rodriguez chops Arroyo's arm, slapping the ball out of his glove, then kicks it down the right-field line, allowing Derek Jeter to score from first. The umpires huddle and call A-Rod out for interference, negating Jeter's run. Yankee Stadium fans react predictably, showering the field with debris and throwing balls and bottles. It takes riot police ringing the field for the game to proceed, and 43 fans are ejected. The bush-league stunt backfires, the rally fizzles, the Red Sox win, 4-2, and it's on to Game 7. Afterwards, A-Rod graciously concedes, "Maybe looking back, I should have just run him over."

October 20

Game 7: The Yankees become the first team ever to blow a 3-0 lead, with 56,129 mightily paying fans at Yankee Stadium to consecrate the biggest choke in sports history. The suspense is over early. Joe Torre bypasses Javier Vazquez and Orlando Hernandez to give the crucial start to 38-year-old Kevin Brown, a $100 million hurler with back problems who lasted only two innings in Game 3. He doesn't even get that far today. In the top of the first inning, David Ortiz burns Brown with a two-run homer, and he's gone after loading the bases in the second inning. In comes Vazquez, and Johnny Damon promptly scorches him with a grand slam that makes it 6-0. The crowd is sullen as the Red Sox coast to a 10-3 victory to take the series they were counted out of four days ago. A fan named Julian Kaiser speaks for the rest when he tells the *New York Times,* "The worst thing is forever we'll be associated with a 3-0 deficit. That we blew it. It's not the end of the world, but almost."

Yankees Goats: In a sense, this list starts and ends with Rivera, though officially he has two saves and a 1.29 ERA. Plenty of other Yankees make key contributions to the collapse, notably Kevin Brown and Paul Quantrill. First baseman Tony Clark goes 3-for-21 with nine strikeouts, and Derek Jeter hits a weak .200, going the whole series without more than one hit in a game.

2005 Division Series

The 2004 choke had a lingering effect on the Yankees, who, like Bobby Cox's Atlanta Braves, won their division almost every year, nine in a row, but went nowhere in October except home to count their money and play golf. The lineup was loaded—Jeter, A-Rod, Bernie Williams, Gary Sheffield, Robinson Cano, Jason Giambi, and more. They picked up Randy Johnson in 2005, Johnny Damon in 2006, and Bobby Abreu in 2007, when they also brought back Andy Pettitte and Roger Clemens. All it did was set them up for frustration. In 2005, they had the same 95-67 record as their opponents, the Anaheim Angels, who featured free agent acquisition Vladimir Guerrero and 21-game winner Bartolo Colon.

October 5

Game 2: After Mike Mussina beats Colon in the series opener, the Yankees give Chien-Ming Wang a 2-0 lead in Game 2 at Angel Stadium of Anaheim, but he can't hold it. A-Rod's error in the sixth inning helps the Angels tie it, but it's Wang's own fault in the seventh. After a leadoff single, Wang's lousy throw on a bunt sets up Orlando Cabrera's two-run single that gives the Angels a 4-2 lead, and the 5-3 final leaves the teams even heading to Yankee Stadium.

October 7

Game 3: This is the only slugfest, and with the Yankees' big power, it's surprising that the Angels win. They perform the impossible feat of knocking Randy Johnson out in three-plus innings with a nine-hit, five-run assault. Garret Anderson drives in five runs, three on a homer in the first inning. The Yankees get Johnson off the hook, going ahead in the fifth inning, which makes Aaron Small the losing pitcher when he's the first of three Yankees relievers to give up two runs in the 11-7 Anaheim victory.

October 10

Game 5: When a 3-2 Yankees win sets up the showdown game, it's Mussina against Colon again. Bartolo is hurt and leaves in the second inning, and it's rookie Ervin Santana who handles the Yankees until a seventh-inning exit with a 5-3 lead. All the damage is done off Mussina, five runs in less than three innings. The Yankees get three hits in the ninth inning but can't score. After Jeter's leadoff single, A-Rod hits into a double play, and two more singles are wasted when Hideki Matsui grounds out to end the 5-3 defeat and the Yankees' season.

Yankees Goats: Mussina and Small stand out among the pitchers, but the big bust of the series is Alex Rodriguez. He goes 2-for-15 (.133), doesn't drive in a run, strikes out five times, hits into two double plays, and makes a crucial error in Game 2. Bernie Williams (.211) and Hideki Matsui (.200) drive in one run apiece, and when the middle of the order disappears, you go home.

2006 Division Series

Once again, the Yankees win their division by ten games, post the best record in the AL, lead the majors in runs scored, and embarrass themselves in the first round of the playoffs, losing to the wild card Detroit Tigers. Their balanced offense features Ivan Rodriguez, Magglio Ordonez in right field, and Carlos Guillen at shortstop, and their pitching staff includes the AL Rookie of the Year, Justin Verlander. After Chien-Ming Wang wins the opener, the fun begins.

October 5

Game 2: Johnny Damon's three-run homer off Verlander in the fourth inning gives the Yankees a 3-1 lead, and that's the end of their postseason party. The 56,252 fans at Yankee Stadium spend the rest of the afternoon sitting on their thumbs. The Tigers score in the fifth inning on Curtis Granderson's sacrifice fly, tie it in the sixth on Guillen's homer, and go ahead in the seventh on Granderson's RBI triple off Mike Mussina, who lasts long enough to take the loss and is now 5-7 in the postseason as a Yankee. The Tigers' bullpen allows the Yankees only one hit over the final 3 2/3 innings to even the series with a 4-3 win.

October 6

Game 3: At Comerica Park the next night, 43,440 fans gather to behold the geriatric showdown between 43-year-old Randy Johnson and 41-year-old Kenny Rogers. Rogers stands tall while Johnson bends and breaks, resulting in a 6-0 win for the Tigers. Rogers pitches into the eighth inning, scattering five hits and striking out eight Yankees. The Tigers rip four hits off Johnson in the second inning, scoring three runs, and knock him out in the sixth on back-to-back RBI doubles by Rodriguez and Sean Casey. The Division Series is Johnson's jinx; in his final postseason appearance, he drops to 2-8 in the DS for four franchises.

October 7 **Game 4:** With the season on the line, Joe Torre turns to his fourth-best starter, Jaret Wright, whose 16-12 record and 4.99 ERA over his two seasons as a Yankee don't bode well. Sure enough, Wright gives up homers to Ordonez and Craig Monroe in the second inning, and a bad throw by Alex Rodriguez in the third inning helps the Tigers make it 4-0. The Yankees fold their tents, and it's 8-0 before they score. The 8-3 final leaves fans dancing in the streets in Detroit, while the New York writers hasten to speculate about who will be run out of New York first, Torre or Rodriguez.

Yankees Goats: Alex Rodriguez is the deserving fall guy for this disaster. "This kind of showing is not why a gross amount of cable revenue is being paid to Alex Rodriguez, who just may need to move on," George Vecsey writes in the *New York Times*. How bad was he? Despite a hot September, he starts the series batting sixth in Torre's order. In Game 3, he goes hitless in the cleanup slot and is now 1-for-11. Torre drops his $25 million-a-year third baseman to eighth in the lineup for Game 4, and he still doesn't get a hit, dropping to .071. He's part of an infield trio, joining Robinson Cano and first baseman Gary Sheffield, who go a collective 4-for-41 with one RBI. Meanwhile, the pitching staff posts a 5.56 ERA against the Tigers, while Mariano Rivera logs one mop-up inning in Game 1 and then sits.

2007 Division Series

Guess what? Joe Torre returned, Rodriguez did not move on, and the Yankees took a different route toward disaster. Instead of running away with their division, they appeared to be dead in the water, not getting over .500 for good until after the All-Star Game. They got hot down the stretch to secure the wild card spot, the kind of hot finish that often precipitates a run to a championship (like the Nationals in 2019). As soon as October rolls around, however, it's deja vu all over again, and Torre's troops look helpless while watching their hopes go down the drain. This demise comes at the hands of the Cleveland Indians, led by center fielder Grady Sizemore, catcher Victor Martinez, designated hitter Travis Hafner, and 19-game winners CC Sabathia and Fausto Carmona.

October 4

Game 1: Johnny Damon, the only new Yankee in a lineup of aging All-Stars, leads off the series with a home run off Sabathia, and that's about the only thing that goes right in two games at Jacobs Field. It begins with the swift demise of Chien-Ming Wang, winner of 19 games each of the last two seasons. Tonight he lasts into the fifth inning, drilled for eight runs on nine hits, and Kenny Lofton drives in four runs in the 12-3 romp that deflates the Yankees' hopes.

October 5

Game 2: Having offended some stray deity, the Yankees are assailed by the Fourth Plague when midges swarm around rookie reliever Joba Chamberlain, driving him nuts long enough to aid the Indians in an 11-inning, 2-1 victory. Tom Withers of the *Associated Press* calls it "a low-budget, late-night horror flick: 'The Bugs Who Ate the Yankees.'" It's calm enough for seven innings, with the Yankees leading, 1-0, and Andy Pettitte pitching out of several jams, with help from Chamberlain in the seventh inning. In the eighth, television close-ups show the bugs covering Chamberlain's sweaty face and neck as he peers through the cloud in an effort to find home plate. He can't. He walks the leadoff batter and hits the next guy. Delays for dousing with bug spray only make it worse, but Joe Torre leaves the 22-year-old out there as if it's a fraternity hazing. A sacrifice moves the runners up, and still visibly tortured, Chamberlain uncorks a wild pitch that brings in the tying run. The bugs are gone when Hafner's bases-loaded single off Luis Vizcaino settles things in the 11th inning.

October 8   **Game 4:** After the Yankees win the first game in the Bronx, Joe Torre goes again with Chien-Ming Wang. Not for long, mind you, just long enough to finish their chances. Later Torre wonders whether he should've given the hook to Wang after Grady Sizemore starts the game with a home run. They score again in the top of the first, yet Torre waits until Wang loads the bases with nobody out in the second inning to get his ass out of there. Mike Mussina, making his first appearance of the series, lets two of the runners score, and by the time he exits in the sixth inning, the Indians lead, 6-1. The final score is 6-4, and the last three outs of Torre's tenure with the Yankees are made by Derek Jeter, Alex Rodriguez, and Jorge Posada.

Yankees Goats: Wang's shortcomings are vividly exposed by the Indians as he posts an ERA of 19.06 in his two losses. Chamberlain lingers, traumatized and doomed, misused by the Yankees, coddled and ruined while still in his twenties. On offense, Alex Rodriguez again drives in just one run, as does Derek Jeter, whose .176 average looks better than Jorge Posada's RBI-free, .133 performance. Torre, after losing 13 of his last 17 postseason games, avoids the Yankees' awkward attempt to let the door hit him on the ass on the way out. He lands on the Dodgers for three final seasons, manages a pair of Division Series sweeps before fading in the LCS, and retires from managing at age 70.

2010 League Championship Series

After failing to make the playoffs in his first season as Yankees manager and winning a title in his second, Joe Girardi spent the next eight seasons in a gradual descent into Bronx oblivion. Here's the start of the decline. The Yankees lead their division all summer until losing eight of their last eleven games to drop into the wild card slot. After sweeping the Twins, they advance to the LCS against the Texas Rangers, who are already satisfied from winning their first postseason series in nearly four decades of existence. A solid offense revolves around left fielder Josh Hamilton, third baseman Michael Young, and designated hitter Vladimir Guerrero, though their pitching staff is mostly no-names. It doesn't matter because, after the Yankees win the first game, the Texas offense engulfs the Yankees like a prairie fire.

October 16

Game 2: Phil Hughes is lit up for five runs in the first three innings, and it's smooth sailing for Colby Lewis and the Rangers, 7-2. They're just getting started on Hughes, 18-8 during the season and an easy winner over the Twins. He's gone here after giving up a double and triple to start the fifth inning.

October 18

Game 3: Following the split in Arlington, they play a quiet game at the new version of Yankee Stadium. Andy Pettitte, now 38 years old, faces southpaw Cliff Lee, playing for his fourth team in two seasons. Lee went 4-0 for the Phillies in the 2009 postseason and just beat Tampa Bay with two great starts in the ALDS. The Rangers get to Pettitte in the top of the first inning when

Michael Young's single is followed by Josh Hamilton's home run. Then they sit back and watch Lee work. The Yankees are hitless until Jorge Posada's two-out single in the fifth inning, and in the sixth, Lee becomes the first pitcher to record three straight 10+-strikeout games in one postseason. He keeps his death-grip on that 2-0 lead through eight innings, allowing two hits and fanning 13 (he also two-hit them for eight innings in September at Texas). In the top of the ninth, David Robertson gives up five hits as the Rangers score six times, giving Lee one inning off for great behavior in the 8-0 win.

October 19

Game 4: The Yankees lead this one, 3-2, after five innings before the Rangers explode for four home runs to win going away, 10-3. Bengie Molina's three-run blast off A. J. Burnett puts the Rangers ahead in the sixth inning. Josh Hamilton launches a pair of solo shots, giving him four in the series, and Nelson Cruz concludes the festivities with a two-run shot off Sergio Mitre. "At this point, they've been a lot better than us," admits Derek Jeter, reminiscing about striking out three times against Cliff Lee. The Yankees have been outscored in the last three games, 25-5.

October 22

Game 6: After CC Sabathia wins Game 5, the teams return to Arlington for a rematch between Phil Hughes and Colby Lewis. It's an echo of their previous game, as Hughes again is kayoed in the fifth inning. It's 1-1 when Joe Girardi orders Hughes to walk Hamilton intentionally with two outs. The move backfires as Vladimir Guerrero burns Hughes with a two-run double. David Robertson comes in to serve up a two-run homer to Nelson Cruz. It's 5-1, and the Yankees end with a whimper, not a bang. Five of them strike out in the last two innings as the Rangers win, 6-1, to reach the World Series.

Yankees Goats: The stinkiest goats are clearly Hughes and Robertson, who combine for a 13.50 ERA. When you're outscored, 38-19, there's plenty of blame left over for a quintet of "hitters." Mark Teixeira goes 0-for-14 before exiting with a Game 4 injury. Right fielder Nick Swisher hits .091, designated hitter Marcus Thames .125, left fielder Brett Gardner .176, and even Alex Rodriguez does his mediocre part with a .190 average and two runs batted in, both in the Game 1 win.

2011 Division Series

The Yankees bring back memories of Joe Torre's last years in pinstripes, topping the AL with 97 wins yet fizzling out in the first playoff round to another team lacking the Yankees' credentials. The Detroit Tigers are led by recycled stars Miguel Cabrera and Victor Martinez, though their biggest threat is posed by starting pitchers Max Scherzer and Justin Verlander, the Cy Young Award winner with a Triple Crown season: a 24-5 record, 2.40 ERA, and 250 strikeouts. The Yankees get a big break when Verlander wastes 25 pitches before a storm rains out Game 1, suspended until the next day, and he doesn't start again until Game 3. It almost matters.

October 2

Game 2: Max Scherzer, a 15-game winner for the first time this season, takes charge at Yankee Stadium to square the series. Scherzer takes a no-hitter to the sixth inning and allows just two hits before leaving in the seventh. It's 4-0 by then, with Miguel Cabrera's home run off Freddy Garcia the big hit, and the bullpen holds on for a 5-3 win. After the Yankees score twice in the bottom of the ninth, Robinson Cano grounds out with the tying runs on base to end it.

October 3

Game 3: At Comerica Park, Verlander shows his heart over eight tough innings to outlast the Yankees, 5-4. It's 4-2 when Brett Gardner's two-run double ties it before Verlander fans Derek Jeter to end the threat. Verlander is rewarded when Delmon Young's homer off Rafael Soriano restores the lead. He tallies 120 pitches in eight innings of work, striking out 11 and picking up the win when Jose Valverde teases the Yankees by walking two men in the ninth inning before ending the game with a strikeout of. . .Jeter once more, with feeling.

October 6

Game 5: The Yankees win Game 4 in Detroit to send the series back to Yankee Stadium for its exciting conclusion. Doug Fister (8-1 for the Tigers after a July trade from Seattle) faces Ivan Nova (16-4 during the season and the Game 1 winner) and a cast of thousands. Nova is rocked in the top of the first inning by back-to-back homers by Don Kelly and Delmon Young, and he's gone after two innings. Joe Girardi's parade of pitchers includes Phil Hughes, Boone Logan, CC Sabathia, Rafael Soriano, David Robertson, and Mariano Rivera. The only one who matters is Sabathia, who gives up a run after yet another misguided intentional walk. Miguel Cabrera is passed to get to Victor Martinez, whose single gives the Tigers a 3-0 lead. That's just enough. The game rides on the bottom of the seventh inning, when the Yankees, trailing 3-1, load the bases with one out. Joaquin Benoit strikes out Alex Rodriguez, walks Mark Teixeira to make it 3-2, and strikes out Nick Swisher to end their last threat. Jose Valverde finishes off the 3-2 clincher by delivering a final strikeout of Alex Rodriguez.

Yankees Goats: Several goats emerge from the finale—Nova, Sabathia, A-Rod, and Swisher. A-Rod is the series standout with a horrid 2-for-18 performance (.111) and no extra-base hits. Teixeira and catcher Russell Martin also fail to hit their weight, while Teixeira and Swisher drive in one run apiece. "No regrets," says A-Rod, whose teams make the postseason eleven times but the World Series only once.

2012 League Championship Series

Guess which team led its league in wins in 2012 and didn't get to the World Series. The Washington Nationals. Oh yeah, and the Yankees, again. Joe Girardi's 97-win team gets past the Orioles in a tight, low-scoring Division Series, emerging for another shot at the Tigers in the LCS. It isn't even fair this time around. The Yankees, who batted .211 against the Orioles, are overpowered by the Tigers' hurlers—and they don't even face Verlander and Scherzer until Game 3. The result is a pathetic .157 average; the Yankees manage 22 hits while striking out 36 times in the Tigers' impressive sweep.

October 13

Game 1: The Yankees' high point of the series comes in the bottom of the ninth inning at Yankee Stadium, when two-run homers by Ichiro Suzuki and Raul Ibanez pull them even, 4-4. A half-hour later, in the top of the 12th inning, Derek Jeter dives for an infield single and somehow breaks his ankle. The Tigers score twice to win, and they never look back.

October 14

Game 2: Anibal Sanchez, 4-6 after a mid-season trade from Miami, shuts the Yankees down on three hits over seven innings. Hiroki Kuroda is better for six innings, holding the Tigers to one hit, but the Tigers get a run in the seventh, and Joe Girardi's night goes horribly wrong after Kuroda strikes out the first two Tigers in the eighth inning. Omar Infante singles, and on Austin Jackson's single, the throw comes to Robinson Cano at second base, who tags Infante. Umpire Jeff Nelson calls Infante safe, and in these pre-replay days, all Girardi can launch is a futile squawk. He brings in Boone Logan, who quickly gives up an RBI single. Girardi has a chance to see the replay in the clubhouse before the next pitching change, a chance to inform Nelson that he really did blow the call. Nelson ejects Girardi, Joba Chamberlain gives up another run-scoring hit, and the final score is 3-0.

Game 3: At Comerica Park, the Yankees are helpless against Justin Verlander, even though he strikes out only three of them. Through the first eight innings, the Yankees' only hits are a pair of singles by Ichiro, and Verlander leads, 3-0. Eduardo Nunez leads off the ninth with a homer, and after Verlander gets one out, he yields the mound to Phil Coke. The ex-Yankee gives up a couple of singles but strikes out Raul Ibanez to put the Tigers up, 3-0.

October 16

Game 4: It looks like a great match-up on paper: CC Sabathia, 74-29 over the past four seasons, facing Max Scherzer, midway through his own four-season stretch of 70-24. Actually it's no contest as the Tigers out-hit the Yankees, 16-2, in an 8-1 joyride that completes the sweep. Scherzer allows both hits but strikes out ten before leaving in the sixth inning with a 6-1 lead. Sabathia is knocked out in the fourth by a pair of two-run homers, by Miguel Cabrera and shortstop Jhonny Peralta.

October 18

Yankees Goats: These numbers say it all: six Yankees—Derek Jeter, Alex Rodriguez, Robinson Cano, Curtis Granderson, Eric Chavez, and Brett Gardner—combine forces to go a whopping 3-for-59 with 20 strikeouts and zero runs scored or driven in. Amazingly, the Yankees score just one run in the whole series before the ninth inning!

2015 Wild Card Game

Joe Girardi's reign went into decline after the 2012 debacle, and the Yankees played exactly one postseason game from 2013 through 2016. They finished third in 2013, and in 2014 and 2016 they won a mere 84 games, their worst winning percentage since 1992. Their only sniff at the postseason came in 2015, whose format required that two wild card teams duke it out in a one-game playoff to see who'd get to play a real series. The Yankees finished six games behind the Blue Jays in their division and faced the Houston Astros, recent arrivals in the American League thanks to Bud Selig extorting that as the price for new ownership. The Astros actually hit more homers than the Yankees, with five players between 22-27, but their leader is second baseman Jose Altuve, a 5'6" sparkplug who led the AL in hits and stolen bases.

October 6   It's all on the line at Yankee Stadium with 50,113 on hand, and Masahiro Tanaka (12-7) faces southpaw Dallas Keuchel, who's about to win the Cy Young Award after going 20-8 with a 2.48 ERA. Keuchel silences the crowd with six shutout innings, allowing three puny singles. Homers by Colby Rasmus and Carlos Gomez make Tanaka the losing pitcher, and Altuve singles in a run later to make the final score 3-0. The Yankees expire meekly, with their offense against the Houston bullpen consisting of one walk in the final three innings. Alex Rodriguez, making his final postseason appearance, goes 0-for-4 and whiffs twice.

Apart from the 2009 title season, Alex Rodriguez hit .202 in the postseason as a Yankee. He played in 36 games in seven losing series plus this wild card game, going 35-for-173 with 48 strikeouts, 4 home runs, and 15 RBI. Projecting his numbers over a 162-game season, you get 36 doubles, no triples, 18 home runs, 68 RBI, and 216 strikeouts.

2017 League Championship Series

After leading the division at the end of July, the Yankees settled into second place behind the Red Sox. They won the wild card game from the Twins, beat the Indians in five games, and reached the LCS for the first time since 2012. There they ran into the Houston Astros, winners of 101 games just four years after losing 111 in their first season in the AL. Batting champion Jose Altuve is still their driving force, but the Astros hit 238 home runs this year, and the lineup is scary from top to bottom. Their late-season acquisition of Justin Verlander is even scarier after he goes 5-0 down the stretch and beats the Red Sox twice in the Division Series.

October 13

Game 1: Dallas Keuchel gets another shot at the Yankees and does not waste the opportunity. This time he gives them four puny singles in seven innings, striking out ten. Their one chance comes in the first inning, when Greg Bird is thrown out trying to score from second on Aaron Judge's single. The Astros get the runs they need in the fourth inning on RBI singles by Carlos Correa and Yuli Gurriel. Bird's homer with two outs in the ninth inning isn't enough in the 2-1 loss.

October 14

Game 2: Heeeere's Justin! His performance since joining the Astros is unreal: six starts, a 7-0 record, 42 2/3 innings, 24 hits, 7 runs, and 46 strikeouts. It's better than that today. After Correa's home run, the Yankees get even in the fifth inning on back-to-back doubles by Aaron Hicks and Todd Frazier. That wakes Verlander up, and the Yankees don't get another hit until the ninth inning. Verlander strikes out 13, but it's a 1-1 tie to the bottom of the ninth, with Aroldis Chapman on to pitch. Altuve singles with one out, raising his postseason average to .565, and he races around the bases on Correa's double. The relay to the plate might beat him, but the short-hop eludes catcher Gary Sanchez, and the Astros have another 2-1 victory.

Game 6: After a Yankees sweep in New York,
October 20
it's back to Minute Maid Park for another date with Verlander. It's business as usual for him, not allowing a Yankee past first base until the sixth inning. Luis Severino stays with him until the fifth inning, when three walks help the Astros score three runs, capped by Altuve's two-run single. Verlander leaves after seven shutout innings, and Aaron Judge's home run in the eighth makes it 3-1. Altuve matches that one leading off the home eighth against David Robertson, who gives up three more runs as the Astros win, 8-1.

Game 7: Joe Girardi's contract is about to
October 21
expire, and he's been on the firing line all season. He has one chance to save the season and is happy to go with CC Sabathia, 14-5 in a comeback campaign and the Game 3 winner. In their first Game 7 since 2004, the Yankees face Charlie Morton, 14-7 during the season. The Yankees can't solve him, getting two crummy hits in five innings. Evan Gattis breaks the ice with a fourth-inning homer off Sabathia, and it turns out that he breaks the bank as well. With a 1-0 lead, Astros manager A. J. Hinch replaces Morton with Lance McCullers, Jr. (whose father was a Yankee in 1989-1990), who started Game 4 and allowed just two hits in six innings. The first batter he faces here gets a hit—and that's it. He walks a guy later but smokes the Yankees for the final four innings, striking out six to clinch a 4-0 win. For the second time this century (see 2001), the Yankees lose a series in which the home team wins all seven games. That's what they get for sneaking in as a wild card.

Yankees Goats: Chapman and Severino get the votes in the bullpen, but the biggest lapses are on offense. Outfielders Aaron Judge, Aaron Hicks, and Brett Gardner strike out 28 times in 75 at-bats, and Todd Frazier is the only Yankee who *doesn't* average more than one strikeout per game. Center fielder Hicks is awful, 2-for-24 without an RBI, Starlin Castro doesn't drive in a run either, and Gardner hits only .148 with one RBI. Of course, in the Yankees' universe, the biggest goat of all is Joe Girardi, who bites the dust shortly after watching his team fade into the sunset of the season.

2018 Division Series

Even though the Yankees won 100 games for new manager Aaron Boone, they still finished eight games behind the Red Sox to lose their division for the sixth straight season. They paid again this year, when eliminating Oakland in the wild card game brought the hollow reward of facing the juggernaut Red Sox. Batting champion Mookie Betts was the AL's MVP, J. D. Martinez led the league with 130 RBI, and Xander Bogaerts and Andrew Benintendi also had big years.

Game 1: Despite going 7-0 after a summer trade to the Yankees, J. A. Happ is no Justin Verlander, and he lasts just two-plus innings at Fenway Park. Martinez slugs a three-run homer in the first inning, and Happ leaves after Betts' double and Benintendi's bunt single. Chad Green comes in to let the inherited runners score, and that's the difference. The Yankees chip away at the 5-0 deficit, Chris Sale exits with a 5-2 lead, and five relievers hold on. Aaron Judge leads off the ninth inning with a homer off Craig Kimbrel to make it 5-4, but Kimbrel fans Brett Gardner, Giancarlo Stanton, and Luke Voit to shut the door.

October 5

Game 3: After the Yankees win the second game, the Red Sox enjoy a field day at Yankee Stadium against Luis Severino and five relievers, all of whom give up runs. Severino is knocked silly in a seven-run fourth inning that makes it 10-0, allowing Nate Eovaldi to coast through seven innings. It's 14-1 when Aaron Boone lets catcher Austin Romine pitch the ninth. He gives up a

October 8

two-run homer to Brock Holt, who completes the cycle while driving in five runs in the 16-1 spree.

Game 4: It's curtains for the Yankees in front
October 9
of 49,641 fans at the Stadium. Once again, CC Sabathia gets the honor of losing the final game of a series, gone after a three-run third inning that starts with a hit batter. In the fourth, Red Sox catcher Christian Vazquez homers off Zack Britton to make it 4-0, and again the Red Sox just hold on. Rick Porcello pitches five strong innings, and it's 4-1 to the bottom of the ninth. Kimbrel gets in trouble again on two walks, a single, and a hit batter, but Gary Sanchez makes the second out on a sacrifice fly, and Kimbrel gets second baseman Gleyber Torres on a groundout to eliminate the Yankees and move one step closer to another title.

> Sabathia became the first Yankees pitcher to lose three deciding games, though none came in a World Series. Waite Hoyt lost two World Series finales, while Andy Pettitte lost one of each. Future Hall of Famers to surrender the farm were Red Ruffing (1942), Whitey Ford (1963), Goose Gossage (1980), Mariano Rivera (2001), and Mike Mussina (2005).

Yankees Goats: It's a team effort when you're outscored, 27-14, in a series. Happ, Severino, and Sabathia all take their lumps, and the bullpen doesn't help. The offense bats .214, and Judge is the only outfielder with an extra-base hit. After bopping a record 267 homers during the season, the Yankees get four in this series—three of them in their lone win.

2019 League Championship Series

For much of 2019, the Yankees and the Houston Astros are on a collision course, which occurs in the LCS. After crashing 306 homers during the season, the Yankees win their division for the first time since 2012, then sweep the Twins (with their 307 homers) in the Division Series. The 103-win Yankees meet the 107-win Astros, whose lineup is now loaded with the additions of MVP candidate Alex Bregman, Rookie of the Year Yordan Alvarez, and George Springer. Their pitching is just as scary, with Verlander (21-6), Gerrit Cole (20-5), and this year's late-season acquisition, Zack Greinke (8-1).

October 13

Game 2: After the Yankees win the first game at Houston behind Masahiro Tanaka, the Astros go to work. The starters are Verlander and James Paxton, who's gone in the third inning. It's 2-2 through five innings, with Aaron Judge's two-run homer the only damage off Verlander, who pitches seven innings. The bullpens take over, but both managers remain alert enough to over-manage in extra innings. In the bottom of the tenth, Aaron Boone brings in CC Sabathia to retire the leadoff hitter, a lefty. Then he brings in Jonathan Loaisiga to face a pair of righties, both of whom he walks. Here comes a lefty, and here comes southpaw J. A. Happ, and pretty soon it's the top of the 11th and Hinch's turn. When righty Joe Smith walks a man with two outs, Hinch brings in another righty to face lefty Brett Gardner, who singles. Out strolls Hinch, and he brings in a third righty to pitch to righty Gary Sanchez, who takes a called third strike to end the threat. In the bottom of the 11th, Carlos Correa takes all the strain off the managers by belting Happ's first pitch to the opposite field for the game-winning homer.

Game 3: After striking out 326 batters in his

October 15

first full season with the Astros and humiliating Tampa Bay in two Division Series starts, Gerrit Cole is primed for his big dream start at Yankee Stadium. He doesn't have his best stuff, walking five Yankees, but he has enough stuff to shut them out for seven innings. Jose Altuve's first-inning homer off Luis Severino and Josh Reddick's in the second give Cole a cushion, and they add two runs in the seventh inning off the bullpen. A Gleyber Torres homer is the extent of the Yankees' comeback as the Astros go ahead with the 4-1 win.

Game 4: It's Tanaka vs. Greinke, and George

October 17

Springer strikes the first big blow, a three-run homer in the third inning. A. J. Hinch manages as if the game matters, lifting Zack Greinke with a 3-1 lead after he puts two men on base with one out in the fifth inning. It must be the key spot, because after Ryan Pressly walks a man to load the bases, he strikes out Torres and Edwin Encarnacion, and the Yankees are never in it again. Carlos Correa's three-run blast in the top of the sixth off Chad Green makes it 6-1, and the final score is 8-3.

Game 6: After the Yankees somehow beat

October 19

Justin Verlander, it's back to Minute Maid Park for Exhibit A on the sad state of starting pitchers today. Apparently there isn't a starter capable of working for either team—with the season on the line—so it's "a bullpen day," baseball pot-luck with both managers employing seven pitchers in a struggle that lasts more than four hours thanks to 200 *warmup* pitches! Chad Green starting for the Yankees matters only because he surrenders a three-run homer to Yuli Gurriel. None of the 14 pitchers is allowed to retire more than eight batters, and it happens that Roberto Osuna takes a 6-4 lead to the ninth inning, when DJ LeMahieu's two-run homer ties it. The fans settle in to watch all night as Aroldis Chapman enters in the bottom of the ninth. After a two-out walk to George Springer, Chapman fires a high-outside fastball that the 5'6" Jose Altuve reaches for and jerks out of the park in left-center, the series-winning hit, leaving Chapman planted on the mound with one of the greatest shit-eating grins in major league history.

Yankees Goats: Start with Chapman and Happ, the walk-off losers, and work your way back to Chad Green and those three-run homers which crush the Yankees. As always, there are plenty of busts on the offense. Edwin Encarnacion, Gary Sanchez, and Brett Gardner (34, 34, and 28 homers during the season), bat .056, .130, and .136 respectively, all of them joining Aaron Judge in striking out at least ten times in the six-game loss. Houston, they had a problem.

With the Yankees on this current negative run, having just passed their first decade since before Babe Ruth without making it to the World Series, it's tempting to hope they keep getting to the postseason just so they can get crushed, embarrassed, outclassed, and even humbled before a nationwide audience. On the other hand, there's the corner of your mind that wants them to lose every game they suit up for until the end of time and beyond, just so their fans will recognize once and for all that the universe is not Yankees-centric. Either way, there are wonderful losses yet to behold. First, we have to get through the minefield of the off-season, when the Yankees not only perpetrate many of their foulest deeds but also commit many of their most lame-brained blunders. The fact that the ballgames are in abeyance just gives the front office more free time to screw things up.

Part III

The Off-Season

Bad Trades

When Joseph L. Reichler went to list the "worst trades" in New York Yankees history in his book, *The Baseball Trade Register*, he found just one worth noting before 1976. Part of their long success was pillaging talent from less affluent franchises, notably the Boston Red Sox of the 1920s and the Kansas City Athletics of the 1950s. According to historian Jeff Katz, when Roger Maris was traded from Cleveland to the Athletics in June 1958, the players in the *Yankees' clubhouse* exulted, "All right—we just got Roger Maris!" They knew he'd be there soon enough, and so he was, after the 1959 season.

Of course, every general manager makes flawed judgments and ill-advised deals, and that's why I'm here, to celebrate about twenty of the Yankees' worst. Of course, the most ill-advised trade in franchise history didn't even involve management. Do you remember it?

Bad trades come in three categories: great players you never should've gotten rid of, over-hyped bums you wonder why you wanted in the first place, and appealing players you almost got until something wrecked the deal. The most plentiful group is the first, usually untested, younger players you give up to get a presumably more reliable commodity, though sometimes it's a discarded star who has the last laugh.

They Left

January 22, 1918 New Yankees manager Miller Huggins makes a blockbuster trade, giving the St. Louis Browns five players plus $15,000 for second baseman Del Pratt and future

Hall of Fame pitcher Eddie Plank. The problem is that Plank is 43 years old and has already retired. He confirms this, saying, "I will not go to New York next season. . . . When I announced last summer that I was through with baseball at the end of 1917, I meant just that." Huggins played in St. Louis in 1917; didn't he know Plank's intentions? Plank stays on his farm, and the Yankees languish with Pratt for three seasons in New York before unloading him. Meanwhile, Urban Shocker, a right-hander with a 12-8 record in 39 games for the Yankees in 1917, goes to St. Louis and wins 107 games there from 1920-1924, including a 27-12 record in 1921.

February 5, 1942 The Yankees trade 24-year-old outfielder Tommy Holmes to the Boston Braves for two players who are both done in New York after one season. Holmes has languished in the Yankees' farm system for five years, including the last three with their top farm team in Newark, batting over .300 every year and amassing 910 hits, but he can't crack their crowded outfield of Joe DiMaggio, Charlie Keller, Tommy Henrich, and George Selkirk. By 1943, they're all off fighting the war, while Holmes is in the second season of an 11-year career that produces a .302 lifetime average. In 1945, Holmes is second in the MVP Award balloting after batting .352 and setting a National League record with a 37-game hitting streak that stands until conspicuously broken by Pete Rose in 1978.

December 16, 1953 Trying to avoid the inevitable, the Yankees trade Vic Power to the Athletics, parting with the dark-skinned Puerto Rican who just led the American Association with a .349 batting average. The Yankees, eventually the thirteenth of sixteen major league franchises to integrate, have faced ongoing criticism, including charges of racism by Jackie Robinson a year earlier. GM George Weiss declares, "We showed our good faith toward Negro players by bringing up Power and [Elston] Howard" in September. He doesn't mention that neither man was given an opportunity to play even though the Yankees had a 13-game lead with two weeks left in the season, and the Yankees don't break the color barrier until 1955. Meanwhile, Power hits .284 in a 12-year career and, the slickest first baseman of his generation, wins seven straight Gold Glove Awards (1958-1964).

November 26, 1962 Talk about swift payback for a premature move. Bill "Moose" Skowron, Vic Power's teammate at Kansas City in 1953, has been the Yankees' first baseman since 1956. A steady, unsung regular, averaging 21 home runs a year, the popular Skowron is traded to the Los Angeles Dodgers for 14-game winner Stan Williams. The Yankees can't wait to hand the first base job to Joe Pepitone, so away goes 31-year-old Moose. Williams gives the Yankees ten victories in two seasons. Skowron zaps his old buddies in the 1963 World Series, batting .385 with three key RBI as the Dodgers sweep the Series. In Game 1, his two-run single off Whitey Ford caps a five-run second inning, and the next day, he homers off Al Downing.

December 8, 1966 Roger Maris, who never liked playing in New York, gets his long-sought exit from the Yankees, traded to the Cardinals for third baseman Charley Smith. Yankees fans never took to him, partly because he lacked charisma but mainly because he had the effrontery to break Babe Ruth's record of 60 home runs instead of Mickey Mantle, "The Commerce Comet" with feet of clay. The unforgiven Maris, hobbled by injuries, hit just .233 with 43 RBI in 1966, one of roughly 25 reasons why the Yankees finished last. "I expected to be traded ever since 1962," says Maris, relieved to return to the Midwest. He gets to the World Series in both of his St. Louis seasons, leading them to the championship in 1967 by hitting .385 in the Series with seven RBI. As for Charley Smith, the Yankees are done with him after he bats .224 in two seasons with ten home runs.

Only those of us who were eyewitnesses to the 1961 Yankees can appreciate fully the atrocious way that Roger Maris was treated by the New York fans, press, and team officials. A small-town kid who didn't ask for attention, he was overwhelmed by the daily press and the national media, and the team did little to lessen his discomfort. Yankees fans hated him because only Mickey Mantle had a right to break Babe Ruth's record. I grew up ten miles from Yankee Stadium, and all the budding Yankee bullies were pissed at anyone who exceeded The Mick at anything. No wonder Maris wanted to leave.

December 2, 1971 The Yankees want infielder Rich McKinney, who smacked eight home runs for the White Sox in 369 at-bats. This is appealing because *the entire* 1971 Yankees infield (Danny Cater, Horace Clarke, Gene Michael, and Jerry Kenney) totaled only nine home runs in 1,834 at-bats, a feat of frailty not accomplished since the Deadball Era. To get McKinney, they trade Stan Bahnsen, their 1968 Rookie of the Year, a 54-game winner over the past four seasons just entering his prime at age 27. Bahnsen is solid with the White Sox, winning 51 games the next three seasons. Predictably, McKinney peaked in Chicago with his eight homers and .271 average. As a Yankee, he bombs out with one home run in 121 at-bats in 1972, while Bahnsen goes 21-16 for the White Sox. McKinney is the player to be named later in a trade that winter, concluding his New York legacy.

November 10, 1978 Sparky Lyle gets his wish as the Yankees trade him to Texas in a ten-player deal. He has labored the whole season as an unhappy camper, lobbying to get moved after losing his job as the #1 man in the bullpen to newcomer Goose Gossage. How would *you* feel? Lyle won the Cy Young Award in 1977, only the second reliever to win it. But Gossage is the high-priced free agent who must be given the chance to justify his salary. After a couple of bad outings in May, Lyle becomes a middle-innings reliever, and he gets tired of being replaced by Gossage, who gets the saves. Ironically, one player the Yankees get in the big deal is 20-year-old Dave Righetti, who will replace Gossage in 1984. Lyle gets the last laugh in his book, co-authored with Peter Golenbock, *The Bronx Zoo.*

October 21, 1981 Here is an unjustly forgotten candidate for the worst trade in franchise history, made by a justly forgotten general manager, Cedric Tallis. After hitting .322 in his fifth year in the minors, 23-year-old outfielder Willie McGee is traded to the Cardinals for Bob Sykes. Sykes, bothered by arm trouble for years, never pitches an inning for the Yankees, who release him a year later. Could they have used McGee? By 1985, he is a batting champion and MVP, batting .353 with 216 hits and 56 stolen bases. In 1999, he concludes his career with two batting titles, three Gold Glove Awards, and 2,254 hits. Nice move, Cedric.

November 26, 1986   After a seven-win rookie season with the Yankees, Doug Drabek is traded to the Pirates in a deal involving six pitchers. The 24-year-old right-hander went 7-8, but in his last half-dozen starts, he was 4-1 with a 2.27 ERA. Bye-bye. The three pitchers the Yankees receive (Rick Rhoden, Pat Clements, Cecilio Guante) are all gone after winning an aggregate 39 games in two seasons in New York. In 1990, when the Yankees finish last, Drabek wins the Cy Young Award for the Pirates with a 22-6 record and a 2.76 ERA. He wins 92 games for them from 1988-1993 with a sub-3 ERA, leading them to three division titles.

December 12, 1989   After batting .317 in four seasons in the Yankees' farm system, untested first baseman Hal Morris is traded to the Cincinnati Reds for pitcher Tim Leary. In two late-season tenures, Morris played 30 games for the Yankees, with just five starts. He becomes the Reds' first baseman for the next eight years, batting .305 overall and .340 in 1990, helping them win the World Series. And Tim Leary? Yankees fans usually leave the room when people start talking about him. In 1990, he went 9-19, leading the American League in losses, and his record with the Yankees was 18-35 with a 5.12 ERA. The Yankees became so desperate to end their bad trip with Leary that they traded him before the end of 1992 to Seattle for the enduringly unknown Sean Twitty.

They Arrived

March 31, 1981   Looking to add speed to their lineup, the Yankees trade four players—Ruppert Jones, Tim Lollar, Joe Lefebvre, and Chris Welsh—to San Diego for Jerry Mumphrey, who stole 52 bases in 57 attempts in 1980. They think he's the next Mickey Rivers, but they're wrong. Despite hitting over .300 in 1981 and 1982, he steals a mere 27 bases and is thrown out 15 times for the Yankees before being dealt away in August 1983. After being a steady victim of George Steinbrenner's verbal abuse, Mumphrey happily skips town. In 44 games with the Padres, he bats .330, and in 1984 he makes his only All-Star team.

December 12, 1985 Most Yankees fans don't even remember acquiring Britt Burns, probably because he never pitched for them. He was a fine pitcher for the White Sox, going 70-60 from 1978-1985, a big lefty coming off an 18-11 record in 1985. The Yankees trade Ron Hassey and Joe Cowley to get the 26-year-old Burns, knowing he has a hip problem but believing the White Sox trainer who crows, "There's no reason why he can't pitch seven more years." Following May 1986 surgery on his arthritic hip, Burns begins to realize that he won't even pitch seven more innings. The degenerative condition isn't going away, but Britt Burns is, along with his $750,000 salary. Just like my father, the Yankees got a lemon, not a Cadillac.

January 15, 1997 A dream begins, the wishful yearning of a starry-eyed Japanese youth named Hideki Irabu to play for the New York Yankees. Claimed today by the San Diego Padres, Irabu and his agent kick and scream like Mickey Mantle whining "I want my Maypo!" in that advertisement, until he gets his wish—a trade to New York on **May 29, 1997**. There Irabu met reality.

Irabu got hammered early and often, and he went 5-4 with a 7.09 ERA as a 28-year-old rookie in 1997. The fans turned against him, and George Steinbrenner made him a favorite target. After Irabu failed to cover first base in an exhibition game on **April 1, 1999**, Steinbrenner labeled him forever, saying, "He looked like a fat, pus-sy toad out there, not covering first base." Pretty soon, Irabu's goals shrank as his waistline expanded, until the 240-pound toad battled a rumored demotion to the minor leagues, frequent booing at Yankee Stadium, constant hounding by the Japanese press, and his failure to dazzle American League hitters.

On **November 22, 1999**, the dream ends as Irabu is deported—that is, traded to Montreal. His three-year Yankees career brought a modest 29 wins and a mediocre 4.80 ERA. The final straw came in the 1999 ALCS, when he was hammered in Boston for 13 hits and eight runs in less than five innings. GM Brian Cashman says, "Maybe he gets a chance to start fresh, in a new country. In New York it's a tough situation."

Exiled from his beloved team, Irabu could not recapture his shattered dream. He was out of the majors after 2002 (34-35, 5.15 ERA), went back to Japan for one decent season but got hurt and returned to the United States, settling in Southern California. His businesses failed; his marriage faltered, and a stint in an independent league in 2009 didn't help. Nor did the drinking. On **July 27, 2011,** the 42-year-old Irabu hanged himself.

Be careful what you wish for.

They Just Said "No!"

Much has been written about the dry period the Yankees experienced between 1978 and 1996. A lot of blame is placed on George Steinbrenner's spendthrift efforts to buy more pennants after it paid off in 1977-1978, along with causing the decade of instability resulting from his love-hate affair with Billy Martin I-V. A subtler reason was the reluctance of many stars to take the bait and sell their souls to the Yankees. Between 1979 and 1985, four big trades, any of which might have transformed the Yankees, were all but made when the plug was pulled. Twice, players exercised their newly-won right to veto a trade, declining to go to New York. Twice, the Yankees chickened out, and wait till you hear why they lost out on Andre Dawson.

February 3, 1979 Born in Panama, Rod Carew grew up in New York City and played ball as a teenager in McCombs Park, in the shadow of Yankee Stadium. While he played out his option with the Twins in 1978, they asked him which teams he'd like to be traded to. He mentioned a couple of teams, but not the Yankees. The Yankees offered to trade Chris Chambliss, Juan Beniquez, and two other players for Carew, who just won his seventh batting title, but George Steinbrenner calls it off today because he got word that Carew was quoted in a newspaper calling him an "ape" or a "gorilla" or something. Carew, it turned out, either referred to not wanting "to play in that [Bronx] zoo" (citing Sparky Lyle's book) or likened Steinbrenner to the proverbial 3,000-pound gorilla that sits anywhere it wants. Says Steinbrenner, "If he doesn't know what it means like to play for a team like the Yankees, okay, that's fine, he can go someplace else." Carew, who knew all about what that meant in 1979, got his wish when the Angels ponied up four players and let him move to Anaheim, 3,000 miles away from the Bronx.

December 15, 1980   Think about how close the Yankees came to a title in 1981, and then think about how this little adjustment in personnel might have changed things. It was a simple deal that reflected the times, coming just months after a contentious near-strike. The players had won some battles in the uphill war against the owners, and some players had "no-trade" clauses that changed the labor landscape. Instead of the Steinbrenners of the world telling players "you just got traded to Podunk," they would have to consult with the player's agent to see if the player might condescend to go there or perhaps to this other team, just upwind from Podunk. In this case, the Yankees wanted to trade pitcher Rudy May to the Kansas City Royals for Hal McRae. May, a journeyman southpaw, didn't want to leave the Yankees. McRae, the best designated hitter in the 1970s, didn't want to go *to* New York. So they *both vetoed* the deal. That tickles me. McRae was good enough to drive in 133 runs in 1982, while May went 13-22 in the rest of his stay with the Yankees and allowed the final run of the 1981 World Series on a Pedro Guerrero home run.

October 26, 1985   The Yankees have a blockbuster deal in place to make Carlton Fisk a Yankee. George Steinbrenner wants to trade Don Baylor, Ron Hassey, and pitchers Joe Cowley and Marty Bystrom to the White Sox for Fisk, Britt Burns, and infielder Scott Fletcher. The big name is Fisk, who hit 37 homers for the White Sox this season, but he's about to become a free agent, and his agent, Jerry Kapstein, is also Baylor's agent, and they have no-trade clauses, a mine-field of obstacles. Fisk nixes any deal today, declaring his intention of going through the free-agent process, after which he plays eight more years with the Chisox. Instead, the Yankees give away two players for Britt Burns, who never plays again.

December 5, 1985 The Yankees call off a six-player trade with the Expos which would have brought Andre Dawson to New York. You won't believe why. Listen to this proposal: Dawson and pitcher Bill Gullickson, a 43-game winner over the past three seasons, for three pitchers—Dennis Rasmussen, Joe Cowley, and Rich Bordi—who went a combined 21-19 in 1985, plus rookie outfielder Henry Cotto. The Expos want rookie outfielder Dan Pasqua instead, and the Yankees *refuse* to part with Pasqua, a Steinbrenner favorite who hit .209 with nine home runs. Steinbrenner won't make the deal, which is like canceling a big banquet because the caterer won't serve sherbet instead of mousse. Poor Pasqua, born too soon, continued to show power but struck out way too much, at a 2019 rate, and was traded after hitting .233 in 1987. That same winter, Dawson joined the Cubs and earned the 1988 MVP Award, smashing 49 home runs, driving in 137 runs and adding a Gold Glove Award. He could've roamed the Yankee Stadium outfield with Dave Winfield and Rickey Henderson, but no, Steinbrenner just had to keep Dan Pasqua.

They Should Have Just Said "No"

Finally, the *piece de resistance*, the most ill-advised, dastardly trade in New York Yankees history. On **March 4, 1973**, fittingly at separate press conferences, Fritz Peterson and Mike Kekich, half of the Yankees' starting rotation, announced that they have traded wives. . .and children (two apiece). . .and houses. . .and even dogs, no doubt with a delivery man to be named at a later date. It began last summer after they attended a barbecue at the home of sportswriter Maury Allen, and pretty soon the best buds fell in love with each other's wife, Peterson with Susanne Kekich, Kekich with Marilyn Peterson.

"Unless people know the full details, it could turn out to be a nasty type thing," Kekich said in his conference. "Don't say this was wife-swapping, because it wasn't. We didn't swap wives, we swapped lives." The husbands simply changed households. Susanne Whichever added the next day, "We didn't do anything sneaky or lecherous. We are not involved in lechery. Don't make this out to be Bob and Carol and Ted and Alice [the film]. That was dirty and ugly. There isn't anything smutty about this."

There *is* an item, however, in Peterson's profile in the 1971 Yankees yearbook which says that for him, "No day is complete without pulling some kind of a prank on Kekich." If so, this was Peterson's greatest prank ever. On the day of the announcement, Kekich said, "I would like it to work out with Marilyn and me, but I'm dubious." He knew he'd been had.

What passed for a sex scandal in 1973 (and today would be a passing episode on a "reality" show) continued to unfold over the next few weeks. On **March 11**, the left-handers revealed more. Kekich said that Mrs. Peterson wanted to call the whole thing off the night before they did it. She asked her husband, "How can you do this to me?" Fritz Peterson admitted, "That is the only thing I didn't tell Mike about throughout the whole situation." Just that little detail about Fritz's wife not being so sure about his pal Mike. But Fritz was sure about Susanne, and they've been married since 1974. Mike Kekich and Marilyn were history before long. So Peterson's scouting report was legit. Quite the prank. He and Kekich haven't talked in a long time.

About the time attention was waning, on **March 19**, Commissioner Bowie Kuhn butted in for no reason, suddenly piping up about how, as the "conscience of the game," he was "appalled" by what they did. Ralph Houk chirped, "Why did he wait two weeks before speaking out? He has to wait for public opinion to run the full gamut, doesn't he, to decide which side to jump on?" Yankees GM Lee MacPhail wryly wondered why Kuhn bothered: "What would you expect him to say to them: Don't do it again?"

In the short term, both men wrecked their careers. Peterson, 31 years old, went 8-15 for the Yankees in 1973 and was traded the following season. Kekich, 28, made just five appearances with a 9.20 ERA before getting traded in June, and he won just seven more games in the majors.

Bad Free Agents

With just a few exceptions, there were no free agents in the major leagues until 1976. Free agency is a risky business on both sides of the equation; careers shipwrecked in their prime are as plentiful as the diminished returns on aging millionaires. Since the Yankees under George Steinbrenner were the most conspicuous consumers of free agents, they had to *caveat* more than other *emptors*. I wrestled a long list down to a dozen wonderfully wretched free agent signings, from Don Gullett to Jacoby Ellsbury, and we'll work our way through a feast of regret featuring the two biggest disasters—Dave Winfield and Alex Rodriguez.

Before the amateur draft began in the mid-1960s, teams could sign anybody, wasting money on teenagers instead of on established players as they do in the free agent era. So let us begin with several cautionary tales of young men who made deals with the Devil and got only money out of it.

Bonus Babies

November 16, 1948   The Yankees outbid a dozen other teams to sign their first "bonus" player. They shell out $50,000-75,000 to 23-year-old pitcher Paul Hinrichs at a time when even Joe DiMaggio is only making $65,000. A divinity student, Hinrichs doesn't have a prayer in the majors. He spends two mediocre seasons in the Yankees' farm system (with a 1950 salary almost as large as Yogi Berra's), hampered by injuries, is taken by the Red Sox in the Rule 5 draft, and is history after a 21.60 ERA in four appearances with them in 1951. He does better in divinity, with a long career as a Lutheran minister. God knows he couldn't play in the majors, but the Yankees didn't.

June 25, 1951   San Francisco phenom Ed Cereghino was ballyhooed for his fastball and his knuckleball—when he was 14! Today, with seven no-hitters and 150 victories on his resume at age 17, he signs with the Yankees for a $74,000 bonus. Life is sweet, until he starts pitching for a living. After an 11-3 record at the Single-A level, he gets worse as he goes along, winning in double figures three times but racking up a dismal 14-31 record in his final four seasons. All in the minors. The Yankees keep throwing good money after bad despite his 9-16 record and 5.08 ERA for New Orleans in 1958, until Cereghino, who by now has four kids and a lovely home, finally walks away, goes to college, and becomes a high school principal.

November 25, 1960   Going under for the third time with a pitching prospect, the Yankees shell out $65,000 to Howard Kitt, an 18-year-old, left-handed pitcher from Long Island who's a sophomore at Columbia University. In his last year of high school, he went 18-0 with an ERA of 0.05. How can he miss? Very easily, it turns out. Like many lefties, he's wild. In two stints in AAA, he walks 65 batters in 53 innings. His last year in pro ball is 1965, and he never comes close to being the successor to Whitey Ford that the Yankees daydreamed he

would be. He does, however, learn the value of money. He gives up baseball, gets a Ph.D., and becomes an economist.

A few decades later, mistakes cost much more. On March 24,
2001, Drew Henson agrees to skip his senior year as the quar-
terback for the University of Michigan when the Yankees offer him a six-year, $17 million contract. "During the past year,"
says Henson, a Heisman Trophy candidate, "I have come to
the realization that my passion is baseball." Joe Torre gushes,
"He's a future superstar, no question." In 2002 at Columbus,
the third baseman hits .240 and commits 35 errors. After a major league career consisting of one hit in nine at-bats, he takes
the rest of his money (including a $6 million salary in 2006)
and scrams.

November 28, 1966 Charlie Sands and Frank Tepedino weren't
bonus babies, but the 18-year-olds were the
first two choices of the last-place Yankees in the annual "unrestricted
draft" of minor leaguers not protected on the parent clubs' 40-man ros-
ters. Neither one does anything for the Yankees as they stagnate in the
standings for another decade. Sands, a catcher, gets one at-bat for the
Yankees. Tepedino, a first baseman-outfielder from Brooklyn, lasts long
enough to get 507 at-bats, but only 77 for the Yankees, batting .221 with
no home runs.

They Escaped

January 22, 1982 Reggie Jackson officially leaves the Yankees,
sometime after wearing out his welcome. No
free agent impacted the Yankees more than Reggie Jackson. The 1977
Yankees were mostly the same bunch who got swept by the Reds in the
1976 World Series, except for Jackson, who signed a five-year deal for $3
million back when $3 million meant you were a helluva ballplayer. Jack-
son drove in 207 runs in the next two seasons, lived up to his own hype as

the straw that stirred the drink, pissed off captain Thurman Munson and half his teammates, and fought with his manager on national television while leading the Yankees to yadda yadda. From 1977-1980, he hit .289 and averaged 29 home runs and 102 RBI, but by 1981, the grind of matching egos with George Steinbrenner, combined with the summer strike, wore him down. His average dropped to .237, and the Yankees planned to use him mainly as a designated hitter (where he hit .227 in his career), while he wanted to wander the outfield like a real ballplayer. That hurt the feelings of 35-year-old Reggie, who took his bat and his candy bars and went home when California Angels owner Gene Autry waved a four-year, $4 million offer at him. In 1982, when the Yankees finished fourth in the East, Jackson played right field every day and hit 39 home runs for the Angels, who conquered the West and got within one win of the World Series.

December 21, 1983 Rich "Goose" Gossage gets richer, signing a three-year, $4 million deal with the San Diego Padres. After six seasons in the Bronx, he wants to go far away. George Steinbrenner thought he had a good shot at keeping Gossage and blames the defection on Gossage's agent, Jerry Kapstein. There was speculation that Gossage's decision depended on who would manage the Yankees in 1984; reportedly he wasn't any more thrilled with Billy Martin III than he was with Martin II or Martin I. Kapstein said that didn't matter. Gossage, in his announcement, gets to the heart of the matter: "I will not return to play for George Steinbrenner." As a Yankee, Gossage posted a 2.10 ERA and averaged 25 saves; in 1983, he went 13-5 with a 2.27 ERA. In two World Series, he pitched 11 innings and gave up no runs on just three hits, but he tells reporters, "Even if we win, it's no fun. The last time we won [1981], we got apologized for, which is ridiculous. We didn't lose that World Series. They lost it upstairs." Mellowed in San Diego, he reflected on the Bronx Zoo: "When I got into the car last year to go to the ball park, it felt like I was going to a funeral. . .It seems like you just got kicked over there instead of being appreciated."

December 31, 2003   David Wells loved playing for the Yankees more than just about anybody. He splurged with some of his bonus money on a genuine Babe Ruth jersey, saluted The Babe's monument before every Yankee Stadium start, and emulated him by expanding the girth above his belt. As it turned out, one of the few things he loved more than following in Ruth's jock-steps was getting more money to wear some other uniform. He first signed with the Yankees as a free agent and gave them a stellar 34-14 record in 1997-1998. He went 18-4 in 1998, including a perfect game, was the ALCS MVP, and won Game 1 of the World Series, but his reward for all that was a trade to Toronto for Roger Clemens. A 20-game winner there, Wells found himself a free agent again in 2001, agreed to a deal with Arizona, but jumped at the Yankees' last-minute offer of a two-year deal. Again he compiled an outstanding 34-14 record. He gave the Yankees an oral commitment to sign for 2004, but the Padres' incentive-laden offer could bring the 40-year-old fatso up to $7 million. Bye-bye, Yankees. He signs today with San Diego. Brian Cashman notes the symmetry: "It looks like he is going to do to us what he did to Arizona. What comes around, goes around, I guess."

January 12, 2004   "Clemens Comes Out of Retirement to Play for Astros," read the headlines in Texas, and there is consternation in the Bronx. It was tough for the Yankees to watch Roger Clemens ride off into the sunset after the 2003 season, but they couldn't blame the 41-year-old for retiring to, as he insisted, savor the splendor of family life back in Houston. He spent the whole 2003 season on a retirement tour, honored around the league and at Game 4 of the World Series, after he threw the final pitch of the final game of his career, leaving after seven innings with a 3-1 deficit. When the Houston Astros announce today that they have signed Clemens to a one-year, $5 million deal, the Yankees are stunned. "Did I talk to him about retiring?" asks Brian Cashman. "Yeah. He said he was taking it to the house." Exactly. To his house in Texas, where he stays except when he consents to pitch for the Astros. The Yankees are left with a forlorn cry of "Shane! Shane! Come back!" They could have used Clemens' Cy Young Award season of 2004 and his 1.87 ERA in 2005. Instead, Shane didn't come back for four years, with his speed gone in 2007. He got toasted for an eight-run second inning two days before his 45th birthday and faded away with a 6-6 record and 4.18 ERA.

Three Who Eluded Capture

December 2, 1992   GM Gene Michael announces that the Yankees are withdrawing their five-year, $38 million offer to free agent Barry Bonds. Bonds (that is, his agent, Dennis Gilbert) said he wanted six years for $43 million, and Michael calls their bluff. "We have to draw the line somewhere," says Michael. "I have no regrets saying we did not offer him a sixth year." The next day, ownership partner Joe Molloy says the offer is still on the table. A week later, Bonds signs with the Giants: six years, $43.75 million, less per season than the Yankees' offer. Let's check the scoreboard. In the next five years, Bonds won another MVP Award and finished in the top five three other seasons. The sixth year would've been 1998, when Bonds hit .303 with 37 home runs and 122 RBI, drew 130 walks, stole 28 bases, and scored 120 runs. Oh yeah, he won his eighth Gold Glove Award. So what if the Yankees won 114 games anyway that season. Bonds would've hit a home run every other day at Yankee Stadium, smashing Roger Maris' record, would've stayed after 1998, and soon would've been joined by Clemens and A-Rod. Think of it, picture all of them together, the Three Musketeeroids—striding through the clubhouse, punctured arm in arm, proclaiming "all for 'cream,' and 'clear' for all!"

December 9, 1992   The Yankees hadn't played a postseason game in more than a decade when that bleak winter of 1992-1993 rolled around. Besides pursuing Bonds, the 1992 MVP, they made an even more desperate attempt to sign two-time defending Cy Young Award winner Greg Maddux. The Yankees wined and dined Maddux, showed him the spiffiest suburbs in New Jersey, took him to see "Miss Saigon" on Broadway, and more, trying to dazzle a guy who grew up in Las Vegas. They offered him a five-year deal for $28 million, only $10 million less than they offered The Great Barry Bonds. Finally, the Yankees' owners even sicced Donald Trump on Maddux to sing the praises of living lavishly in the Big Apple. That's probably what clinched the decision: on this date, Maddux shocks the Yankees by signing with the Braves for $6 million less. Take that, you philistine plutocrats! Maddux turns down their money, heads south, and picks up three more Cy Young Awards in a row. His record for the Braves the next five years is 87-32. A collateral effect is that, spurned by Maddux, Steinbrenner put the kibosh on offering big contracts to pitchers a year later, ending talks about acquiring Randy Johnson, who earns $26 million from the Mariners by going 75-23 over the next five seasons. When the Yankees finally land Johnson in 2005, he's 41 and has a bad back, but he still wins 34 games in two seasons.

December 16, 2010 Cliff Lee's two-year odyssey ends today, but much to the surprise of the Yankees, he disembarks in Philadelphia, not New York. The stakes have changed since they courted Greg Maddux, and this time the insufficient offer is for seven years at more than $20 million *a year*. Lee the refugee won the Cy Young Award in 2008 for the Indians with a 22-3 record. They traded him the following summer to the Phillies, where he went 4-0 with a 1.56 ERA in their postseason run to the title, including two wins in the World Series. For that, he got traded again over the winter, this time to Seattle. There he went 8-3 with a 2.34 ERA—and got traded in July 2010 just the same. Now with the Rangers, he pitched an LCS game that October at Yankee Stadium. While he was making a 2-0 lead hold up for eight innings of two-hit ball with 13 strikeouts, his wife, Kristen, was harassed by Yankees fans, prompting one of the Texas owners to call them "violent" and "apathetic," though Lee denied the report of someone spitting on her. Lee's few months in Philadelphia in 2009 were enough for him and Kristen to want to settle there. He signs for the Phillies at $25 million a year, winning 41 games in three-plus seasons before injury ends his career.

They Came, They Saw, They Conked Out

There's nothing like a free-agent bust to rile up the hometown fans, some overrated early-achiever or charismatic zilch who gets a gazillion bucks to demonstrate how difficult it is to play baseball well. Expectation is commensurate with salary, and in surveying the history of free agency, now closing in on a half-century of misadventure, it's easy to see that the disappointments have far outnumbered the triumphs, for the Yankees and everyone else. Here are a dozen free agent disasters, and every name will make Yankees fans cringe. They shared one thing: none played as many seasons for the Yankees as hoped for or expected. Most didn't come close. The dozen contracts covered 63 years, but the Yankees got just 34 full seasons out of the bunch. The closest was Dave Winfield, who stayed for the whole ten years he signed for (missing 1989 due to injury), which turned out to be worse than the rejects. He was the one guy George Steinbrenner wanted to get rid of most of all, and he seemed to stick with the Yankees out of spite. So here they are, the dirty dozen, the most disastrous Yankees free agent signings.

November 18, 1976   In the first free-agent draft, the Yankees think they've struck gold when they sign southpaw Don Gullett. He's only 25 years old but has compiled a record of 91-44 (almost identical to Babe Ruth's) and a 3.03 ERA in seven seasons with Cincinnati. In 1976, a shoulder injury limited him to 20 starts, but he went 11-3, pitched two-hit ball in the first game of the NL CS, and beat the Yankees in Game 1 of the World Series, 5-1. The Yankees snag him with a six-year deal worth $2 million. President Gabe Paul says, "We feel Gullett is a modern-day Whitey Ford," and despite shoulder problems which force him to miss all of August, he has a Ford-like 14-4 record in 1977. But he's horrible in the 1977 postseason, going 0-2 in three starts with a 6.75 ERA, and things get worse in a hurry in 1978. Recurring arm woes keep him sidelined until June, and after only eight appearances, his arm is history. In his final start, on July 9, he faces nine batters, giving up three hits and walking four men. Doctors say it's a torn rotator cuff, in those days a death sentence for a pitcher (a year later, it retired Catfish Hunter at 33).

Surgery doesn't help, and despite a lot of hard work, Gullett's career ends in frustration. His last game in the majors came before his 27th birthday, and the Yankees got exactly 203 innings of work for their $2 million investment.

December 15, 1980 Fasten your seat-belts; it was a bumpy ride. On this date, the Yankees claimed victory in the Dave Winfield sweepstakes, signing him to a ten-year contract. They needed him because their outfield was getting old; Lou Piniella turned 36 that year, Reggie Jackson and Bobby Murcer 34. Winfield was 29, a 6'6", five-tool star who finished third in the MVP balloting in 1979. Clearly, the Yankees saw him as the right-handed counterpart to Reggie—but one who could run, field, and throw. Winfield's base salary with the Yankees was $1.3 million a year, with an annual cost-of-living increase, an attendance clause, and other incentives. Winfield's agent assured everyone, however, that the key factor was George Steinbrenner's pledge to help Winfield establish a charitable foundation, focused on health, educational, and recreational programs for children, with an annual $300,000 donation.

Their relationship was stormy from the start. On **January 24, 1981**, before Winfield even suited up, Steinbrenner threatened to call off the deal after learning that the cost-of-living clause would cost more than he thought, forcing a last-minute compromise. Over the course of his decade with the Yankees, Winfield experienced way more lawsuits than pennant races, as he and Steinbrenner filed mutual charges of failing to meet obligations to the foundation.

Let's start with Winfield on the field. He hit like gangbusters the first three months of 1981, cooled off after the two-month strike, and froze completely in October. In the five-game Division Series win, he hit .350 but didn't drive in a run. In the LCS, he hit .154, mainly contributing a two-run double to a 13-3 victory. His performance in the World Series resembled a professional swan dive off the Brooklyn Bridge. In Game 1 against the Dodgers, he walked with the bases loaded, and that was his high point in the six-game Series loss. He managed a single off Jerry Reuss in Game 5, and he piled up five walks, but he wound up 1-for-22, a

.045 average that branded him forever to Steinbrenner as a flaming choke artist who cost them the title. It didn't matter that Winfield averaged 106 RBI from 1982-1988, or that he hit .340 one year. With him as their big gun, they never topped the American League East for the rest of his tenure.

The Winfield-Steinbrenner working relationship went south after the embarrassing 1981 World Series. After making the first three quarterly payments to Winfield's foundation, Steinbrenner said no more. "Winfield's a good athlete," said the owner, "but he's no Reggie." Winfield sued him, and they settled out of court. Steinbrenner resumed the payments and got a seat on the foundation's board. And the Yankees played on, but they didn't get anywhere. On **September 14, 1985,** during an eight-game losing streak that helped the Yankees miss the postseason by two games, Steinbrenner uttered his enduring judgment: "Where is Reggie Jackson? We need a Mr. October or a Mr. September. Winfield is Mr. May." As Winfield put it in his 1988 book, *Winfield, a Player's Life,* "In New York, performance isn't even judged day to day; it's play to play. And George Steinbrenner has the shortest memory in town."

Things got worse the following spring when Steinbrenner entered the clubhouse during a Players' Association meeting and Winfield, the player rep, kicked him out. Steinbrenner took that as insubordination and told Winfield he'd trade him anywhere he wanted. Winfield said, "I like it here." The more Steinbrenner threatened and badmouthed him, the more Winfield blew it off. He got some payback in his book, writing, "There are only two kinds of moves on the Yankees. The ones made because George is displeased, and the ones made because he soon will be. Sensing this, the players begin to doubt their manager. They can't believe any more than the press or the fans can, that any manager's moves are his own."

Steinbrenner had his own payback in mind. Enter Howard Spira, a gambler and general lowlife. Imagine that you're the boss and you really don't like one of your department heads. You're paying him a lot and not getting results, and now he's giving you a hard time because you have second thoughts about the money you promised to his charity. One day a stranger calls and tells you nasty things about your disgruntled employee that will enable you to say to him, "screw you and your charity!" Does it bother you that the snitch is an admitted con man and degenerate gambler? Nope—not if the dirt is dirty enough and your name is George Steinbrenner. In that case, you tell the guy, "Listen, I'll be down in Tampa in a few weeks. Let's meet." On **December 30, 1986,** Steinbrenner and Howard Spira did meet, and eventually they hatched a plot to destroy Dave Winfield and his foundation. Spira got busy, concocted some dirt on Winfield, and sold it to Steinbrenner for $40,000.

In 1989, Winfield suffered a herniated disc, and surgery kept him sidelined all year, giving him and Steinbrenner more time to try to ruin each other. Steinbrenner had stopped making the foundation payments again in 1987, and even after Winfield (his lawyers, I mean) went to the trouble of getting *three court orders* covering $450,000 in arrears, Steinbrenner didn't pay up. Winfield sued him; Steinbrenner counter-sued. On **January 10, 1989,** the shit hit the fan. Spira confirmed that he had supplied Steinbrenner's ammunition in his expanding war against Winfield. Among Spira's assertions were that Winfield and his agent loaned him money to pay off his gambling debts, charged him loan-shark interest, and threatened to wring his neck if he didn't pay it back. Most people considered the source and focused instead on Steinbrenner's culpability.

Spira went astray when he tried to parlay the $40,000 into $150,000. Steinbrenner balked at such bald extortion, complete with phone calls that Spira secretly taped. On **March 18, 1990,** Steinbrenner admitted paying Spira $40,000 but said it was "because I cared about this guy, who in my opinion was a lost human being." I'll meet him halfway, just as Commissioner Fay Vincent did. When the smoke cleared, Vincent banished Steinbrenner from his ownership role for two years, simply because of his inability and/or unwillingness to say to Spira, "Hey, you're a wacko. I don't care what you say about him. Go away!" That's what Winfield told Spira when Spira approached him first with an offer to provide dirt on Steinbrenner, which prompted Spira to turn to Steinbrenner instead.

While the prosecution of Spira unfolded, Winfield returned to action in 1990 but struggled early, going hitless in 23 consecutive at-bats in late April, and found himself being platooned. On **May 11,** the Yankees traded Winfield and his .213 average to the Angels for pitcher Mike Witt. After a snit and assorted renegotiations, Winfield agreed to go to Anaheim, where he resurrected his career. He even got back to the World Series in 1992 with the Blue Jays, when he became "Monsieur Octobre" in Canada by doubling in the Series-winning runs.

Spira was indicted on **March 23, 1990,** and I'll spare you the details of the ugly court case except for Steinbrenner's crocodile-tearful testimony on **April 23, 1991,** complete with quivering voice and nose-blowing. On **December 10, 1991,** Spira was sentenced to 2½ years in prison for attempted extortion. His exited the proceedings with these immortal words: "My father really should have worn a condom. He did not deserve Howard Spira as a son." Yet George Steinbrenner felt that *he did* deserve Spira as a friend.

December 23, 1981 One big reason why Winfield's Yankees never got back to the World Series was the front office's failure to solve the outfield problem. In 1981, along with Winfield came Jerry Mumphrey, whose stolen base total went from 52 to 14 as a Yankee. Now, with Reggie Jackson about to escape to California, Steinbrenner perceived a need for speed. The Yankees acquired Reds stalwart Ken Griffey in a November trade, and today they signed another Reds outfielder, free agent Dave Collins, who stole 79 bases in 1980. Surely, with Collins, Griffey, and Mumphrey at the top of the lineup, Winfield should drive in 150 runs. They gave Collins a three-year deal for $2.5 million, and he promptly stopped getting on base, much less stealing. His sorry 1982 stats: a .315 on-base percentage, 41 runs scored, and 13 steals in a whopping 21 attempts. That prompted a trade the following winter that the Yankees ultimately regretted even though it did kick Collins over the border to the Toronto Blue Jays. Along with him went 19-year-old prospect Fred McGriff. Collins stole 91 bases in two seasons with the Blue Jays and retired in 1990 with 395 in his career. The biggest name the Yankees got in return was Dale Murray. And the Yankees still had a mediocre outfield, since Griffey and Mumphrey combined for just 21 steals in 1982.

November 10, 1982 Here's what they did about it. Hours before trading Collins, they signed free agent Steve

Kemp to a five-year, $5.5 million deal. The 28-year-old had reached stardom with the Tigers in 1979 with a .318 average, 26 home runs, and 105 RBI, and he drove in 96 runs for the White Sox in 1982 before becoming a free agent. How could it go wrong—a left-handed power hitter coming to Yankee Stadium in his prime? How? Because he stank, hitting 19 home runs and driving in 90 runs for the Yankees—in two seasons. Down the stretch in 1983, he went 3-for-38 to drop his average to .241, and in 1984, he was strictly a platoon player, driving in 41 runs in 94 games before they dealt him away.

December 27, 1984 You barely had time to catch your breath between big Yankees deals for big-deal Yankees in the 1980s. Two weeks before dumping Kemp, they made a big trade that brought Rickey Henderson to New York, and today they sign free agent pitcher Ed Whitson to a five-year, $4.4 million deal. Whitson, 29, went 14-8 for the San Diego Padres this season and stood tall in winning Game 3 of the NLCS against the Cubs before getting kayoed early in his World Series start. He got off to a horrendous start as a Yankee—a 1-6 record and 6.23 ERA in his first eleven starts—and the fans never warmed up to him. Only a ton of run support gave him a 10-8 record with his 4.48 ERA, and things got worse in a hurry in 1986. After a third-inning exit in his first start brought choruses of boos from the Yankee Stadium faithful, manager Lou Piniella announced that Whitson would start only on the road. It didn't matter; by this time, he would have sucked in any role on the Yankees. He allowed 77 men to reach base in 37 innings before a **July 9** trade back to San Diego, where he pitched the best ball of his career in 1989-1990. In exchange, the Yankees got Tim Stoddard, another lump like Dale Murray.

November 19, 1990 It was a short, strange trip for Tim Leary with the Yankees, who were temporarily dazed by the right-hander's one good season, a 17-11 record, six shutouts, and 2.91 ERA for the 1988 Dodgers, plus two good outings in the World Series. It didn't bother them that he was 28-45 otherwise, was coming off an 8-14 season in 1989, had already failed to last with four teams, and was about to turn 31. They acquired him from the Reds, trading away Hal Morris. In 1990, Leary led the major leagues in losses with a 9-19 record for the Yankees, with a 1-9 record at Yankee Stadium that made the fans there yearn for the good old days of Ed Whitson and Andy Hawkins. He also led the majors with 23 wild pitches and had a 4.11 ERA, so most GMs wouldn't even ask him for a forwarding address. But this Yankees team had finished last by seven games in 1990, and they were hoping this was some hallucination from which they would emerge into their old Yankees-centric universe. So on this date, the Yankees serve up a three-year, $5.95 million offer which Leary jumps at. Guess what? He pitched even worse in 1991, going 4-10 with a 6.49 ERA, but bless 'em, the Yankees gave him another chance in 1992, 15 more starts before they couldn't take it any more and traded him to Seattle for a non-prospect. Not many Yankees resumes sparkle with this kind of shine: 18-35 with a 5.12 ERA for a $6 million man.

December 24, 2002 This was the free agent signing that prompted Boston Red Sox president Larry Lucchino's venomous "The evil empire extends its tentacles even into Latin America." The tentacles snared 6'4" Cuban right-hander Jose Contreras, who defected in October and set off a bidding frenzy. The Yankees thought they won the sweepstakes when they landed him with a lure of $32 million over four years. But bringing the 31-year-old to New York didn't work. In 2003, shoulder problems cost him two months and he finished at a promising 7-2 with a 3.30 ERA. His pitching went to hell in a hurry in 2004, as he allowed 23 runs in his first 21 innings. He made a few good starts, but in late July, after allowing 15 runs in two starts, he was dumped into a canoe and pointed toward Cuba. That is, he was traded to the White Sox, who welcomed his 5.64 ERA in exchange for Esteban Loaiza. Contreras went 28-16 for the White Sox in 2005-2006, while Loaiza gave the Yankees exactly one win before leaving as a free agent.

December 20, 2004 The 2005 Yankees were an offensive powerhouse, second in the majors in runs, home runs, and batting average, with big numbers posted by Alex Rodriguez,

Derek Jeter, Gary Sheffield, Jason Giambi, Robinson Cano, and Hideki Matsui. With the 21st century bringing skyrocketing salaries, it seemed like a no-brainer for the Yankees to invest $39.95 million in a four-year deal with free agent Carl Pavano. The 28-year-old right-hander starred for the Florida Marlins in the 2003 postseason and went 18-8 in 2004 with a 3.00 ERA. How can he miss? Here's how. He hurts his shoulder his first year and is done after June; misses the second year because of the shoulder problem, but just in case, breaks two ribs in a car crash; blows out his elbow the third year in his third start, has ligament replacement surgery, and pitches in exactly seven games in the final year of his contract. For their $40 million, he gave them a 9-8 record and a 5.00 ERA in 26 starts. Two years later, unburdened, he was good enough to go 17-11 for the Twins.

December 28, 2004 Brian Cashman got on a bad streak in the mid-ohohs in his quest for pitching to back an all-star lineup. Eight days after signing Pavano, he went off for another $21 million to sign Jaret Wright for three years. Can you blame him? Highly regarded ever since his postseason excellence as a rookie in 1997, Wright seemed to come into his own in 2004 with the Braves, going 15-8 with a 3.28 ERA in 32 starts. The day before his 29th birthday, he became a Yankee with a bright future. Right. Four starts into his career in the spotlight, he injured his shoulder and missed four months, wrecking that season with a 5-5 record and 6.08 ERA in 13 starts. There went the first $7 million. In 2006, he pitched in 30 games and was consistently mediocre, never making it through seven innings. After he finished at 11-7 with a 4.49 ERA, he punctuated his season by getting drilled and taking the loss in the deciding game of the Division Series. On November 12, 2006, the Yankees gave him to the Orioles, paying $4 million of his 2007 contract just to be rid of him, receiving reliever Chris Britton, who lasted 35 2/3 innings with the Yankees to end his career.

December 27, 2006 This deal made Yankees fans want to stage an intervention for Cashman. After losing out on the colossal bidding war for Japanese ace Daisuke Matsuzaka, the

Yankees eagerly snared the consolation prize, Japanese southpaw Kei Igawa, a 27-year-old who went 75-43 in the last five seasons. The process rivaled international diplomacy, with teams bidding on how much to pay the pitchers' Japanese teams to release them from their contracts. If you won that auction, you could try to sign the player. In one sense, the Yankees got a bargain, coughing up a mere $46 million—$26 million to the team, $20 million to Igawa for five years—compared to the $103 million the Red Sox hemorrhaged on Matsuzaka. In a more important sense, the Yankees screwed themselves. For their investment, the Red Sox got 15 wins from Matsuzaka in 2007, a winning start in the World Series, and an 18-3 season in 2008 before arm problems wrecked him. And Kei Igawa? The Orioles hammered him for seven runs in his major league debut, and it soon became clear that Igawa was seriously over-matched. The Yankees let him pitch 14 times in 2007 but only twice in 2008 before demoting him to the minors, where he played out the rest of his $20 million deal before seeking asylum back in Japan. For their $46 million, the Yankees got a 2-4 record in 16 games with an ERA of exactly 6.66, showing the power of that curse.

December 13, 2007   On the same day that the Mitchell Report was released, naming Yankees pitchers Roger Clemens and Andy Pettitte among the many who used dubious substances to improve performance, the Yankees made a ten-year, $275 million commitment to Alex Rodriguez, whose previous PED abuse now seems a mere prelude to his New York excesses. Since acquiring Rodriguez in a trade with Texas in 2004, the Yankees had failed to reach the World Series, but they reinvested in him. This deal paid off in 2009, when A-Rod led the Yankees to their final World Series title, but he gave them only one season of solid production after 2010. During the final seven years of a contract that paid him at least $20 million per season, A-Rod developed an unprecedented love-hate relationship with the Yankees and their fans, to the point where a **November 5, 2014** *New York Times* headline announcing his 2015 return from a one-year suspension read: "With Alex Rodriguez Coming Back, Things Look Bleak in the Bronx." Let's see how this dream alliance crumbled.

The big issue, A-Rod's illicit use of PEDs, was compounded by his staunch denials. It began just three days after the Mitchell Report, when he went on *60 Minutes* and declared that he had never used "steroids, human growth hormone, or any other performance-enhancing substance." On **February 7, 2009**, *Sports Illustrated* reported that he had tested positive for steroids in 2003, before he joined the Yankees, giving him room to insist that although that might have been true, he had been a good boy since he moved to New York. If only.

For several years, most of Gotham's attention focused on A-Rod's poor postseason performances, though his personal life also got roasted. His wife, Cynthia, filed for divorce in 2008, shortly after their second daughter was born, citing infidelities. The New York tabloids had a field day catching him out on the town with Madonna, though more recently he has gotten engaged to a younger singer, Jennifer Lopez. Custody battles, lawsuits, and publicized private nastiness went on for years, alienating more of the public.

The issue of his PED usage never went away, and early in 2013 it came to a head. On **December 3, 2012**, the Yankees announced impending hip surgery for A-Rod, which ultimately limited him to 44 games in 2013. While he was sidelined, the mess down in Florida which he had hoped to avoid came to light. Investigations had been going on about a Florida clinic, Biogenesis, and a fake Dr. Anthony Bosch, a "Dr. Playgood" who provided A-Rod and many other top athletes with custom-designed regimens combining a variety of cutting-edge PEDs. The story gradually came to light while A-Rod recovered from surgery. He didn't help his cause by tweeting in late June that he was ready to start rehabbing, prompting Brian Cashman's classic reply: "Alex should just shut the fuck up."

On **August 5, 2013**, the hammer fell on A-Rod, a 211-game suspension (one of 13 Biogenesis customers suspended at least 50 games) for his use of "numerous forms of performance-enhancing substances, including testosterone and human growth hormone over the course of multiple years." A-Rod appealed the suspension and was allowed to play the rest of the season, returning to action that day and hitting a lackluster .244 for two months. The legal battle over the suspension raged through the off-season, with both sides looking more despicable all the time. On **January 11, 2014**, an arbitrator reduced the suspension to 162 games, conveniently banning him for the 2014 season.

All the sordid details came out, such as this stark *New York Times* description by Steve Eder on **January 14**: "Alex Rodriguez took an energy cocktail on Mondays and a therapy cocktail on Fridays. He used a special cream in the morning, and a testosterone cream in the evening. He took testosterone lozenges before games 'as needed.'" No wonder the outlook seemed "bleak in Bronx" as A-Rod's return loomed early in 2015. As *Times* reporter Juliet Macur put it, "He is a player who lied about his steroid use, then admitted it (2009), then publicly said he was absolutely clean (2013-present) — it's a witch hunt, he declared — and then turned around to privately testify to federal agents that why, yes, he had used drugs, a lot of drugs, in recent years, and thanks for asking."

A-Rod did rebound in 2015 to hit 33 homers, but reverted to form, going hitless and fanning twice in their wild card Game loss. He struggled through 2016, knowing he couldn't perform any more, and faced the truth on **August 12, 2016**, announcing his retirement, one year shy of the end of his contract. The last few seasons of mediocrity succeeded in keeping him from breaking Barry Bonds' hallowed career home run record (falling shy of 700) and dropped his lifetime batting average, Mantle-style, from .306 after 2008 to .295 lifetime.

December 7, 2013   Last but not only not least, but actually the Yankees' second-most expensive free agent disaster, I give you Jacoby Ellsbury, signed on this date to a seven-year, $153 million contract. He thought he'd follow in the footsteps of Red Sox stars who slipped out of town and sneaked into the Bronx, enjoying further success like Wade Boggs and Johnny Damon. He was wrong. Known more for speed than power despite his 30-30 season in 2011, the 30-year-old center fielder put up exactly one good number as a Yankee, 39 steals in his first season, though even that was a comedown after he topped 50 in a season three times for the Red Sox. He also peaked as a Yankee in 2014 with a .271 average and 71 runs scored. A plague of injuries—oblique muscle, back, hip surgery—caused him to miss the 2018-2019 seasons, and the Yankees released him on **November 20, 2019**. But they didn't want to pay him, withholding $26 million because they claimed he had sought outside medical treatment without consulting them. This ongoing battle between the Yankees and Ellsbury's agent, Scott Boras, will keep court reporters and Yankees-haters well-armed for the foreseeable future, as the Yankees attempt to renege on a contract mocked in a *New York Post* headline as the "Worst $153M Ever Spent." Just part of the Yankees' "rich" tradition.

Bad Behavior

We've covered plenty of bad behavior during the season, but there's a difference between your catcher starting a brawl on a baseball diamond in the heat of a pennant race and your manager getting in a fight with a marshmallow salesman a week *after* the World Series that makes the off-season so special. There are no distracting game details, no cushion of a winning record when pinstripes turn to prison stripes. Reporters and other investigators have all the extra time they need to compile those massive and damning accounts like the ones that sliced like ginzu knives through Alex Rodriguez's PED denials.

Settle back and recall how comfortable it felt by the fireplace when you first read about the wayward misadventures of these wanton Yankees. There are fights and assorted violence for you; arrests and illegal acts; suspensions; accidents, and more—a feast of nastiness and humiliation.

Billy Martin: The Champ

I would be remiss if I didn't have Billy Martin lead off the winter shenanigans, although the time he broke his ankle probably wasn't his fault. Rabid dogs backed off when he got in one of his moods, and he relished any chance to fulfill his self-image as a Western gunslinger. Some of his many fights were covered earlier, but his two most infamously brief fights occurred in the off-season.

March 12, 1952   The Yankees lose second baseman Martin for six weeks after he breaks an ankle. The galling thing is that it doesn't happen when Martin is executing some aggressive and heroic play on the field. Nope, he does it filming a segment for "The

Joe DiMaggio Show," the retired Clipper's $100,000-a-year audition to become "Mr. Coffee". DiMaggio invites his teammate of 85 games to be a guest on his television program. Show us how you slide, Billy. Sure, Mr. DiMaggio. Martin sizes up the makeshift baseline and bag, makes his charge, catches his spikes in the dirt, jams his right ankle into the bag, and breaks it in two places. Let's go to a commercial. Martin's season doesn't begin until May 14, and he winds up playing only 109 games in 1952.

February 18, 1954   Martin is perplexed when his draft board denies him a hardship deferment even though "I have more dependents now than when I got out on the dependency claim" in 1952. He spent five months in the army in 1950-1951 before getting discharged to support five people. Now his hardship has swollen to six with the birth of daughter Kelly Ann: his mother, stepfather, sister, daughter, and estranged wife. In fact, it was his daughter's birth in January which triggered the review by his Berkeley, California, draft board. They tell him to suit up; he appeals, and is told again to suit up. He winds up spending all of 1954 and much of 1955 in military service. Martin's mother confesses that she waited more than a week to tell him that his induction notice had arrived, explaining on **March 3, 1954**: "He already had so many worries I just didn't have the heart to tell him about it."

June 15, 1957   On this darkest day of Martin's playing career, he is exiled from the Yankees to Kansas City in a six-player deal. It is one month since the infamous fight at the Copacabana, for which Billy is the fall-guy. For a change, he didn't start the fight, but it was *his* birthday, and it proved to GM George Weiss that he was a "bad influence" on Mickey Mantle and Whitey Ford. Their talents aren't expendable, so off goes Martin to Kansas City, distraught over being separated not only from his drinking buddies but also his mentor in the dugout, Casey Stengel, not to mention from that annual World Series check. This launches a five-year fizzle during which Martin plays for seven teams, long enough to start two more fights before retiring (from playing, not fighting).

November 11, 1978   On this bar stool, Billy Martin, 5'11½", 170 pounds, who blew his first stint as Yankees manager a few months ago. On that stool, Ray Hagar, 5'9", 170 pounds, a reporter for the *Reno Evening Gazette*. Martin is in town for a basketball game, and Hagar thinks he's interviewing him. It turns out that he's pissing him off instead with those questions about the fracas with Reggie Jackson in June that got Martin I dumped. Martin later admits slugging Hagar but protests, "I didn't know him, never punched a writer before. Why would I want to fight him?" He clarifies the moment of crisis to another reporter, saying that Hagar "deliberately wanted me to hit him. His questions got bad at the end." Martin gets in several shots to Hagar's zero, leaving Hagar with three chipped teeth, a gash above his eye, and the basis for a lawsuit that is settled out of court. Midway through the next season, practically on the anniversary of his confrontation with Jackson, the reign of Billy Martin II begins.

October 23, 1979   He's still Martin II when he engages in his signature snafu, his celebrated visit to a bar in Bloomington, Minnesota. According to Martin biographer Peter Golenbock, after six scotches, Martin gets into a baseball argument with, of all things, a marshmallow salesman, Joseph Cooper, prompting Martin to toss three $100 bills on the table and say, "Here's three hundred dollars to your penny I can knock you on your ass and you won't get up." Cooper puts up his penny and they head for the lobby, Martin leading the way. Martin's version is that after he left the bar alone, Cooper "must have followed me out of the bar, because as I was walking in the lobby I turned around and saw this guy laying on the floor. He fell and cut his lip." Not quite; actually, Martin sucker-punches him, putting a 20-stitch cut in his lip and making sure to collect the penny. Soon enough, the truth emerges, and five days after the fight, Martin II is fired. On **October 30**, Cooper puts it all in perspective. "He was ahead of me, and I was behind. As we walked through the archway into the lobby, he abruptly turned and hit me in the mouth. I assume all of his fights have been sucker punches. . .Any man in that position that would jeopardize his career with something as foolish as this—what can I say?"

December 25, 1989 Billy Martin has hated Christmas since his impoverished, fatherless childhood, and he's mad at his fourth wife, Jill, so he's in no mood to stay home. Instead, he spends the day drinking vodka at a Binghamton, New York bar with his close friend Bill Reedy until it's time to go home to dinner. On the way, driving without a seat belt, Martin misses a turn and takes the hillier route he normally uses to avoid the police who wait on his regular road to nab him for a DUI. At the base of the hill across from his driveway, the car slides into a left turn, and Martin stubbornly tries to power through it. Instead, he loses control, and the car hurtles into a ditch, striking a pole. Martin is killed instantly. Seriously injured, Reedy initially claims that he was driving, having taken the fall for his buddy before. But Martin's friends know that no matter how drunk he was, he wouldn't have let anybody else drive. Reedy changes his story once he realizes there is nobody to protect, and he doesn't care if people don't believe him. All that matters is that his friend, the five-time Yankees manager, is dead at 61. George Steinbrenner shares a touching memory: "When I first hired [Martin], his mother called me and asked for an autographed picture, and I sent it. He told me that 'every time you'd fire me, my mother put the picture in the john. When you hired me, she put it above her dresser.'" Martin's mother died two weeks before he did.

Other Fights

November 7, 1933 Here's a fun couple for you. Ben Chapman's estranged wife, Ola, takes him to court, charging him with cruelty and non-support after he leaves her stranded in Birmingham, Alabama, with only $2.87 to her name. For his part, Chapman accuses her of "extravagance and nagging conversation" and says she annoyed him so much that "he was unable to perform at his best on the diamond, and [she] frequently had threatened to commit suicide."

March 26, 1955 Unless you're a public figure, you can't know how unnerving ever-present photographers must be. Still, it makes news when high-paid folks snap, and Casey Stengel is the guilty party in this one, back in an era when—what liability insurance?—photographers were allowed on the field during the game. This photographer is blocking Casey's view, and he requests that the gentleman park himself somewhere else. The photographer goes into the dugout, and a moment later he's on the way to the police station to press charges. Casey faces two counts: cursing the photographer and kicking him in the leg. On **March 28,** Casey issues a semi-apology: "Maybe I was a little mad and I yelled at him. Maybe I didn't say 'please' to him. . .but it was a tense game, and I didn't want anyone in our way." He doesn't mention the kick or that it was *an exhibition game*. The charges are dropped anyway.

A different approach is taken by Hideki Irabu on **March 7, 1998**, when he is confronted by critical Japanese reporters outside the Yankees clubhouse. Someone is filming them, so Irabu charges at him—showing remarkable reflexes for a fat toad—and wrestles him for the camera. Then he demands that the still photographers hand over their film. He exposes it all to ruin their shots, then throws the videotape to the floor and stomps on it, Godzilla-style.

February 14, 1961   Savor this tender tale of a Valentine's Day gone awry in a different era. Relief pitcher Marshall Bridges is at spring training in Fort Lauderdale, Florida, while his wife and three children are at home in Mississippi. He's at the Negro Elks Club one evening when he starts talking to the 21-year-old woman sitting next to him at the bar. Here's what the woman, aptly named Carrie Raysor, tells police: Bridges "tried to pick me up . . .He put his arm around me and pulled me over, and I don't like that kind of mugging. . .and when he kept bothering me, I took out my gun and shot him." The bullet hits him below the knee and lodges in his calf, fracturing his fibula and tearing a muscle. Bridges pitches only 23 more games for the Yankees, who exile him to Washington after the season. Raysor goes on trial a year later for aggravated assault, but charges are dismissed when Bridges doesn't show up.

October 15, 1981   You'd think that sweeping Billy Martin's Oakland team to get into the World Series would mellow out the Yankees. Not this bunch, the remnants of the "Bronx Zoo." At the team "family" party thrown by George Steinbrenner to celebrate the pennant, Reggie Jackson and Graig Nettles get into a scuffle and shoving match. Nettles brought eight family members to the party, and while they're away from the table, Jackson brought some uninvited guests over and they all sit down. The players are elsewhere when the two families argue over the seats and life in general. The matter of race is touched upon. Nettles' mother weeps. Jackson sees trouble brewing between the two groups and finds Nettles out in a corridor. Before telling him the problem, he takes the precaution of knocking Nettles' beer bottle out of his hand. They scuffle first, knock over some furniture, and are pulled apart. Goose Gossage makes a cameo appearance as a peacemaker, and pretty soon they're both apologizing. And you know which one Steinbrenner blames.

December 18, 1993   Lefty phenom Brien Taylor, who has started to justify his $1.5 million signing bonus by going 13-7 with a 3.48 ERA and 150 strikeouts in 163 innings for Albany in the Eastern League, ruins his career in a brawl. After his brother gets in a fight over a business matter near their home in North Carolina, the 21-year-old Taylor joins his brother on a mission to the other party's home. Much to everyone's surprise, another fight breaks out, and Taylor is tackled and knocked down, landing on his pitching shoulder. His mother (remember Bettie?) says, "He's just had a little soreness," and his agent (try to forget Scott Boras) calls it "a little bruise." The doctors know better: his shoulder is dislocated, requiring surgery. On **December 28**, Dr. Frank Jobe does what he can to repair a torn labrum and torn capsule, but that 98-mph fastball is left somewhere on the gurney. After missing a season, Taylor tries to come back in 1995, and the rest of his career presents an extreme case of "Steve Blass Syndrome," the horrifying inability to throw strikes. Forget that his post-surgery record was 3-15; that's the least of it. In 1996-1997, he pitched 17 games for Greensboro of the South Atlantic League. His record was 1-9 with an ERA of 15.99, and in 43 1/3 innings, he walked (don't flinch) 95 batters and hurled 30 wild pitches. Or as Bettie Taylor must have pictured her son's efforts to locate the strike zone, he "missed it by *that* much." He was mercifully released on **January 20, 1999.**

January 14, 1997 David Wells, that most Ruthian of recent Yankees, picks a dandy time for the fight of his life, breaking his pitching hand four weeks after signing a three-year free agent deal with the Yankees for $13.5 million. George Steinbrenner had interviewed him personally, saying, "I heard all these stories about motorcycles and other stuff, so I wanted to meet with him before we got serious. He was delightful. He's a man's man." The man's man and a friend leave Wells' car "unattended with the doors open," according to a San Diego police spokesman, then can't find the keys. They accuse two men of taking the keys, chase them, and start a fight that shelves Wells for six weeks. No charges are filed in what the District Attorney terms "a misunderstanding that escalated among guys who had been drinking." The escapade occurs while Wells is in San Diego for his mother's funeral. That's the dandy timing.

Arrests and Other Illegal Acts

Novermber 13, 1945 Larry MacPhail, who joined Del Webb and Dan Topping in buying the Yankees from the estate of Jacob Ruppert, has a long reputation as a loose cannon while serving as Yankees president. Today, MacPhail is indicted on two counts of assault and one of disorderly conduct for an October incident in Maryland. Unable to make a long-distance call because of a work stoppage by operators, he stormed into the phone company's office, cursed at the employees, slapped one of them, and pushed another. In a January trial, he is found guilty of the disorderly conduct charge and fined $50, yet found innocent on the assault charges because he apologized to them. Why didn't that ever occur to Billy Martin?

January 29, 1951 And now a change of pace for you. Walter Sherwin, 46, has worked for the Yankees for

20 years, and for the past eight years has managed their Fifth Avenue ticket office. He makes $90 a week. Today he pleads guilty to stealing $43,687 in ticket sales from the office. He says he spent a mere $80 on himself and used the rest to buy a house for the parents of his wife, a showgirl-model-actress who calls herself Gregg Sherwood (formerly Dora Mae Fjelstad), plus a car and jewelry just for her. The 28-year-old divorcee used to date Joe DiMaggio and Dean Martin, and he sensed the need to impress her. She and her folks deny it and turn around to accuse him of posing as the heir to the Sherwin-Williams fortune when he came a-courtin'. Once she figured out that he was just Sherwin and not even a Yankees bigwig, Gregg Sherwood got a Mexican divorce (her second), and she wants nothing to do with him. On **February 20**, a judge lets Sherwin off with probation if he promises to help track down the money nobody is willing to account for. It turns out that Walter got involved in a kickback scheme involving ticket brokers that backfired, and, facing a very risky shortfall, he stole. Meanwhile, his ex-wife, described as a "gardenia blonde" along the lines of Lana Turner, rebounds quickly from jettisoning *the wrong* Sherwin, zeroing in on *the right* Dodge, Horace Dodge, Jr., announcing her engagement to that *real* heir, the only child of the company's founder, in May. Horace is 53 years old and has already married four blonde showgirls, but he dumps the last one after he gets a double eyeful of 28-year-old Gregg, once a contender in the "Miss Plunging Neckline" pageant. Gregg Sherwood marries Dodge, which launches her at last on the trail of her dreams. A decade later, during which they are known as "the Fighting Dodges," Horace files for divorce. Incredibly, a man with an eight-figure fortune admits, "I can't afford the woman," citing $300,000 she wasted in self-indulgences in one year alone, including two-carat diaper pins for the baby. While the divorce action is pending, he dies, leaving her $11 million. She has to sue her 94-year-old former mother-in-law for it and settles out of court for $9 million. Her next move is to marry a former policeman and bodyguard fifteen years her junior, who gets away with shooting a supposed intruder a year later. They get busy spending all that money as she sets herself up as a Palm Beach socialite in a 34-room place, that is when they're not at the 64-room

mansion in Greenwich, Connecticut. It takes a wild decade to blow through the fortune, and by that time, her bodyguard has killed himself. She declares bankruptcy in 1978 and, a year later, admits stealing money from her son's $8 million trust fund (set up after the matriarch's death at 103—don't get me started on *her* life) but stays out of jail when the court sells off her Dodge possessions. She keeps herself going, more sedately, until 2011, refusing to take the plunge for the fifth time, no doubt thinking about what happened to Horace and *his* fifth spouse, who left him a broken man with an eight-figure estate. Throw in Horace's heartbreaking death scene, which I'm sparing you, and the whole mess sounds like a Lana Turner movie (guess what—the icing on the cake—Gregg had a bit part in Turner's 1952 movie—ready?—*The Merry Widow*) and is just a murder or two shy of a Raymond Chandler novel. If you think about it, Sherwin—remember Walter Sherwin, the piker who robbed the Yankees?—gets off easy, simply going to prison for violating his probation and never having to contemplate paying for two-carat diaper pins. Who says you have to be a star athlete to get involved in tawdry romance?

April 3, 1956 In training for the regular season, Don Larsen goes out drinking most of the night in St. Petersburg, Florida, then drives off the road and wraps his car around a utility pole. He bashes in the front end of the car but luckily avoids injury and arrest. He cannot, however, escape the irony that only a few weeks ago, he pledged to change his ways, telling the *United Press*, "I was getting such a reputation for horsing around that even my mother spoke to me about it. . .I'm gonna stick to my knitting this year. No more living it up and stuff like that." That was on **March 5**, weeks ago. He has every reason to be good. After a nightmarish 3-21 season with the Orioles in 1954, he was evacuated to the Bronx via trade, and after a stint in the minors came back to go 8-1 over the final two months of the 1955 pennant race. Now he wrecks his car, but the Yankees are sympathetic. He escapes his actions but not his reputation; six months later, after his ultimate gem in the 1956 World Series, he earns this headline: "Imperfect Man Pitches Perfect Game."

January 20, 1976   A three-year prison sentence is handed down by a court in Barranquilla, Colombia, to Kelly Ann Martin, the 23-year-old daughter of Billy Martin. She was arrested on **November 16, 1975**, while trying to board a plane to Miami with a pound of cocaine in baggies strapped to her thighs. Of course, she didn't know it was cocaine. Some guy asked her to take it to his mother, telling her it was "hard-to-get medicine". As indeed it was. She served half her term, one of nearly 100 Americans then in Colombian prisons on drug-related charges, and was released in July of 1977.

January 29, 1987   Here's a talented pitcher whose weakness for cocaine and alcohol, aided and abetted by MLB, wrecks his life. Presenting Rod Scurry, a southpaw whose addictions became public when the Pirates suspended him in 1985, then sold him to the Yankees late that season. After pitching decently in 31 games for the Yankees in 1986, he endures a dramatic winter. He becomes a free agent, and the Yankees re-sign him on **December 6** to a non-guaranteed, $360,000 deal for 1987. A few weeks into the new year, Scurry is arrested in Reno for drunk and reckless driving. He refuses to take a field test, and his license is suspended, but he doesn't go to jail. Instead, he goes to spring training, where lousy pitching and his lingering woes prompt the Yankees to release him on **March 27**. After a year in the minors, he plays for Seattle in 1988 but is arrested again on **December 22, 1988**, a day after the Mariners release him, for purchasing cocaine. This time he gets away with a suspended sentence, but his drug abuse continues until 1992, when the 36-year-old dies in Reno, going into cardiac arrest while police try to subdue him after answering a call that he was hallucinating about snakes.

November 12, 1992   All kinds of crimes were associated with the sad case of Steve Howe, making it surprising on this date when arbitrator George Nicolau lifts the lifetime suspension of the sullied southpaw. Naturally, the all-forgiving Yankees are eager to re-sign him now that he has escaped the ban imposed in June by Commissioner Fay Vincent. The previous winter was a long one for Howe.

On **December 19, 1991**, he was arrested in Kalispell, Montana, charged with attempting to possess cocaine. On **February 7, 1992**, he pleaded not guilty to two Federal charges, and, awaiting trial, dawdled away his free time by ramming his car into a light pole and leaving the scene on **February 12**, paying a $125 fine when the police caught him because he didn't realize that his license plate fell off. His 1980s rap sheet could fill the back of his Topps card:

- 1982: five weeks of drug rehab after the season
- 1983: suspended by the Dodgers during the season, plus more rehabbing
- 1983: suspended one year by Commissioner Bowie Kuhn after failing drug test in December; missed 1984 season
- 1985: released by Twins after a cocaine relapse
- 1986: suspended twice by Commissioner Peter Ueberroth after continuing drug problems while playing in the minor leagues
- 1988: released by Texas Rangers after violating alcohol abuse after-care program

Vincent's lifetime ban, which came before Howe pleaded guilty and got off without prison time, was Howe's umpteenth comeuppance, having set the record with seven addiction-related suspensions, getting zapped by three commissioners (also a record). Yet Nicolau buys the argument that Howe's addiction is due to "adult attention deficiency disorder," therefore not entirely his own fault, and finds the lifetime ban excessive. Howe pitched only 22 innings for the Yankees in 1992, but they're desperate for a left-handed reliever, and on **December 8, 1992**, they sign the 34-year-old Howe to a three-year deal. If enabling addiction is a crime, this is Grand Enabling. He'll pitch four more seasons for them (one good, three lousy), during which time they'll contribute $7.6 million in salary to his drug-depleted bankroll, enough to buy the really good stuff until they release him and his 6.35 ERA in June 1996. Two days later, he is arrested at Kennedy Airport for carrying a loaded .357 Magnum in his luggage. He gets three years probation for that one, seriously injures himself in 1997 when he crashes his motorcycle while driving drunk, and somehow lasts until 2006 before dying in a car crash on a lonely road in the middle of the night, age 48.

March 31, 1995 Gene Michael, the Yankees GM who drew the line at offering Barry Bonds a six-year contract, neglects to draw the line at his own drunk driving, until he loses control and rams into a utility pole. Actually, in the fine tradition of Steve Howe, Michael doesn't draw the line there either. He keeps driving until the police see smoke coming from a flat tire and arrest him. There wasn't much else for a baseball executive to do in Fort Lauderdale during the strike that spring except watch a bunch of scabs try out, a spectacle which would have driven any good baseball man to drink. Still, this is reportedly "at least" his second such arrest since 1991, and the upshot is that after the season, George Steinbrenner kicks him sideways, keeping him in lesser advisory capacities rather than letting him oversee the championship run of the team he built during his GM tenure from 1990-1995.

February 22, 2000 Another all-star recidivist surfaces on this date, when Darryl Strawberry is busted in Tampa for cocaine possession. He has massive legal problems, since the bust came from testing mandated during his sentencing last spring (18 months of probation). His major league career is over, though that takes awhile to unfold. He's facing a third suspension, and three strikes and you're out these days. Suspended in 1995 for 60 games for cocaine use, he also missed most of the 1999 season after being busted in April. Commissioner Bud Selig lowers the boom on **February 28**, a one-year suspension that combines with health problems to shelve Strawberry permanently. It's the merciful thing; he hasn't managed as many as 300 at-bats in a season since 1991, he had one half-decent season out of five with the Yankees, and his demons aren't going away. They should have seen it coming in the key word he used when they signed him on **January 8, 1998**: "I have high standards and high goals for myself." In the two decades since then, his existence has continued to be punctuated by arrests and addictions, the products of a lifestyle fueled by career baseball earnings of more than $36 million.

March 11, 2002 Do you remember this one? The same year his cousin Mariano debuted for the Yankees, outfielder Ruben Rivera got one at-bat with them as well. One of the players traded to the Padres in 1996 in the Hideki Irabu fiasco, Rivera spent four seasons there. His high point was going 4-for-5 with two doubles against the Yankees in the 1998 World Series. Although his best power numbers were 23 home runs and 57 RBI, his batting averages in those two most prolific seasons were .195 and .208, making him a borderline major leaguer at best. Yet after another unremarkable season in Cincinnati, he was signed as a free agent by the Yankees on **February 14, 2002**, with a non-guaranteed $1 million contract. On this date, just a few weeks later, they release him. Why? Because he stole Derek Jeter's glove and sold it to a collector for $2,500. I dare you to make sense out of it.

Suspensions and Fines

Earlier, we covered suspensions like Alex Rodriguez's and fines like Miller Huggins zapping Babe Ruth $5,000 for insubordination. Here's an assortment, starting with another punishment meted out to The Babe.

December 5, 1921 Commissioner Landis suspends Babe Ruth and Bob Meusel until May 20, 1922, for participating in a postseason barnstorming trip. They violated a rule enacted in 1911 to prevent World Series participants from barnstorming, a rule Ruth also violated in 1916. In addition, they forfeit their World Series shares, roughly $3,300. Says Landis, "This situation involves ... a mutinous defiance, intended by the players to present the question: Which is the bigger—baseball or any individual in baseball." He means they knew they were breaking the rule, but think about the rule. Management's objection was to players organizing their own tours, from which the players (and promoters) would earn income not funneled through the team. Forget about the publicity benefit of letting people all around the country see the best players. Just don't let those peons cash in on their talents in the off-season if we can't get a piece of it. There's also the issue of selective enforcement. On **March 13, 1922**, Ruth signs a contract containing this clause: "Player agrees to abstain from the use of intoxicating liquors and not to remain up later than one o'clock A.M. during playing season."

The only thing less likely than Ruth obeying the clause was the Yankees trying to enforce it. But it provided a weapon they would use in battering down his salary demands.

November 6, 1942 Third baseman Frankie Crosetti is handed a 30-day suspension by Commissioner Landis for going nuts in the World Series. In the ninth inning of Game 3, Crosetti slapped a tag on Terry Moore of the Cardinals, and umpire Bill Summers called Moore safe. As the *St. Louis Post Dispatch* described it, "Crosetti not only argued bitterly over the play but shoved Summers around. Summers, in turn, gave Crosetti a rough push, and then a half-dozen other Yanks got around the umpire and jawed with him for minutes." Crosetti wasn't ejected, but a month later, Judge Landis passes judgment, sidelining Crosetti until May 23, 1943.

February 8, 1983 Here's another case of a needy Yankee needlessly humiliated. Mickey Mantle, an unskilled worker getting by as a part-time batting coach for the team, lands a $100,000-a-year job with an Atlantic City casino, and is promptly ordered by Commissioner Bowie Kuhn to give up the coaching job and sever all ties with the Yankees (whose first owner, ironically, ran gambling houses and whose third owner *built* casinos). Mantle, technically the Director of Sports Promotions at Claridge's, will mostly play golf with high-rollers and appear at special events. Fittingly, he had met the Claridge's president who gave him the job on a golf course in Las Vegas, where the man was an executive for the Del Webb (owner #3) Corporation. In a precedent from 1980, Kuhn, that short-sighted bully who suggests to Mickey Mantle that he ought to do something like making a Mr. Coffee commercial instead, banished fellow Hall of Famer Willie Mays, also for taking a (non-gaming) casino job. Mantle notes this example of MLB's hypocrisy regarding gambling: "Earlier this year, I played in a golf tournament run by a casino, and they had about 45 Hall of Fame baseball players in it. They got paid, too." Both idols were reinstated to the good graces of MLB in 1985, shortly after Kuhn was replaced as commissioner by Peter Ueberroth.

(March 6, 1992) The Pascual Perez saga earned honorable mention on the list of worst free agent signings, originating with a three-year, $5.7 million deal from the Yankees on **November 21, 1989.** As one anonymous Yankee puts it, "That's just ridiculous. Amazing. How is that guy worth that money?" It makes Perez the third-highest-paid Yankee, behind just Dave Winfield and Don Mattingly, but in two injury-marred seasons with the Yankees, he pitches just 17 games. The Yankees avoid the third year of that foolish contract only because Perez is handed a one-year suspension today after failing a second drug test for cocaine. Part of his penalty is forfeiting his $1.9 million salary. Nobody signs him, and his career is over.

(December 20, 2010) Here's a heartwarming story of a sweetheart deal gone bad. The New York State Ethics Commission (yes, it exists) imposes a record fine of $62,125 on Gov. David A. Paterson (D) for soliciting and accepting free tickets to the 2009 World Series from the New York Yankees. David M. Halbfinger reports in the *New York Times*, "The panel said [Paterson] knew he had broken the law and then lied under oath to cover it up. In its ruling, the commission found that the governor's sworn testimony about how he obtained the tickets — and his assertion that he always intended to pay for them — had been refuted by one of his own top aides, and was further undermined by officials with the Yankees, a handwriting expert and documentary evidence —'not to mention common sense.'" Conveniently, Paterson is leaving office in eleven days and can go hide in peace.

Now that I've dipped my toe in politics, I will un-dip it and turn to one winter phenomenon which has distracted fans throughout baseball history: salary disputes. For every Pascual Perez who got millions for no good reason, there were hundreds of players—before the arrival of free agency in 1976—who got reamed by their owners, including the most beloved players in Yankees history.

Salary Squabbles

Baseball fans born in the past fifty years have little concept of the servitude endured by players before the 1976 eradication of the reserve clause. A team signing a teenager owned him *for life*. If a player didn't want to sign the contract offered to him, his alternative was. . .to seek a new profession. Imagine a General Electric engineer being told that if he refused to move halfway across the country to a new office, he could *never again be employed as an engineer*. That's what every major leaguer faced, from the relief pitchers to the future Hall of Famers. When Curt Flood challenged the reserve clause in 1969, he was criticized as ungrateful: he was making $90,000 a year, so why complain? His reply was, "A well-paid slave is a slave nonetheless."

Management had *all* of the leverage. The only thing the players had going for them—their talent on the field—was ignored if it seemed to suggest that the player deserved a big raise. Owners and general managers campaigned aggressively and publicly, finding any reason to malign their players, who were left to defend themselves (they had no agents or lawyers). In those dark ages, management was aided by sympathetic newspapers. Even when Marvin Miller fought the reserve clause to three falls in the 1970s, it was hard to locate support in the press apart from Leonard Koppett, Red Smith, and a few others.

Jacob Ruppert and Ed Barrow

Before I started my research, I thought George Steinbrenner was the Yankees owner who badmouthed his players most obnoxiously. He relished lambasting them, and it rarely helped their performance, but paying them millions of dollars bought Steinbrenner the right to some public grousing. Thus my nominee as the most heartless and despicable owner is Jacob Ruppert. A four-term Congressman connected to Tammany Hall, Ruppert inherited the most successful brewery in the country and on **January 1, 1915,** he and engineer Tillinghast l'Hommedieu Huston purchased the Yankees. Within a decade, Ruppert bought out Huston, built Yankee Stadium, survived the shock of Prohibition, and built the biggest dynasty in sports, for which he was as deserving of Hall of Fame status as any owner.

The Yankees had the most talent, the biggest bankroll, and the biggest profits through most of Ruppert's ownership of the Yankees. Though he was believed to be hugely rich, he was worth a disappointing $10 million when he died in early 1939. Some historians have said that Ruppert was quite generous; after all, Babe Ruth *did* make more than President Hoover, and Lou Gehrig still had the biggest salary in the majors the season he had to quit after eight games. My question is: does having the biggest bankroll equal generosity? It's like bragging that you drew the "biggest crowd" of the season when it was only a dozen more people than the next-biggest and there were tons of empty seats. Ruppert, like other owners of his time, didn't pay his players a nickel more than he had to, but his style and his philosophy set him apart to me.

In public, he was gruff and rather humorless, all business. In private, he was a different man. A lifelong bachelor who wound up leaving one-third of his estate to a former showgirl-companion, he became known as a spendthrift with a penchant for collecting ("everything but a wife," quipped Virginia Irwin in the *St. Louis Post-Dispatch* on **February 13, 1946**) and for investing in hare-brained schemes. Collections included Chinese porcelain, exotic animals, yachts, first editions, horses (he bred them as well as St. Bernards), 65 items bequeathed to the Metropolitan Museum of Art, and much more. As for his bad investments, Irwin reported, "Col. Ruppert apparently could be depended on to buy stock in anything from a farm to raise silkworms to a scheme to grow edelweiss on top of the Empire State Building. The inventory of his estate listed 45 issues of valueless stock."

That's the part I can't forgive. Ruppert wasted millions—getting taken in *completely* at least 45 times—but wouldn't pay his players, the heroes of their generation, what they were actually worth. Economist Michael Haupert has calculated that the Yankees paid Babe Ruth a paltry percentage of the income he generated for the team. Ruppert paid handsomely for a "priceless" blue macaw valued at a hundred bucks after his death, but he begrudged any extra $1,000 he had to pay to Ruth, Gehrig, DiMaggio, and other stars. Ruppert's henchman, GM Ed Barrow, did the negotiating, while Ruppert took potshots as needed to batter the recalcitrant future Hall of Famers into submission. As you read these accounts, note the disparity between the tones of the parties and see if *you* can figure out why Ruppert chose to belittle them rather than celebrate them with conspicuous generosity. Why did he reward the crackpots and con artists while punishing the immortals?

March 4, 1919 As an appetizer, here's Tillinghast L'Hommedieu Huston announcing that he refuses to raise salaries after the end of World War I, which had reduced salaries: "Baseball will have to be put on a strictly business basis and the sooner the better. It's about time the players learned something about the business end of this game." What he means is "take it or leave it—that's how it works." Salaries had dropped steadily since competition from the Federal League ended in 1915, and besides, the Yankees finished fourth in 1918 with their sixth losing season in seven years. Winning should change his tune.

February 13, 1922 Huston is outraged at his players' salary requests following the first pennant in franchise history. "They were fabulous [Webster's Dictionary: "almost unbelievable; incredible"]," Huston raves, "almost beyond belief. And that despite the fact that we have been what we consider liberal in every case. We couldn't pay some of the salaries asked and still run our club." Here are the numbers. Their profit in 1921 was $176,000, and salaries for 1922 rose $76,000 from 1921, so there was plenty more money to go around. Instead, the other $100,000 went to Boston in the latest lopsided trade.

February 9, 1923   Jacob Ruppert finds it necessary to deny reports that a lot of Yankees are facing salary cuts even though the team just won its second straight pennant. Nobody has been cut, though only a few have received significant raises. He can't help adding, "Two or three will be compelled to take their work more seriously if they are to draw down the same salary." In 1922, their profit rose to $270,000, and the salary budget for 1923 rose by just $20,000, but of course there was the excuse of losing the World Series again. Another $100,000 goes to the Red Sox in deals that bring Joe Dugan and Herb Pennock to New York. They help the franchise win its first World Series title in 1923, so surely the players have earned bigger pieces of the pie. Hold that thought.

January 31, 1924   On the day 1924 contracts are mailed out, the New York Times reports, "It will be a case of 'read 'em and weep,' for it is rumored that very few raises will be dealt out to the men who won the last world's series." Indeed, the figures reveal the innate cheapness of Jacob Ruppert, now sole owner of the Yankees. The team made a profit of $464,885 after taxes in 1923. In 1924, the total team payroll went up—by exactly $3,743.97. Can you justify that? If only the players had cultivated a patch of edelweiss he could invest in, they might have found themselves in clover. Sadly, they were merely future Hall of Famers. Let's get down to cases.

February 10, 1922   The experience of Waite Hoyt (Hall of Fame 1969) was typical. Liberated from the Red Sox, he won 19 games in his first season with Yankees and pitched three complete games in the 1921 World Series without giving up an earned run. Asked today if he has signed his 1922 contract, Hoyt says, "I have not and don't intend to until the figures are changed. I received the papers through the mail and discovered that the salary called for $200 less than I drew last season." He made $4,200 in 1921, and when the smoke cleared, he signed for $6,000. In 1922, he won 19 games again and gave up one earned run in his only Series start. That brought a raise to $10,000, where his salary stayed for the next four years. From 1923-1927, Hoyt won 84 games without making more than $11,000 in a season. In 1927, he went 22-7 with the lowest ERA of his career, then won his World Series start, but the Yankees offered a minimal raise. On **March 14, 1928**, he declared that it was time for a rare two-year deal, at $20,000 a year. A stalemate ensued, and he held out until **April 10** before signing for two years at $16,000 a year. His salary peaked the year he turned 29—winning 23 games plus two in the World Series—though he lasted another decade.

(February 10, 1927) Babe Ruth has made $52,000 a year for the past five seasons, and he is steamed when the Yankees send him a 1927 contract calling for the same old salary. Ruth has cleaned up in vaudeville all winter and threatens to leave baseball entirely to open a string of gymnasiums if the Yankees don't wake up and give him the $100,000 he deserves. Do you think he deserved it? In 1926, his best season since 1921, Ruth hit .372 and led the American League with 47 home runs, 153 RBI, 139 runs, 144 walks, a .516 on-base percentage, and a .737 slugging percentage (for an OPS of 1.253—plus 1.448 in the World Series). On **February 26**, Ruth releases a long letter that could have been ghost-written by a time-traveling Professor Haupert, which he sent to Jacob Ruppert explaining why he deserves a two-year, $100,000-a-year contract. Ruth writes: "The New York club has profited from five of the best years of my baseball life. During that period my earning power to the club has greatly increased, while my salary has remained unchanged. . . .If I were in any other business. . .rival employers could bid for my services. Baseball law forces me to work for the New York club or remain idle, but it does not prevent a man from being paid for his value as a 'business getter'. . . .The New York club plays more exhibition games than any club in baseball, but I receive nothing for such games. All your exhibition contracts oblige me to play and as you do not have to guarantee the appearance of any other player, it is evident what other managements think of box office values." That wakes them up, and he signs for $70,000 plus a share of the revenue from exhibition games.

December 4, 1931   Here's Ruppert in a nutshell. He makes a blustery declaration that Babe Ruth will never get another $80,000 salary [his salary in 1930-1931]. "Baseball—no, not even the Yankee management—cannot afford to pay such a salary." He insists that Ruth "isn't the big drawing power" of the Yankees and snorts, "I suppose Gehrig didn't help draw all those big crowds last summer?" Okay then. Does this mean that Gehrig will be rewarded for surpassing The Bambino as the big drawing card? Are you kidding? Ruppert and Barrow batter the less assertive Gehrig down to the same $25,000 he got in 1931, when he set the American League record with 185 RBI. No doubt Ruppert told Gehrig, "They don't come to the park to see you, they come to see the big guy. He's the colorful one." Ruth actually is forced to take a cut to $75,000 after hitting .373, driving in 162 runs, tying Gehrig for the league title with 46 home runs, and leading the majors with a .495 on-base percentage and .700 slugging percentage. So it goes in the Bronx, while Ruppert struggles along, purchasing a 36-story building that year on the corner of Fifth Avenue and 44th Street. Yes, *the Yankees* posted a modest profit of $56,000 in 1931. It wasn't the Yankees' supposed struggle to survive that *compelled them* to drop the combined salaries of Ruth and Gehrig by $5,000 after the two colossuses combined to drive in 347 runs in 1931. It was Ruppert's greed.

December 22, 1932   Visiting the Wishful Thinking Department, Babe Ruth is delighted that President-elect Franklin Roosevelt has proposed an amendment to repeal Prohibition. Ruth figures that he and Yankees owner Jacob Ruppert, a brewer, will get even richer when Prohibition is lifted, declaring, "the Colonel would be so tickled he'd never even hear how much I was asking. . . .Just give Colonel Jake Ruppert the right to make good beer again and I'll have no trouble signing any contract with the Yankees." Reality sets in soon enough as Ruppert and the Yankees bewail their financial woes in the grip of the Depression, and on **January 17, 1933**, Ruth is "plenty burned up" because the Yankees don't want anybody knowing they're ripping him off. "I don't mind telling you and the world the offer is $50,000, a cut of twenty-five grand," Ruth pouts, "and that's some wallop. . .I'll never sign for that." For the record, Ruth hit .341 in 1932 with 41 home runs and 137

RBI, then starred in their World Series sweep of the Cubs. But it's the Depression, and the Yankees managed to record a loss on paper of $4,730 in 1932, ironically after deducting over $50,000 in depreciation on the players who just won the World Series. Ruth sounds defeated on **January 19,** moaning, "I fully expected to get a reduction this year and wouldn't have said a word had the club been just a little reasonable about it. But lopping $25,000 off at one smack is no cut. That's what you fellows might call an amputation." No matter. "The Sultan of Swat" is forced to sign for $52,000, a 31% reduction in salary—after hitting his celebrated "Called Shot" at Wrigley Field, for heaven's sake. Ruppert must have been counting his dimes, because he soon finances the 1934 South Pole expedition of Admiral Byrd in return for having a World War I surplus ship re-christened the *Jacob Ruppert* for the voyage. Land ho, Babe!

March 1, 1935 Lefty Gomez (HOF, 1972), one of the funniest men in baseball, is in a sour mood, mystified by the Yankees' failure to offer him a raise. "I don't know what you have to do in this league to get a raise. I led the American League last year and had my best season since I joined the club. I think now that I deserve a substantial increase." If that sounds like a vague protest, try this: in 1934, he won the pitching Triple Crown, going 26-5 with a 2.33 ERA and 158 strikeouts, one of the best pitching seasons of the decade. He wants to double his salary to $27,000 a year and eventually settles for a two-year deal at $20,000 a year. . . **February 13, 1937**: Gomez is more himself when he comments on the Yankees' "starting point" salary offer of $7,500, a reduction from $20,000 in 1936, when his record was 13-7: "I think, though, they might have started at some figure I could see without the help of a microscope." This is before the 25% maximum salary cut, so Gomez does some hard bargaining just to sign for $13,500. In 1937, he wins the Triple Crown again (21-11, 2.33, 194 Ks), and for this his salary is jacked up all the way back to $20,000, the most he ever makes in a season.

March 4, 1936 Red Ruffing (HOF, 1967), after winning 35 games the past two seasons, thinks he deserves a raise from $12,000, reasonably up to $15,000. Nope. Manager Joe McCarthy tells him today that he can't work out with the team until he signs. This holdout lasts three weeks until Ruffing caves and signs for the same $12,000. A year later, he's more stubborn. **March 13, 1937**: A 20-game winner in 1936, Ruffing wants extra salary for his hitting. In the last two seasons, he hit .339 and .291, including an impressive 14-for-35 with 10 RBI as a pinch-hitter. "Whenever they need a pinch-hitter, they call on me first. Joe McCarthy must think I'm pretty good at it, or he wouldn't call on me. But what do I get for it? I won a couple games for other pitchers with hits last year and they said 'thanks.' But they don't pay my salary." A career .269 hitter with 36 home runs, he declares, "I'm going to be paid for hitting or I'll sit right here and stick it out if it's the last thing I ever do." It almost is. Neither side budges, and the season starts without Ruffing, who is suspended until signing in May for $15,000. From 1937-1939, his records are 20-7, 21-7, and 21-7 (and he pinch-hits 53 times), and he goes 3-1 in five World Series starts. Ruppert and Barrow reward him with a raise every year, all the way up $24,000 by 1940, what he should have made years earlier.

That 1936-1937 off-season is a tough one for Ruppert, who feels put upon by the salary demands of players who just won the World Series— but only their second in eight years. Preparing to head to Florida on **February 15, 1937**, Ruppert issues an ultimatum: sign before I leave New York or else. He declares, "If they are not signed before the team assembles at St. Petersburg that will be their hard luck. . .they will have to live at their own expense." That doesn't bring them to heel, so on **February 24, 1937**, Ruppert goes off to the *Associated Press*: "Gehrig gets $31,000 or nothing. I don't believe any ball player is worth more than that today. Connie Mack once said that $25,000 was too big a salary, and I'm going him $6,000 better." Well, aren't you something! Mack said that twenty years ago, when the country was embroiled in World War I. "We gave DiMaggio a good raise over last season," Ruppert reminds us. That's true enough, raising his rookie salary of $8,500 to $15,000, but Ruppert can't help demeaning him. "He ought to be satisfied. Besides, how do we know what he'll do as a second year man?" He'll drive in 167 runs in 1937, and we'll hear Ruppert's take on that sophomore season.

Ruppert tries misdirection on **March 14, 1937,** insisting, "I want no discontented players on my ball club. They must all be satisfied. I would rather lose a pennant than have a dissatisfied player on the club, and no player can be contented if he feels he is signing for less than he actually thinks he is worth." The implication—that because he wouldn't think of causing such discontent, he must therefore have given everyone a fair contract—must have made Red Ruffing and Lefty Gomez do spit-takes with their beer when they read it.

What about Lou Gehrig's outrageous demand for more than $31,000? Gehrig first earned $25,000 in 1928, and that remained his salary through 1934. Over that seven-season stretch, Gehrig's averages were .349, 38 home runs, 140 runs, and 141 RBI—and he never got a raise! When Ruth said he was "plenty burned up" from battling Ruppert and Barrow early in 1933, here's what Gehrig told reporters: "In a few days I'll drop around to the office to see if we can't get the matter adjusted." He got his cut adjusted, right back to the same $25,000, and all his congeniality got him was a financial screwing. Finally, after Gehrig won the Triple Crown in 1934, Ruppert raised him all the way to $31,000 for two years. How did Gehrig do? In 1936, he hit .354, drove in 152 runs, led the league in runs, on-base percentage, and slugging percentage, and paved the way to their World Series title. What was his thanks? Headlines like "It's $31,000 for Gehrig Or Else."

February 3, 1937   After Gehrig rejects a contract offer lacking a raise, he is blasted by Ruppert, who says, "Gehrig comes into my office and says he should get more than $31,000. But he does not mention that he also got $31,000 in 1935 when he had a poor season. So I remind him of it. I also reminded him that. . .he and [Lefty] Gomez ruined our pennant chances in 1935 by their Japan trip." How the 1934 postseason trip affected the 1935 season is unclear, but in what Ruppert calls a "poor season," Gehrig hit .329, led the league in runs scored and walks, finished second in RBI, and was third in home runs and slugging percentage. Ruppert gets in another high lather on **February 11,** moaning, "I can understand how a man and his club can be a few thousand dollars apart, but when a player asks $19,000 a year more than he received the previous season, that is another matter. . . .I've taken a definite stand on this matter, and I'm ready to put a ball club on the field this Spring no matter what happens."

A 2020 arbitrator would laugh in Ruppert's face and award Gehrig every penny he sought, but not in Ruppert's day. Note Gehrig's view of Ruppert's arithmetic: "Has it occurred to the Yankees that in twelve years they have not had to employ a reserve first baseman? Only last year the Yankees, through their farming system, sold three first basemen for the reported price of $105,000." Good point, and one more reason to deplore Gehrig settling for $36,000.

January 21, 1938 Joe DiMaggio (HOF, 1955), Jacob Ruppert's final salary ingrate, rejects a $25,000 offer after meeting with Ruppert and Barrow. DiMaggio, despite Ruppert's skepticism, had an incredible sophomore season, leading the league in home runs, runs scored, and slugging percentage, batting .346 and driving in 167 runs. While the Yankees have the nerve to offer him the same $15,000 he made in 1937, he asks for $40,000, and the battle is joined. Ruppert chirps to a reporter about his offer to DiMaggio: "I think you'd be satisfied with it." Well yeah, but the reporter didn't knock in 167 runs in 151 games. The holdout is a bitter one. On the train to Florida on **March 13**, Ruppert shouts at reporters that DiMaggio is "an ungrateful young man . . . I've offered him $25,000 and he won't get a button over that amount. Why, how many men his age earn that much?"

DiMaggio cools his heels at home in San Francisco and is angered when manager Joe McCarthy says the Yankees "can get along without DiMaggio". DiMaggio responds on **March 31**: "The contract they sent me for $25,000 is gone with the wind. Just say I've lost it. They're going to pay my price or else." The stalemate lasts past the start of the season, when DiMaggio gives in, signs for $25,000, and misses the first dozen games.

DiMaggio's salary squabbles with Barrow continued after Ruppert's death. Barrow, on his first day as Yankees president, **January 18, 1939**, assured everyone that "We'll try to carry on the way we know he [Ruppert] would want us to," continuing the policy of signing players for the smallest salaries that could be wrenched out of their egos, to maximize profits. In 1941, coming off his second straight batting title, DiMaggio had to hold out for six weeks to get a modest $5,000 raise. You might remember how his 1941 season went, with a .357 average, a 56-game hitting streak, and his second MVP Award. On **March 6, 1942**, DiMaggio rejected a crummy "final" offer of, get this, a $2,500 raise. "All things considered," he said. "I feel justified in looking for an increase. I do not consider $2,500 a fair raise." Eventually, he carved out a raise from $37,500 to $43,750 and went off to war a year later.

Dan Topping and George Weiss

Apart from CBS, the only Yankees owners (1964-1973) to lose money, the most hands-off owners in franchise history were Dan Topping and Del Webb. They bought the club in 1945 with Larry MacPhail, who went nuts during celebrations of the 1947 World Series title, prompting them to buy him out. Topping was a jet-setter and Webb was busy building Las Vegas and Phoenix; they wisely left the Yankees in the hands of GM George Weiss. A successful minor league owner before joining the Yankees in 1932 to create their farm system, Weiss saw how Ruppert and Barrow conducted salary "negotiations," and as GM from 1948-1960, he built, oversaw, and manipulated the stars of the Yankees' greatest dynasty. Weiss added a new wrinkle during their championship run from 1949-1953, the notion that World Series money was assumed to be part of a Yankee's yearly income, releasing the Yankees from the obligation to pay higher salaries. A decade later, assistant GM Dan Topping, Jr. told holdout Jim Bouton he could "always count on" World Series money. Bouton replied, "Fine. I'll sign a contract that guarantees me $10,000 more at the end of the season if we don't win the pennant." Sorry, Bulldog, that was always a one-way loophole, just one of Weiss' many ploys.

February 27, 1951   Weiss is frustrated by Yogi Berra's holdout, insisting that Berra "is far out of line and the difference between his figure and ours is so great that further argument is ridiculous. When he comes down out of the clouds, we will be happy to bargain with him." Berra, a holdout last year, was hammered down by

Weiss' critique that he hadn't driven in 100 runs (his totals were 98 and 91). So the 25-year-old has a breakout season in 1950, finishing third in the MVP voting with a career-high .322 average, 28 home runs, and 124 RBI. Now he wants $40,000, and Weiss won't budge from $25,000. Eventually Yogi signs for $28,500, a raise of $11,000 that is, incredibly, the biggest boost of his career. In negotiations after his three MVP seasons (1951, 1954, 1955), he got raises of $4,500, $10,000, and $8,000. Leo Durocher's "nice guys finish last" applied more to contract negotiations than to the game on the field.

January 2, 1953   The Yankees always disdained and short-changed the immortals who brought them World Series glory. Nothing surpassed George Weiss' eternal disdain of Mickey Mantle's career as a half-empty glass and consequent insistence on punishing him for not winning a Triple Crown every season. An article today indicates that Mantle's demand for a $25,000 salary has stunned Yankees officials so much that they refuse to admit that either side has even made an offer. In 1952, Mantle hit .311 with 23 HR and 87 RBI, and he probably drooled at his salary of $10,000. In Game 6 of the 1952 World Series, his eighth-inning home run provided the winning margin; in Game 7, he homered to break a 2-2 tie and also drove in the insurance run that gave the Yankees their fourth straight title. After those heroics, he has the audacity to think he deserves a big raise. Imagine! Weiss cuts the 21-year-old down to size, signing him for $17,500. Mantle won't reach the lofty $25,000 plateau until 1955.

January 28, 1958   Nothing is more cold-blooded than how the Yankees treat Mantle and Yogi Berra this winter. Mantle is coming off his second straight MVP season, when he hit .365 with a ridiculous .512 on-base percentage, plus 34 home runs. He made $60,000 in 1957 and wants a fairly modest raise to $75,000. No dice. In fact, Casey Stengel gets in a low blow, chirping "Mantle should work out in center field. He's missing balls over his head. Needs some practice on that." There you have it; that must be why, days after announcing record advance ticket sales, the Yankees refuse to share that $1.7 million windfall with their two biggest stars. Three-time MVP Yogi Berra, despite 24 HR and 82 RBI in 1957, can't do better than a $5,000 salary cut from $65,000. Mantle's modest $5,000 raise—after two straight MVP Awards!— is balanced in the team's books by cutting Berra.

January 16, 1959   Mickey intends to fight hard for a salary increase to $85,000, declaring, "I thought I had a pretty good year, but I don't think they did." Yankees publicity director Bob Fishel agrees that "by Mantle standards, Mickey didn't have a good year," and George Weiss agrees, sending Mantle a contract with a pay cut. Let's check the ledger. Mantle slammed 42 home runs to lead the league in 1958, also led in total bases, runs, and walks, compiled a .443 on-base percentage and a .592 slugging percentage, and was fifth in the MVP balloting. On the other hand, Weiss notes, his batting average dropped from .365 to .304, and he failed to drive in 100 runs (he had 97). But for goodness sake, George, Mantle just led the American League in Wins Above Replacement (WAR) for the fourth straight season! Mantle fights the cut and forgets about the $85,000, but it still takes until the end of February to pry a token $5,000 raise out of Weiss, to $70,000.

March 4, 1960   Well, this time Mantle *did* have a bad season, with 1959 figures of .281, 31 HR, 75 RBI, and a .904 OPS, and he figures he's in for a cut. Instead, Weiss proposes the old Ruthian amputation, a cut of 20-25%. Today, their battle goes public, courtesy of the *Associated Press*. "This is the year Mantle must learn the facts of life," Weiss leads off. "He must learn that he can't bulldoze us into accepting his terms." Mantle, home in Dallas instead of attending spring training, replies angrily, "I don't know what he means by bulldozing. . .I sent them a nice letter when they sent me that contract back in January and told them what I'd sign for. I didn't hear from them for a month. Now, they say it's important. Seems to me it was important then, too." The Yankees refuse to telephone Mantle, who refuses to travel to Florida "with no reason". Boys.

Here's another Weiss tidbit: "We have been pampering this boy for nine years and I think it's about time he acted like a man." Yes, that's what he said: the Yankees, those benevolent pamperers, have been bulldozed by Mickey Mantle. In 1992, Mantle told Dave Anderson of the *New York Times*, "When I asked Weiss for $65,000 [in 1957], he told me I was too young to make that kind of money. Then he threatened to show my wife reports from private detectives he had gumshoe me and Billy Martin. He threatened to trade me to Cleveland for Herb Score and Rocky Colavito." Sign right here, son. Do you suppose that this was the only time Weiss blackmailed him? Way to bulldoze 'em, Mickey! He takes a $10,000 cut.

Don't think that the Yankees' front office concerned itself only with underpaying their superstars. They treated their lesser lights just as shabbily. On **February 23, 1954** with pitching mainstay Vic Raschi resisting a salary cut after a 13-6 season, the Yankees solve the problem by abruptly selling him to the Cardinals for $85,000. Weiss blasts his players today as "independently wealthy men through the winning of five pennants and world championships, [who] have become too complacent," at a time when few players earned enough from baseball to avoid taking part-time winter jobs to support their families. During the run, Raschi's records were 21-10, 21-8, 21-10, 16-6, and 13-6, the best winning percentage in the majors over that stretch, plus four World Series victories. His mistake, being 34 years old, allows Weiss and the Yankees, as one newspaper headline puts it, to "Use Raschi Sale To Jar Bombers". Says Weiss, "Some of the players don't seem to realize, or will not admit, that the club itself had something to do with our winning streak." You see how that scam worked; Weiss could tell *every* player, "you were just one of 25 players, so how important could *you* be compared to 24 guys?"

January 23, 1957   Don Larsen boldly tries to cash in on his World Series perfect game, seeking a raise from $13,500 to $27,500. "If they don't do better than the offer they sent me," Larsen says, "I may end up tending bar." In two years with the Yankees, Larsen has gone 20-7 with a 3.19 ERA, plus that Game 6 daydream against the Dodgers. The Yankees offer him $17,000, and George Weiss explains, "Don will get every consideration in his new contract for having pitched his masterpiece. But we have an entire season to think about, too, and how many games did he win—eight or nine?" Actually, it was 11 in 1956, 11-5 in 20 starts and 18 relief appearances totaling 179 2/3 innings. Weiss can laugh off the empty threat to quit, and Larsen signs for $17,000, the highest salary of his Yankees career.

January 21, 1959   Whitey Ford (HOF, 1974) is shocked that the Yankees "cut me eight grand" even though "I didn't think I had a bad year." You judge: Ford had a 14-7 record, and his 2.01 ERA and seven shutouts *led the major leagues*. The Yankees want to slash his $34,000 salary to $26,000, and he has to fight hard to get $31,000. George Weiss tells Joe Trimble of the *New York Daily News* that sometimes he cuts a player's salary not because he had a bad year, but "to make him think about himself," from which Trimble concludes that "Mickey and Whitey are being chastised for some of their off-field fandangos," mainly fandangos on the rocks. In the 1960s, after Ford perfects his technique of cutting the baseball with a fake wedding ring, he cheats his way up to a peak salary of $60,000.

January 25, 1960   Bob Turley, who went from 21 wins in 1958 to eight in 1959, reacts to being offered of a 24% pay cut, 1% less than the maximum allowed: "I got a contract one degree from all the way. I can't understand it. They might as well have gone all the way." His 1959 salary was $30,000, so they offered $22,800. Turley adds the kind of thing that passed for wisdom in those days of brainwashed ballplayers: "I always understood that if you weren't too tough on them in a good year, they wouldn't be too tough if you had a bad one. It was kind of rough. I didn't expect that much of a slash." How sad. Turley signs for $23,000, a slash of 23.3%.

March 9, 1964   New GM Ralph Houk is tired of Jim Bouton holding out for a $20,000 salary, twice what he made in 1963, when he went 21-7 with a 2.53 ERA and six shutouts. Houk announces that he told Bouton yesterday—Bouton's birthday—that if Bouton doesn't sign in two days, the $18,500 salary offer will go down by $100 a day. "I'll probably have to give in," Bouton concedes, "but I'm going to check thoroughly to see if I have any recourse. I think this is grossly unfair." He calls AL President Joe Cronin, who won't help. Marvin Miller hasn't arrived on the scene yet. All Bouton can do is tell the *Associated Press*, "They are worried about what they might have to pay if I became a super star. I'm worried about what happens if I get hit by a truck or lose my stuff." Bouton signs the next day, and after an 18-win season plus two victories in the 1964 World Series, he reaches a peak salary of $30,000. Later, learning that Dick Radatz, a Red Sox reliever who had a comparable year in 1963, got a $41,000 contract for 1964, Bouton concluded, "The bastards were *stealing* my money."

March 2, 1974

Here's a bonus, an easy bar bet to win. Bet a Yankees fan that he can't tell you the first Yankee to make *more* than $100,000 in a season. Give him five guesses or ten or whatever, because he won't come up with Bobby Murcer. Joe DiMaggio and Mickey Mantle were both in their thirties before getting paid $100,000, a figure never attained by Yogi Berra ($65,000 max) or Whitey Ford ($60,000), their other recent Hall of Fame electees. Murcer, 27, signs today for $110,000. This after hitting .304 in 1973 with 22 home runs and 95 RBI, the kind of season that got Mickey Mantle a $10,000 *cut*. There's a catch, of course. From Murcer's contract: "If in the judgment of George Steinbrenner, Bobby Murcer has what is considered by George Steinbrenner a good 1974 season, Murcer will be paid an additional five thousand dollars. The decision of Mr. Steinbrenner will be final." Is that clear enough? No wonder he had a lousy season in 1974; his average dropped 30 points, and he hit just ten home runs after averaging 26. Instead of five grand, Murcer got a ticket out of town, a trade to the Giants.

Ugly Exits

The "farewell tours" of Derek Jeter and Mariano Rivera in recent years represent the way long-standing stars wish they could exit the game, though it was jarring to see Jeter honored at Fenway Park, like Julius Caesar fielding tributes at Carthage. Getting other franchises to salute their retiring stars is one way of making up for the ugly and frequently heartless exits experienced by many of the Yankees' biggest names of the previous century.

Players

December 26, 1928 Joe Dugan, the third baseman in the "Murderers' Row" lineup who earned three World Series rings in his six years in New York, is steamed. Two weeks ago, Ed Barrow told him he'd get an unconditional release, allowing him to negotiate with all teams as a free agent. The newspapers said so. Now they announce that he's been sold to the bottom-dwelling Boston Braves. "I went to see Colonel Ruppert at once," Dugan complains, "and he certainly did not treat me very cordially. He told me I had been sold to the Braves and that I would have to play there whether I liked it or not." Dugan doesn't like it, saying "I think I deserved something better from the Yankees after the years of service I had given them." He plays 60 games for the Braves, sits out a year, and ends his career with a sour 17 at-bats for the 1931 Tigers, done at age 34.

February 26, 1935 The Yankees give Babe Ruth his unconditional release, refusing to let him manage in "The House That Ruth Built." Unlike most early Hall of Famers, Babe's dream of managing will go unfulfilled. Ruppert says tersely, "Ruth was determined to sign only as a player-manager, and in this capacity our lists were closed to him." Indeed. Ruth painted himself into a corner in 1934, his playing ability fading, by insisting that the Yankees owed him a chance to manage. However, they wouldn't fire Joe McCarthy, who stayed another decade, and Ruth refused to start managing in the minors, so he had no recourse but to skip town. Lured to the lowly Boston Braves by an empty promise that he'll eventually manage, he's through after 72 at-bats in the National League. No farewell tour, just a lot of bad press for being irresponsible, ungrateful, and washed-up. His main post-career activities will be publicity and golf.

January 26, 1943 Another great Yankee who was exiled into oblivion was Vernon "Lefty" Gomez, unceremoniously dumped today, sold at age 34 to the lowly Washington Senators. Winner of 189 games for the Yankees, he added a perfect 6-0 mark in seven World Series starts. After a fine 15-5 record in 1941, he slipped to six wins in 1942. Instead of signing him again for $10,000 in this first full year of rosters depleted by World War II service, the Yankees jettison him, getting $10,000 for him from the Senators. He pitches once for them and retires.

March 3, 1951 Joe DiMaggio stuns teammates by announcing that he will retire after the 1951 season. Persistent foot injuries have limited the "Yankee Clipper" to 215 games the last two seasons. Casey Stengel snaps, "I can't hold a gun at his head and say 'You've got to play ball.' Of course, I'd hate to see it happen." It does happen on **December 11, 1951**: DiMaggio announces his retirement at 37. Apart from his well-publicized foot and heel problems, he cites woes in both shoulders and a buckling right knee as factors. "I no longer have it," he admits, adding that night baseball shortened his career by two years. "I would like to loaf," he says, "But I'm not that well-fixed."

He goes on to fulfill his true destiny as "Mr. Coffee," but not before one more painful exit. **October 27, 1954**: After just over nine months of marriage, Marilyn Monroe divorces DiMaggio. The California divorce, the second for each, isn't contested by DiMaggio even though he says he's still crazy about her.

August 25, 1956   Phil Rizzuto, the folk hero of the Yankees' broadcast booth for shtick like marking plays in his scorebook "WW" for "wasn't watching" and touting the cannoli at his favorite bakeries, displays a similar slowness on the uptake when invited up to the front offices to consult with the brass on the Yankees' roster for the upcoming World Series. Rizzuto is 38, hitting just .231, and hasn't started a game since July 1, losing his shortstop job to Gil McDougald. Discussing one player at a time, Rizzuto agrees that they're all essential. But someone has to be dropped. Eventually it dawns on the "Scooter": "I'm the guy." That's the slow-torture way the Yankees let him know he's being released after a dozen seasons as their sparkplug.

> More than once, Yankees officials have been too cowardly to dismiss a player face-to-face. On **December 20, 1921**, a reporter breaks the news to Roger Peckinpaugh that he has been traded to the Red Sox. Peckinpaugh, 30, the Yankees' starting shortstop since 1913 and their captain since 1914, just scored 128 runs to help secure their first pennant, and his response to the reporter is timeless: "I am too stunned to make any definite statement. The deal is entirely news to me, but it seems that no matter how good a player one is or how loyal service he gives the New York team his position is never safe."

March 1, 1969   In a somber end to a faded career, Mickey Mantle announces his retirement. "I can't hit any more," he says simply. "I feel bad that I didn't hit .300. But there's no way I could go back and get it over .300 again. I can't hit when I need to. I can't go from first to third when I need to. There's no use trying." Third on the all-time home run list (behind Babe Ruth and Willie Mays), Mantle saw his lifetime batting average drop to .298 in 1968, when he hit only

.237. He had almost quit three years earlier. On **January 16, 1966**, as Mantle, 34, headed to the Mayo Clinic, he chronicled physical woes including an array of leg miseries, a new shoulder ache that hampered throwing, plus what the *New York Times* termed "increasing moods of melancholy". Ralph Houk talked him out of quitting. That day, Mantle's lifetime batting average was .306. It was still .305 after 1966, and even a lousy 1967 left him at .302. He stuck around just long enough to give himself a full dose of regret. Mickey, Mickey, not so fine.

March 29, 1975 Mel Stottlemyre, the backbone of their pitching staff for a decade, is released three days before the Yankees would have to pay him half his 1975 salary. No surgery exists yet to repair his torn rotator cuff, so his career is over at age 33. He came to spring training determined to pitch again and expected the Yankees to give him time to come around. Phil Pepe writes in the *New York Daily News*, "A gamut of emotions swept through Mel Stottlemyre. . . . There was a trace of bitterness, mixed with hurt, anger, insult and shock. Mostly there was shock." Says Stottlemyre, "If I had known it was going to happen here, I wouldn't even have come to spring training." When the shock wears off, the bitterness remains, partly at the financial hit but mostly at George Steinbrenner for not handling the release himself, denying him the warm and fuzzy retirement he deserves as the last remaining Yankee from a pennant-winner. He will boycott the Yankees for twenty years because of that snub before returning as Joe Torre's pitching coach.

March 21, 1996 "Donnie Baseball," Don Mattingly, says he won't play this year because he's just too tired of spending so much time away from his family. In a conference call with the press, Mattingly calls it a semi-retirement, saying he could play if he felt up to making the effort. After all, he hit .417 in the 1995 ALDS loss to Seattle. Hardly mentioned are the back problems—which began when he was in high school—that have also plagued the 34-year-old Yankees captain, who says he might return in 1997. But he doesn't. His career is over, like so many other great Yankees—Gehrig, DiMaggio, Mantle, Ford—in his mid-thirties.

Managers

The Yankees franchise history is rife with ugly firings of managers, but leave it to that maniac Larry MacPhail to break the mold by taking a manager who wants to quit and holding him hostage. **July 23, 1945**: Joe McCarthy wants out as manager, a post he has manned since 1931. Suffering from nervous exhaustion, badly needing to dry out, and thoroughly disenchanted with his fourth-place team, McCarthy tenders his resignation. MacPhail refuses to accept it and tells McCarthy to go home to his upstate New York farm to think it over. McCarthy rests awhile, returns, and stays until May of 1946, when he gets a note from his doctor and MacPhail finally excuses him from managing.

October 18, 1960 After winning ten pennants and seven World Series titles in a dozen years, Casey Stengel is fired. The most successful and popular manager in franchise history, Stengel has lost three of his last five World Series after winning five in a row, but that isn't what got him fired. Later he'll remark famously, "I'll never make the mistake of being seventy again." Today, he says the Yankees owners "told me my services were no longer desired because they want to put in a youth program. . . .That was their excuse—the best they've got." Columnist Cleveland Amory expresses the average New Yorker's reaction: "The Yankee bosses are for the birds. . . .You can take the whole bunch—Topping, Webb and Weiss—and dump them in the East River." Casey lets the real boss have the last word: "Mrs. Stengel still thinks I'm a wonderful manager." Casey keeps managing until he's nearly 75, becoming more beloved with the lowly Mets than he was with the highfalutin' Yankees.

October 16, 1964 After 359 days on the job, Yogi Berra is fired without even a rumor, the second time in five seasons the Yankees unload a leader who loses a tough seven-game World Series. Ralph Houk discloses that the decision to dump the two-decade Yankees darling was made before the Series began. Good thing Yogi didn't win the Series and embarrass them! Houk explains, "The loss of the seventh game had absolutely nothing to do with it. We just felt that it would be better for Berra and for the Yankees to have this new arrange-ment." Houk does not explain how it's better for Yogi to get the pink slip after a first-year pennant. The Yankees want to kick him upstairs to a phantom scouting post, but the Mets offer him a coaching job. On **November 8**, a reporter catches up with Yogi and asks if he has made up his mind yet about that Mets' offer. Yogi's Yogi-like reply: "Not that I know of." When he finds out, he joins the Mets.

October 28, 1979   Five days after sucker-punching marshmallow salesman Joseph Cooper, Billy Martin II is fired, the fifth time he has been fired as a manager, twice in the last fif-teen months. After replacing Bob Lemon in June, Martin got the team to play better but couldn't get them higher than fourth place, so he gets less slack than usual. Just to make sure Martin gets the message, George Steinbrenner announces the hiring of the next manager: Dick Howser, a Yankees coach for the past decade. "Everything happened in the last 36 hours," says Howser. "I knew George was very serious when he called me Sunday morning and sent a plane for me."

November 21, 1980   Dick Howser is out after one roller-coaster season in which he took that fourth-place team and led them to a 103-win season. Sadly, the Yankees are swept by the Royals in the ALCS, a taboo in George Steinbrenner's mind. He says of Howser, "He might be overly impressed with 103 wins. A hundred and three wins is like kissing your sister. It's nice, but it doesn't pack the wal-lop that kissing your girlfriend does."After Howser twists in the wind for three weeks, Steinbrenner stages one of the clumsiest press conferences in baseball history. Howser, with two years left on a $100,000-a-year con-tract, announces his resignation to accept an offer to join a real estate operation in Florida which he can't refuse but which he can describe only vaguely. Steinbrenner insists that Howser could have returned, but Howser's comment that "I'm not bitter about this thing" suggests oth-erwise. The proof is that Howser returns to managing during the 1981 season—for the Royals.

December 16, 1983 Billy Martin III's latest joyride as manager comes to a grinding halt as George Steinbrenner fires him again. Martin thought he was safe with a third-place record of 91-71 and a five-year, $2 million deal, but not with this boss. He'll keep paying Martin to be an "adviser" for trades. Fittingly, the change is made while Martin is recovering from hemorrhoid surgery [insert your own joke here]. The new manager is Martin's old teammate, Yogi Berra, who will last one season plus 16 games before being replaced by. . .yep, Billy Martin IV.

April 28, 1985 Yogi Berra is fired just 16 games into the season, a swift two months since getting the kiss-of-death vote of confidence from George Steinbrenner. Yogi's last sight as manager is Joe Cowley walking in the winning run in the bottom of the ninth inning at Chicago. It's their sixth loss in seven games and gives them a 6-10 record in Yogi's second season back at the helm. The Yankees went 87-75 in finishing third in 1984, despite a 9-17 start. This time, George panics. What pisses Yogi off is that Steinbrenner lacks the decency to tell him in person; flunky GM Clyde King lowers the boom after the game. Berra vows to boycott Yankee Stadium and Steinbrenner, sticking to his guns despite numerous requests (usually by mail) to return. Finally, on **January 5, 1999**, seeking closure before Y2K destroys the world, Steinbrenner shows up at the new Yogi Berra Museum in New Jersey and begs forgiveness, telling him, "I know I made a mistake by not letting you go personally. It's the worst mistake I ever made in baseball." Berra forgives him. Now, did that have to take so long?

October 31, 1988 Dallas Green gives himself the kiss of death with this statement after being hired as manager: "I don't think George Steinbrenner is any worse than anybody else in baseball. He's better than a lot of them because he can put everything else aside for winning." To prove Green right, with the Yankees in sixth place, Steinbrenner puts him aside, firing him on August 17, 1989.

Green's successor, Bucky Dent, gets the full kiss of death from Steinbrenner on **January 25, 1990**: "Bucky [Dent is] going to be my manager all year ... If they get off to a bad start or a great start, or a great start and can't hold it together, he's still my manager." They get off to a bad start—by May 3, they're 7-13—and can't hold even that together. On **June 9**, after the Yankees' eighth straight loss drops them to 18-35, Steinbrenner dumps him one-third of the way through his first full season as a manager.

October 29, 1991   After managing in the Yankees' farm system for ten seasons, Carl "Stump" Merrill (5'8", 185 pounds) got his big chance late in 1990, replacing Bucky Dent. Now his ugly tenure ends mercifully as he is fired following a 71-91 season. He's replaced by another career minor leaguer, William "Buck" Showalter, who as of 2020 has managed 20 seasons in the majors without winning a game later than October 5. This is Steinbrenner's 17th managing switch since 1977. Says GM Gene Michael, after getting overruled for the second straight year, when asked if Showalter was his first choice: "He is now."

October 18, 2007   Mark Feinsand's lead in the *New York Daily News* puts it all in perspective: "Joe Torre brought the Yankees to four world championships and 12 postseasons, yet the Yankees left him twisting for 10 days before presenting him with a low-ball offer he could refuse." Torre detailed it in his 2009 book, *The Yankee Years*. He spent his lame-duck 2007 season fighting dissension and rumors that he'd be fired, so his priority was getting a two-year contract. Even if he left after a year, he'd have peace of mind during that season. The Yankees refuse to offer him more than a one-year deal with a one-third drop in salary. He meets in Tampa with seven executives who convince him that only his long tenure with the team got him *that* lousy offer. Off he goes to Los Angeles to manage for awhile before a further decade spent fronting for the commissioner. Torre might have seen this disrespectful treatment looming back on **February 17, 2001**, when he sought a contract extension after four World Series titles in five years, and

George Steinbrenner scoffed, "He was in three other jobs, and he got fired from all of them. Suddenly you became a genius?"

October 26, 2017   A decade later, the Yankees again resist the temptation to summon some class in dismissing a long-tenured manager. Joe Girardi is done after ten seasons, just when his Yankees are ready to rise again. After winning a World Series title in 2009, Girardi never reached the Series again, and he struggled from 2013-2016 when his team, as usual flashing by far the largest payroll in the universe, averaged just 85 wins and didn't even make the postseason. They bounced back in 2017 thanks to Rookie of the Year Aaron Judge but fell one win short of making the Series. Several columnists noted that Girardi's firing was surprising because there was no clear candidate to replace him; one list of eight candidates made no mention of Aaron Boone. Yet Boone got the job, and it remains to be seen how ugly his exit will be.

Broadcasters and a GM

November 2, 1960   George Weiss, who molded three decades of the Yankees' dynasty, is forced to resign as general manager, kicked upstairs to a part-time consulting post. In a delicious denouement, the 66-year-old Weiss, a Yankee since 1932, is hit on the ass by the same door Casey Stengel used two weeks ago when Weiss fired *him* for being too old at 70. The Yankees unveil a new policy: nobody over 65 works here. Tough luck for George Weiss, the man who brought Stengel, Joe DiMaggio, Mickey Mantle, and so many others to Yankee Stadium. Co-owner Dan Topping toes the corporate line: "Call it a youth program or whatever you want to call it, but we've got to think of the future. No man can go on forever." Weiss soon follows Stengel across the river to the Polo Grounds, the home of the brand-new Mets, as GM.

November 24, 1964   When the Hall of Fame created the Ford Frick Award for broadcasters in 1978, they named

two initial winners of the award: Mel Allen and Red Barber. Both South-
erners, they captured two generations of New York baseball fans. Another
thing they shared was ignominious exits from the Yankees landscape.
Today, the Yankees confirm that they are not renewing the contract of
Mel Allen, the "Voice of the Yankees" for a quarter-century. Allen was
part of the Yankees' first broadcasting team in 1939 and has been with
them ever since except for a gap during World War II. Typically, the Yankees won't say why they're firing the man whose voice has been synony-
mous with their success and who called the games for a dozen
championship teams. Maybe unceremoniously dumping Allen brought
the bad karma that kept them from winning another title until 1977. Or
maybe they were sparing him the anguish of describing their two-year
free-fall into last place. On **December 17**, the Yankees reveal Allen's
replacement: Joe Garagiola. Allen goes on to greater national fame as the
long-time voice of "This Week in Baseball".

September 22, 1966   Here's my nomination for the low point in
franchise history. On a cold, rainy Thursday
afternoon, the last-place Yankees and the White Sox try to make up a
game that has been rained out twice already. Exactly 413 paid customers
dot the landscape of Yankee Stadium to watch a dull, 4-1 Chicago victory.
On the WPIX telecast, legendary broadcaster Red Barber orders the cam-
eraman to pan the near-empty stadium, but the director won't allow the
humiliating image on television, as if viewers haven't noticed already; as
my father put it, "look at all the people who aren't there." Incensed, Barber describes the scene and lectures the home viewers on their abandonment of the team in its time of need, telling them, "I don't know what the
paid attendance is today—but whatever it is, it is the smallest crowd in
the history of Yankee Stadium, and this crowd is the story, not the game."
For his honesty, Barber, a Yankees announcer since 1954 after 15 years
with the Dodgers, is fired four days later. On **September 26**, Mike Burke
of CBS invites him to breakfast, but Barber doesn't even have time for the
proverbial cup of coffee before he gets the ax. "There is a time to come
and a time to go," Barber muses to reporters, "and my time came at

8:40 AM." The 58-year-old lands nicely at NPR, where he enjoys a long run of popularity.

August 23, 1995   Phil Rizzuto, the 77-year-old Yankees legend who has been broadcasting their games for 39 years, bids his fans a tearful farewell. "I've cried wolf enough," he says of past threats (or was it promises) to quit. "I've overstayed my welcome." He is distraught over the decision the week before that caused him to miss the funeral of his old buddy Mickey Mantle in Dallas. He already had his plane tickets, but WPIX, his employer since 1956, chose to send Bobby Murcer to represent the station at the funeral, preferring to put Rizzuto on the air to reminisce about Mantle, his old teammate. "When I saw the services [on television]," Rizzuto confesses, "I realized what a big mistake I had made." He had to leave the booth during that telecast, and now he's gone, taking his box of cannolis and heading home to New Jersey for good. Holy Cow, what an awful way to retire!

Doing Business
the Yankees Way

BS (Before Steinbrenner)

As the Steinbrenner stranglehold on the Yankees nears the half-century mark, a couple of generations of fans might have the impression that George, "The Boss," invented the notion of the Yankees owner as a ruthless, unrepentant bully. Not so. Those elements were present for seven decades of ownership before he perfected them. From the start, their behavior has gone from bad to worse and from worse to unconscionable. They have run roughshod over every baseball constituency and have victimized every category of fans along the way.

January 9, 1903   American League founder Ban Johnson needs a franchise in New York to compete with the National League Giants. He fears that Giants owner Andrew Friedman's connections with the corrupt Tammany Hall officials who run the city will obstruct construction of an American League ballpark. Striking first, Johnson moves the Baltimore franchise to New York and sells it today to two Tammany stalwarts: Frank Farrell, a bookie who operates a gambling house and a poolroom syndicate; and Bill Devery, a notoriously corrupt police official and "bag man" for a $3 million-a-year crime syndicate. Thus the noble birth of the New York Highlanders, later called the Yankees.

December 20, 1914   Before buying a franchise that's a dozen years old, Ruppert and Huston refuse to take over a team that just finished seventh unless the roster is improved. "We must get five more players," says Ruppert, "before we would consent to take the franchise at the price named." The new owners keep whining until Ban Johnson persuades other owners to dispatch several players to New York, allowing them to finish fifth in 1915. It's a different story on **November 23, 1992**. After losing starting third baseman Charlie Hayes, along with Carl Everett and Brad Ausmus, in the expansion draft for new franchises, the Yankees announce that they want the entire draft declared invalid, because the expansion Florida Marlins haven't compensated the Yankees for infringing on their minor-league territory in Fort Lauderdale. A baseball official describes this stance as "an attempt to throw up mud because they lost Charlie Hayes." The Yankees chose to leave Hayes unprotected, hoping a minor-league prospect would be drafted instead. When they lost Hayes, they freaked.

January 1, 1915   Greeting the new year, New Yorkers learn that the Yankees have been sold to the wealthy duo of New York brewer Jacob Ruppert and Colonel Tillinghast L'Hommedieu Huston, a construction engineer living in Havana. The sale price is $460,000, for a team that has never won a pennant and has finished higher than seventh place only once in the previous four years. Newspaper reports say that other AL owners have pledged to *give* the Yankees, apparently their poor cousins, several players from a list of a dozen or more.

December 10, 1919   The Yankees have been battling Ban Johnson over the Carl Mays mess, and now it becomes a pitched battle. Johnson wants to suspend the pitcher for walking away from the Red Sox, who want to sell him to the Yankees. At the league meetings, Johnson beats down repeated attempts by the Yankees, Red Sox, and White Sox to depose him. "They rode over us with a steam roller," says the defiant Colonel Huston, "and we are going to send the steam roller right back at them." On **February 2, 1920**, Ruppert and Huston sue Johnson for $500,000, claiming he is trying to force them out of the league. They charge him with getting the New York Giants to evict them from the Polo Grounds while simultaneously foiling their attempts to buy land on the cheap to build their own ballpark. Though Johnson holds on to his presidency for eight more years, his power largely vanishes, taken over by Commissioner Landis.

March 7, 1935 David Levy files suit against the Yankees and Yankee Stadium ushers in Federal court for $60,000 over what happened at the stadium on **August 14, 1934**. He was among a group of fans trying to capture a foul ball stuck in the netting when, according to the suit, he was "violently and brutally assaulted [by ushers], struck on the face and head, thrown to the ground with such force that he became unconscious." He was treated at a hospital for a skull fracture and other injuries. In 1937, a jury awards Levy $7,500.

In a similar salute to the atmosphere of menace at Yankee Stadium in the 1970s, a civilian review board reports on **March 14, 1978**, that city police "overreacted" and used "unnecessary force" in response to spectators racing onto the field at Yankee Stadium to celebrate winning the 1977 World Series. Television footage showed one policeman clubbing a spectator and another kicking someone on the ground. The report says, "Absent was any semblance of order or direct control over actions of the police officers."

January 13, 1939 Jacob Ruppert, Yankees owner since 1915, dies at the age of 71. Yankees fans know him for building Yankee Stadium and presiding over the team's first seven championships. Yankees haters should remember him as the man who maintained a substantial fortune through the Depression by using his ready cash to buy chunks of Manhattan real estate, but who used everyone else's struggles as an excuse to shortchange his greatest players.

October 14, 1942 Earle "Doc" Painter, Yankees trainer since 1930, is abruptly fired, but nobody will say why. Manager Joe McCarthy informs Painter by letter and tells the press simply that "I just decided to make a change," as if it were no more troublesome than changing his brand of scotch. Team president Ed Barrow has no comment, and when Painter travels to Buffalo to ask McCarthy why he was fired, "All I got was a promise to recommend me to other clubs." Painter says, "It's no way to treat a man after thirteen years."

January 27, 1945 Del Webb, Dan Topping, and Larry MacPhail each buy one-third of the Yankees, but MacPhail says he'll be running the team, announcing a ten-year agreement with his partners. MacPhail brought night baseball to the majors and brings mayhem wherever he goes. Volatile and unpredictable, he fired Leo Durocher in Brooklyn more than once, always changing his mind the next day. With the Yankees, he alienates Joe McCarthy, the manager since 1931, wins the World Series in 1947 with rookie manager Bucky Harris, and somehow blows both his top and his job with a drunken tirade during the title celebration. Webb and Topping buy him out the next day.

March 15, 1947 Despite warnings from Commissioner Chandler to drop the matter, Yankees president Larry MacPhail files formal charges against Dodgers manager Leo Durocher and GM Branch Rickey. At issue: Rickey's allegation that MacPhail allowed two prominent gamblers to sit in his private box during an exhibition game in Cuba, and a Durocher column about MacPhail trying to entice him to manage the Yankees. MacPhail gets his wish to make trouble for the Dodgers as Durocher is suspended for one year and misses being Jackie Robinson's first manager.

December 6, 1950 In one of the strangest occurrences ever at Yankee Stadium, a two-month hunt ends when turf consultant Walter Grego shoots a fox under the stands in Section 26. The fox was first sighted on October 13, the day before the Army-Michigan football game. Stadium employees chased it, tried to trap it, and lured it with horsemeat, turkey necks, grapes, and mackerel, but they couldn't take it alive. When it jumps at an electrician on **December 5**, they call in a sharpshooter. He nails it with one shot from a 12-gauge shotgun. The Yankees' promotion manager announces that the three-foot-long male fox will be mounted by a taxidermist and displayed in the Stadium press club. An unnamed observer summarizes the Big Hunt: "[The fox] was as dead as Yogi Berra trying to steal home."

November 30, 1952   Jackie Robinson says he has no problem with the players, but believes that the Yankees' management is racially prejudiced. "There isn't a single Negro on the team now and there are very few in the entire Yankee farm system," he says. Six seasons after Robinson broke the "color barrier," only six major league teams have been integrated. Robinson says, "It seems to me the Yankee front office has used racial prejudice. I may be wrong, but the Yankees will have to prove it to me." The Yankees won't integrate their team until 1955, the thirteenth of sixteen teams to get with the program, proving his point.

February 4, 1953   The Yankees announce their home schedule, which will include no lucrative night games for the St. Louis Browns. Though they insist that this is not a "retaliatory measure" against Browns owner Bill Veeck, everyone knows it is. Veeck

One owner who stuck it to the Yankees was Charlie Finley. When Dick Williams quits as manager after leading Finley's A's to their second straight title in 1973, the Yankees want to sign him. They need Finley's permission because Williams is still under contract to Oakland. The Yankees sign him without getting permission, and on **December 18, 1973**, Finley seeks a court order, saying he'll never grant that permission. Two days later, AL President Joe Cronin voids the deal. Finley strikes a final low blow on **March 8, 1974**, giving Williams permission to sign with any team *except* the Yankees. "I would not permit the New York Yankees to hire Williams even if they offered me $10 million," says Finley. Williams signs with the Angels, manages another 15 years, and is elected to the Hall of Fame in 2008 without a "New York" on his resume.

thinks road teams should share in radio and television revenues, and since league policy grants these rights to the home team, Veeck has refused to allow Browns road games to be televised. The Yankees only televise 14 night games, but choose to punish Veeck by not allowing his team any untelevised night games either. The only one they do play in 1953 is a late-season make-up game as part of a day-night doubleheader.

November 29, 1964   For some reason, GM Ralph Houk agrees to appear on a television show hosted by Howard Cosell, titled "The Cold, Cold Yankees," in which Cosell and three reporters grill him on why—as reviewer Jack Gould neatly puts it—"the Yankees were such a cold and distant club, seemingly bereft of all the attractive human qualities." Houk promises that his players will stop hiding in the trainer's room to avoid the press, and Stadium fans will be allowed to display banners, imitating the Mets policy which helped the cellar-dwellers outdraw the pennant-winning Yankees this season by 1.7 million to 1.3 million. Gould notes, "At the program's close, Mr. Houk looked as if he had been through an ordeal. . . and, if anything, confirmed rather than refuted the program's title." That was the Yankees' last known attempt to refute the obvious.

November 9, 1967   Despite finishing tenth and ninth the last two seasons, the Yankees announce a 10% increase in box and reserved seat price, the first increase in nine years. President Mike Burke assures the paying public, "This change was dictated by rising costs in every operating category." Their attendance has gone from 1.7 million in 1961 to 1.2 million in 1967, and the hapless Mets regularly outdraw them. The fans stay away, and in 1972, Yankees attendance drops below one million for the only time since World War II.

The Boss-tard

January 3, 1973   The only Yankees owners who didn't make a fortune from them were the geniuses at CBS. Baseball's first corporate owners, CBS bought 80% of the Yankees in 1964 for $13.2 million, and they sell 100% of the team on this date for $10 million. Eight seasons of mediocrity gave the network a glimpse into its baseball future, and team president Michael Burke organizes a syndicate of a dozen businessmen to buy the franchise. Only one of the other eleven is even identified when the sale is announced, one lone investor who bothers to show up to see how his money is being spent, a shipbuilder named George Steinbrenner, who assures the press, "We plan absentee ownership as far as running the Yankees is concerned. We're not going to pretend we're something we aren't. I'll stick to building ships." If only.

Steinbrenner, of course, requires his own timeline of significant low-points:

January 4, 1973 New Yorkers get the PR intro to the Yankees' new principal owner. George Steinbrenner grew up in Cleveland, booing the visiting Yankees but "in awe" of their aura. He was a varsity hurdler and football halfback at Williams College. He coached high school football and basketball in Columbus, Ohio, and was an assistant football coach at Northwestern and Purdue. Currently a part-owner of the Chicago Bulls, he also owns several horse racing stables. Quite the sportsman, he is also active in numerous civic and charitable efforts. He has put dozens of students through college and has lost count of the number of times he watched "Pride of the Yankees." How could you not love this guy? Especially when he promises that "I won't be active in the day-to-day operations of the club at all. I can't spread myself so thin. I've got enough headaches with my shipping company."

November 14, 1973 The City Planning Commissioner approves an additional $15.9 million funding of the Yankee Stadium renovation, bringing the project's current cost to $49.9 million. That's already more than twice the figure announced by Mayor John Lindsay when he approved the project. When Lindsay made the deal, he knew it would cost over $30 million, but he said $24 million because that was what the city spent on Shea Stadium. When today's funding is announced, there's a report on Lindsay's desk from the Economic Development Administration saying that the cost will rise to $80 million.

Concerned New Yorkers wonder why school repairs are being neglected while all this money is poured into a project to benefit CBS, the huge corporation which owns the Yankees. Mayor-elect Abraham Beame's figure is $53 million. Double that, too, as the price-tag ultimately skyrockets over $100 million. The whole renovation was a scam and a mess. By the time the refurbished stadium opened in 1976, New York City was broke. But at least the Yankees didn't move to New Jersey. As Lindsay callously commented when the deal was announced: "By the time I retire, the stadium will be gutted and the project so far down the road it will be impossible to reverse it."

March 30, 1974 Players charge that less than a year after pledging to be an absentee owner, Steinbrenner is wrecking team morale by violating his vow. "He doesn't really understand baseball," says one Yankee, "but he still gets involved." The complaints range from Steinbrenner abusively yelling at his players from his box seat and badmouthing them to his neighbors, to post-game phone calls to manager Ralph Houk (who later resigned) dictating lineups, to directing roster changes which disrupted the team's unity and chemistry. Steinbrenner himself delivers the perfect metaphor for the madness of his method on **February 19, 1997**: "I don't like things too calm. I worry when things are too calm. I picture a ship in the ocean with no wind and the sails all up. If there's no wind, then it doesn't go anywhere." So all those years, he was just supplying wind.

April 5, 1974 George Steinbrenner, the face of the group that purchased the Yankees in 1973, is indicted on 16 counts—most of them felonies—stemming from illegal contributions made to CREEP, the committee charged with re-electing Richard Nixon in 1972. Steinbrenner is charged with setting up a phony bonus program in his Ohio shipbuilding company. His friends would write checks to various politicians, then submit phony expense accounts to get reimbursed for their efforts. Oh, he also destroyed the records. Subject to 55 years in prison, Steinbrenner winds up pleading guilty to two counts, fittingly the same month that Nixon resigns the presidency. As the *New*

York Times reports, Steinbrenner "acknowledged conspiring to violate Federal election laws and trying to 'influence and intimidate' employees of his shipbuilding company to lie before a grand jury." Steinbrenner gets off easy with a fine, a one-year suspension by MLB, and an 11th-hour pardon by Ronald Reagan on his way out the door.

November 27, 1974 Commissioner Bowie Kuhn suspends Steinbrenner for two years, ruling that he can't "have any association whatsoever with any major league club or its personnel." What bothers Kuhn the most was that Steinbrenner coerced company employees into participating in the scheme which used fraudulent bonuses to disguise donations. Kuhn regards that "as a clear disregard and disrespect for the law," and letting such behavior slide "would undermine the public's confidence in our game." Steinbrenner responds, "Naturally, we are shocked beyond belief by Mr. Kuhn's decision. It is certainly a wonderful Thanksgiving present." Turkey.

December 3, 1975 Columnist Red Smith explains the staggering cost of the Yankee Stadium renovation (currently estimated at $75 million, marked up from $24 million): "[The Yankees] figure the Board of Estimate wouldn't hold still for an expenditure of more than, say, $25 million so you call in an expert and tell him: 'Give us an estimate of about $20 million or so. We'll add $3 million as the purchase price and stay under the limit easily.' The Board of Estimate gives the O.K. . . . Now the city is committed. You let a decent interval elapse and then say, 'By the way, the figure is $46 million now.' After that it's a million here and a million there and it just sort of piles up." He suggests that while they're at it, the city ought to start paying Catfish Hunter's salary, too.

March 22, 1976 Steinbrenner feels the urge to bully a bunch of high-priced athletes, so he orders the Yankees to get haircuts, and even Oscar Gamble has to get rid of his famous ten-inch-high Afro. "I have nothing against long hair per se," says the owner.

"But I'm trying to instill a certain sense of order and discipline in the ball club." Lou Piniella chirps, "I told George to paint a white line around my head, I'll go to the barber and tell him to cut to the white line and the hell with it."

February 23, 1977   Word gets out that the Yankees voted against giving their batboys a share of the 1976 World Series money. Teams traditionally gave the batboys $100 or so. The victorious Cincinnati Reds gave the two visiting-team batboys $200 each, and voted one-quarter shares to the two home batboys, or $6,591 apiece. The Yankees stiffed their batboys, who make $12 a game. Billy Martin said they'd get a check during the winter, but it didn't come. On **February 24**, Sparky Lyle makes a lame attempt to save face, explaining that the players had decided to give the batboys money out of the team fine fund. "We were to pay the batboys and use the rest for a party. . . .I didn't want to keep the money around the house, so I put it in my own checking account. With one thing and another, I forgot to mail it to them." On **February 25**, three of the four Yankees batboys refuse the belated offer of $100 from Sparky Lyle. "If we take that," says one, "it will be like taking tip money instead of really getting a Series share, which we feel was coming to us." Former batboy Walter Gershoff reminds us, "The Yankees were cheapskates, and we want everybody to remember them as cheapskates." You don't have to convince me.

December 29, 1977   *Sports Illustrated* reporter Melissa Ludtke files suit against the Yankees, the commissioner, the American League president, the mayor of New York, and other city officials. The charge—that she was refused access to locker rooms to interview players during the 1977 World Series solely because she is a woman. The Dodgers gave her permission to enter their locker room, but the commissioner's office overruled that offer, and the Yankees wanted nothing to do with her. A year later, a Federal judge rules in favor of Ludtke, opening the doors to equal locker room access for female reporters.

January 6, 1982   The *New York Times* discloses details of a December letter from Steinbrenner to his players who had ruined his winter by blowing a 2-0 lead in the 1981 World Series. He wants them to rekindle their "killer instinct" by reporting to spring training by February 9. "If you feel you are unable to comply, or not interested, or would rather be a part of another organization, I will do my very best to place you anywhere you might be happy." Never mind that this plan violates the collective bargaining agreement, which says that players can't be forced to go to spring training before March 1. First baseman Bob Watson speaks for many: "He's going to have an angry ball-player on his hands in my case." Watson is traded before the end of April. The Yankees go through 48 players and three managers en route to a fifth-place finish in 1982.

November 17, 1982   When Steinbrenner was told by city officials that repairs to Yankee Stadium might not be done by the start of the 1983 season, he hatched a wonderful escape plan to open the season with three games in Denver. Now he has to deal with people who don't think it's such a dandy idea. Yesterday the city went to court to bar the Yankees from playing in Denver. Today, Players Association chief Marvin Miller weighs in, noting that the union has already approved the 1983 schedule, which says nothing about the Yankees playing in Denver. The city has to sue to stop the scheme. Says city lawyer Lorna Goodman on **December 1**: "It's a shame that we have to go to court to force the Yankees to do what their contract says they must do, which is play their home games at home."

March 25, 1983   Steinbrenner is unhappy about his team losing three straight (exhibition) games, and he takes it out on the umpires. Referring to the minor-league umpire who worked behind the plate, he promises, "I'll make sure he never gets to the big leagues." Just for the record, his target, Larry Young, retired in 2007 after 23 seasons in the majors. Young umpired two Yankees World Series games behind the plate; Andy Pettitte won them both, 1-0 and 6-1.

On **April 18, 1983**, George Steinbrenner is fined $50,000 for a comment he made about umpires during a March exhibition game against the Expos. He was standing at the fence behind first base when a close call at first went against the Yankees. He shouted a curse at the umpire, Lee Weyer, and told his companions, "The National League will always give the close play to the National League team." The umpires hoped for a suspension for this slur on their integrity—in an exhibition game—but settle for an apology and the fine.

December 23, 1983   Bowie Kuhn fines Steinbrenner $250,000, the largest penalty imposed to date on a professional sports team. It goes back to AL president Lee MacPhail upholding the appeal made by the Kansas City Royals over the "Pine Tar Game". Kuhn is upset by lawsuits launched by the Yankees to prevent the replay of the protested game, but more so by inflammatory comments made by Steinbrenner, such as "I wouldn't want to be Lee MacPhail living in New York. Maybe he should go house-hunting in Kansas City." Kuhn and Steinbrenner have been negotiating since August, including another lawsuit attempting to prevent Kuhn from holding a hearing. Finally, after the hearing, Kuhn gets his funding for the office Christmas party.

March 30, 1985   Taking a break from criticizing his players, Steinbrenner rips into the team's trainer after Don Mattingly's two-day setback from playing two games in one day while recovering from knee surgery. "He's like a thoroughbred," says Steinbrenner, thinking of Mattingly as part of the owner's racing stable. "You've got to keep him in check. You don't let a high-strung thoroughbred go out the first time in his morning work and tear off a 1:09 six furlongs. That's crazy. That's insanity." Yes it is.

November 15, 1986   Steinbrenner has unexpectedly ordered his general manager to cut the budget and says he isn't interested in signing free agents. Jack Morris, a 21-game winner, is a free agent, but Steinbrenner won't even speak his name. Morris re-signs with the Tigers, while the Yankees sign the likes of part-timers Lenn Sakata and Gary Ward and drop from second place to fourth in 1987. Steinbrenner is doing his part in the collusion policy orchestrated by Commissioner Peter Ueberroth in an attempt to undo free agency. "I want to win," Steinbrenner insists. "I'm going to do everything I can to win. But my house isn't in order, and I have to get my house in order first." This posturing helps the Players Association win a series of lawsuits bringing settlements exceeding $280 million to dozens of players. Steinbrenner spends another decade cleaning house.

March 26, 1987   Yankees fans in the Bronx are screwed by the team's new cable television contract. SportsChannel has the exclusive rights to televise 100 games, but only 4,500 homes in the Bronx get that pay channel. Traditional Yankees station WPIX, which reaches 11 million New York households for free, is limited to televising 40 games. A Yankees fan from the Bronx puts it in focus: "Having the Yankees right around the corner and not being able to watch them is like holding up a glass of water to a thirsty man and not letting him have a drink."

July 30, 1990   Commissioner Fay Vincent lowers the boom on Steinbrenner following an investigation of Steinbrenner's payment of $40,000 to lowlife gambler Howard Spira for his efforts to gather damaging information on Dave Winfield. Vincent bans Steinbrenner from running the Yankees or making day-to-day decisions, forces him to sell enough stock to become a mere limited partner, and essentially places him on baseball's "ineligible list". Vincent states that he "was able to evaluate a pattern of behavior that borders on the bizarre." As *New York Times* columnist Dave Anderson puts it, Steinbrenner's chronic "insistence through the years that every bad decision had to be somebody else's fault" leaves him high and dry now.

February 1, 1992   The trick during George Steinbrenner's banishment is to make it appear that someone else is actually running the team. Today it gets tougher to pretend when the guy supposedly in charge, Daniel McCarthy, is a no-show for a meeting with Commissioner Vincent. Vincent is steamed about a lawsuit filed by CEO Leonard Kleinman and won't consider reinstating Steinbrenner unless the suit is dropped. McCarthy skips the Vincent meeting because he's busy firing Kleinman, who sued Vincent for not giving him a chance to take over when Steinbrenner was banned, simply because Kleinman was involved in the Howard Spira mess which got Steinbrenner banned in the first place. Confused? Try this—Steinbrenner financed Kleinman's suit but now is offering him $750,000 to drop it, an offer he refuses. **March 24, 1992**: The contents of Steinbrenner's February letter to other owners are revealed. "It is an ordeal that I hope no other owner in baseball will ever have to endure," Steinbrenner wrote. "It has been repugnant and distressing to think that what has happened to me could actually happen in this nation of ours." Other owners are confused. The letter reads like a threat to sue Vincent, which would be yet another violation of their agreement. It's enough to make you think that Vincent reinstated Steinbrenner just to dispatch these other bozos.

December 4, 1993   Steinbrenner threatened repeatedly to move to New Jersey, claiming that fans were afraid to come to the Bronx, including this eloquent appeal: "I've heard there are crack houses within three blocks of the Stadium and buildings where mattresses, stoves and refrigerators are thrown out in the middle of the night. Let the city concentrate on making conditions in the Bronx more humane to live in, and when they can show they have the money to fix up the Stadium, we'd consider staying there." Did he mean any of that? The New Jersey threat became a Yankees mantra; as late as **October 24, 2008**, Yankees President Randy Levine, a former deputy mayor under Rudolph Giuliani, insisted that the team would move to New Jersey, even with the new Yankee Stadium nearing completion, if the city didn't approve yet another bond issue. This hold-up, good for $370.9 million, passed on **January 16, 2009**, three months before the stadium opened.

November 1, 1994   The major leagues are in turmoil—a strike since August, no World Series, and no guarantee when the 1995 season will start. But that doesn't stop the Yankees from telling season-ticket holders that they must make their renewal payment in full by December 12 or lose their seats. When asked why they can't merely ask season-ticket holders for a partial payment, a team spokesman says, "It would be a nightmare administratively." In other words, front-office personnel would be unduly burdened and bewildered by having to make a notation of the deposit payment, send a bill for the remainder, and make a second notation when that payment is received. A Yankees season-ticket holder (and lawyer) says, "It borders on consumer fraud. They haven't treated the fans fairly in this. They could have at least let you decide what you wanted. They have nothing to sell. They don't have a product." On **March 8, 1995**, facing the prospect of starting the season with replacement players, the Yankees finally reduce ticket prices. But they won't give their television and radio networks the same consideration. "We have no intention of making a refund," says a team spokesman about the $47 million being paid by the MSG Network and WABC-AM radio. "We have no obligation to give refunds. There's a risk in every agreement."

December 14, 1999 Two weeks before a lawsuit is set to go to trial, the Yankees agree to provide better seating options for disabled fans. In 1998, four fans tried to get the Yankees to change their policy of limiting fans in wheelchairs to 44 pairs of seats—32 pairs in a section with poor visibility and 12 pairs in the most expensive seats. The Yankees refused, so the fans sued. Now the Yankees consent to allot 300 pairs of seats in various sections and price ranges. Once again, it takes a lawsuit for the Yankees to do the right thing.

April 12, 2000 The Yankees consider no constituency too small to escape bullying by management. This time it's the Yankee Stadium ushers who are about to bite the dust. In the golden days, 200 ushers might work a game at the Stadium, but the team has gradually reduced the elderly crew, even though over 100 are still employed by the Mets. Now only eight Stadium ushers remain, and the team doesn't even allow them to escort fans to seats, brush off the seats, or accept tips. All they can do is point, just like the security guards who have replaced them. Today brings the announcement of a final two-year deal with the remaining ushers, whose spokesman, lawyer Dennis Menna, is stupefied by the Yankees' stance during negotiations. "They said they needed the money to pay the salaries of the ballplayers. I couldn't believe it." At this time, the ushers make about $72 per game, or about $46,000 for the whole season—for the whole crew—while the players' payroll is about $92.5 million, the highest in baseball.

January 7, 2003 Steinbrenner sings a different tune. The last-minute 2002 collective bargaining agreement aimed to slow down rampant spending by increasing luxury taxes assessed to splurging owners. The Yankees nevertheless go from $126 million in 2002 to nearly $153 million, 30% more than MLB's second-highest payroll. While firing dozens of office employees, Steinbrenner spends $66 million to acquire Jose Contreras, Hideki Matsui, and Raul Mondesi, and even hands $6 million to Sterling Hitchcock, who won one game in 2002 and matches that total in 2003. Today, Steinbrenner explains why: "It's been two years since we've won it. I'm getting hungry." He challenges fellow owners to emulate his free spending. "You don't need to put it in your pocket like 90 percent of the rest of the owners may do." Will he second-guess himself? Mondesi and Hitchcock are jettisoned in mid-2003, Contreras doesn't last through 2004, and Steinbrenner slides into dementia before the Yankees win another title.

November 20, 2008 With George debilitated, Hal Steinbrenner is named as the new day-to-day boss of the Yankees. Hal, 40, has been unofficially running the business for a couple of years, while brother Hank, 51, has been the loudmouth-piece in their father's mold. Hal shows he can act like a Yankees owner when his first pronouncement is an ultimatum to CC Sabathia to sign that free agent offer, or else.

Spring Training

Baseball diehards spend the winter counting down to the special date marked on their calendars, that day in February when pitchers and catchers report for spring training. We've made it through the doldrums of the off-season and begin to reap the rewards of those first glimpses and sounds of ballplayers playing ball. As teams and teammates prepare for the season, everyone is filled with hope, and seldom is heard a discouraging word. Unless, of course, the Yankees are involved.

January 31, 1961 Dr. Robert Wimbish, the NAACP chapter president in St. Petersburg, Florida, the spring training home of the Yankees and Cardinals, challenges them to fight Jim Crow practices which force separate housing on Negro players. He refuses to continue helping them find housing because "This business contradicts my active fight against discrimination. . . .It's time the management of the clubs takes a hand." **February 1**: Norville Smith, assistant manager of the segregated St. Petersburg hotel where the Yankees stay: "We hope to have [the Yankees] with us for many years to come on the same basis. I mean on the same basis as we've always had them, by making arrangements for some of the players outside." **February 3**: Co-owner Dan Topping, the man who can actually do something about it, as many others have, caves in on the Jim Crow issue: "We do not run the State of Florida. . . .I would like very much to have the whole team under one roof. . .[but] we have every intention of living up to our contract." Elston Howard is on his own.

February 6, 1982   Yankees players receive a letter from the team which says, "The request for early participation in spring training is just that—a request. It is strictly voluntary." Players from other teams receive similar letters from their league presidents, all a result of George Steinbrenner's January 6 letter pressuring Yankees to report weeks early. This solution—singling out the Yankees for a direct clarification—is accepted by the Players Association, which agrees not to file a grievance over this gross violation of the Basic Agreement.

February 29, 1992   Several newer Yankees admit that they wouldn't have come to New York with George Steinbrenner [exiled in 1991] still in the picture. Mike Gallego, Danny Tartabull, Steve Farr, and Matt Nokes are unanimous in their view that the atmosphere on the Yankees is much happier than what they'd heard it was like all these years. Nokes says, "I didn't want to play here, not after all the horror stories I had heard." Gallego adds, "I'd by lying if I said all that wasn't taken into consideration."

March 2, 1949   Joe DiMaggio works out on the first day of spring training and reinjures the heel he underwent surgery on in November. He has to leave camp and winds up missing the first 65 games of the season. I can't help wondering whether someone put a contract out on the surgeon.

March 10, 1982   George Steinbrenner brags about controlling his temper this spring, having recognized that exhibition games "don't mean anything in October." As evidence of his March mellowing, he cites a game the other day when Bob Sykes walked three men in a row before giving up a grand slam. He didn't even storm into the clubhouse to berate Sykes, as he normally would. **March 21**: Despite his promise to regard March games as insignificant, Steinbrenner goes off after an 8-1 loss when the team looks awful. He blames his front-office advisors, saying, "I gave them eight or nine opportunities to tell me this wasn't the way to go. They told me we were constituted good enough to win it. If we're not, nine guys were wrong, and I don't like getting bad advice." Somebody was wrong; this team will finish fifth.

March 16, 1978   Andy Messersmith, acquired during the winter to replace Mike Torrez in the starting rotation, trips over first base during an exhibition game at Sarasota's Payne Field and suffers a shoulder separation. He pitches in just six games for the Yankees in 1978, going winless. His arm is wrecked. The Yankees release him that winter, and after eleven games with the Dodgers, another injury forces his retirement at 33.

March 17, 1998   After Hideki Irabu beans the Toronto shortstop, Derek Jeter knows he's next. "I knew he was going to hit me," Jeter says, referring to Toronto hurler Roger Clemens. Sure enough, Clemens' second pitch grazes Jeter's chest. "I threw an inside fastball," Clemens tells writers. Asked whether he was happy with the pitch's location, he answers, "Yeah."

March 20, 1975   After Yankee Elliott Maddox tells reporters that Texas manager Billy Martin is a liar, the two teams stage a melee in St. Petersburg. Maddox is hit by a pitch his first time up; next time up, he flings his bat toward the pitcher; in his third at-bat, the pitcher hurls a fastball over his head. But it isn't until a Yankees pitcher throws two balls over a Ranger's head that the brawl erupts. The managers square off, and Yankees skipper Bill Virdon winds up on the ground. Naturally, Martin denies instigating the beanball war, claiming, "Our guys were not told to throw at Elliott Maddox. But our guys can read, too. They saw the paper. I think he made our players madder than me." As if that's possible. Yankees teammates told Maddox before the game: "Watch out, Billy's after you." There's your Billy Ball.

March 22, 1962   In the first-ever meeting between the Yankees and Mets, Casey Stengel's upstarts win, 4-3. It is the 71-year-old Stengel's first taste of the Yankees since they fired him after the 1960 World Series, and he manages like it's October. The Mets win in the bottom of the ninth on a triple by Joe Christopher and a pinch-hit single by Richie Ashburn.

April 2, 1931   Joe Engel, the Barnum of the minor leagues, unleashes a *17-year-old girl* on the barnstorming Yankees. Engel signs Virne "Jackie" Mitchell, a southpaw who learned to throw a sinker from future Hall of Famer Dazzy Vance, for his Chattanooga Lookouts and puts her in to face Babe Ruth and Lou Gehrig in the first inning. Ruth swings and misses twice, then takes a called third strike. Gehrig follows by taking three "hefty" swings, according to a reporter, and missing. That's the end of Mitchell's career with Chattanooga; later, she pitches for the House of David. The Yankees go on to lose the 1931 pennant to Philadelphia by 13 games.

April 3, 1919   According to a hilarious account penned by W. O. McGeehan of the *New York Tribune*, Yankees outfielder "Ping" Bodie takes on an ostrich in a spaghetti-eating contest that spices up an exhibition game. In a battle promoted by the Jacksonville Chamber of Commerce, Bodie, a fine specimen at 5'8" and 185 pounds, appears to be the underdog against Percy the Ostrich, but the man was born Francesco Pezzullo in San Francisco, and spaghetti is his strong suit. From McGeehan's round-by-round, tongue-in-cheek coverage:

- Round 2: "Bodie had his plate clean while Percy was still fumbling. Members of the Chamber of Commerce who had wagered heavily on the contest began to look for a chance to hedge."
- Round 3: "The ostrich came back strong. . .and swallowed his second's [Brooklyn manager Wilbert Robinson] watch and chain with the third platter."
- Round 5: "The ostrich came out a bit weary. Bodie's golden smile widened, and he refused the napkin proffered by his solicitous second."

- Round 6: "Percy was tiring visibly. Many women spectators at the ringside started for the door for humanitarian reasons."
- Round 8: "It was plain even to the layman that Bodie was merely toying with his food, while Percy the Ostrich was dying on his feet."
- Round 10: "The ostrich staggered out of his corner with his beak sagging. It was plain that he had little further to go. Bodie grinned."

Bodie won when Percy keeled over in the 11th round while "Bodie was almost finished with his platter." Only members of PETA, which didn't exist then, would care whether this really happened.

April 4, 1929   Katy Field in Waco, Texas, seats 4,000, but 11,000 fans show up to witness Babe Ruth. They overrun the field before the game, and it takes a long time to get them pushed back against the fence from foul line to foul line. Before the game can start, 300 children storm the field and surround Ruth, who signs autographs and plays with them, causing another delay. By the third inning, Ruth is totally engulfed by fans as he takes his position in right field. After Ruth leaves the game in the eighth inning, the crowd goes wild and nobody cares that the Yankees don't finish the game.

April 7, 1925   Babe Ruth has felt like crap for days as the Yankees barnstorm their way north from spring training, beset by fever and chills. This morning, he finally collapses in Asheville, North Carolina, and is carried unconscious from the train station to the hotel. The malady is described variously as a cold, the grippe, a nervous attack, indigestion, influenza, and motion sickness, with venereal disease the unstated favorite. Two days later, on the train to New York, he passes out again, cracks his head on the wash basin, and is unconscious for 90 minutes. Ultimately, what is pronounced an intestinal abscess requires surgery that keeps Ruth sidelined until June 1. The Yankees' season is wrecked with a 15-25 record by that time, and they finish seventh thanks to what is long ballyhooed as "Ruth's bellyache." It's the black mark on Ruth's resume, the only season from 1923-1932 when he hit lower than .323, the only season with fewer than 41 home runs, the only season with fewer than 124 RBI. His dismal numbers--.290, 25 HR, 67 RBI—aren't even close.

April 11, 1966 In an effort to cultivate young fans, the Yankees hold their first "open house" at Yankee Stadium, and 8,500 kids show up for a free view of the team practicing the day before Opening Day. Perhaps because they can tell how bad this group of impostors is, they get restless. Soon the teenagers realize that they have the security people badly outnumbered, providing many opportunities for entertainment. Someone throws a ball at Roger Maris, who flees the outfield. The teens swarm the field, hounding the practicing players for autographs. When batting practice is cut short, a stampede ensues as fans try to swipe gloves and caps from the terrified, fleeing players. The teens steal the bases, tear up the new infield grass, and grab whatever they can for souvenirs. You can't take Yankees fans anywhere nice, it seems. Yet it's far from the worst day that season at the Stadium, where the Yankees go 35-46 en route to a last-place finish.

April 1, 1956 *Damn Yankees*, the Broadway hit based on Douglas Wallop's novel, *The Year the Yankees Lost the Pennant*, wins six Tony Awards, including one for best musical, one for choreographer Bob Fosse, and two for star performers Ray Walston and Gwen Verdon. Wallop's novel appeared early in 1954, when the Yankees had won five straight World Series and it appeared that it would take a bargain with the Devil to make them lose. All it took *that* year for the Yankees to lose the pennant was Cleveland winning 111 games. The play opened on Broadway on 5/5/55, five months before the Yankees lost the 1955 World Series to the Brooklyn Dodgers. It closed two days after the Yankees lost the 1957 World Series to the Milwaukee Braves. In

1958, the film was released, starring Verdon, Walston, and Tab Hunter. The timing of the Broadway revival was perfect, too; on any day during 1994-1995 without baseball because of the strike, you could attend a performance of *Damn Yankees*.

Ah yes, Damn Yankees. Damn near what *I've* been calling them all these years.

Part IV

Search Tools

Cerberus – also known as the "hound of Hades" – was the 3-headed dog who guarded the gates of the Underworld, preventing the dead from leaving, and making sure that those who entered never left. [from greekmythology.com]

Index of Infamy

"I recently asked a lifelong New Yorker why Yankee fans kick people when they are down. 'When else can you kick them?' he wanted to know."
—Burt Solomon

Names, Ranks, and Serial Numbers

Index of Dates